ETHNE, ED. [OR RATHER WRITTEN] BY MRS. E FRANCES FIELD

Publisher's Note

The book descriptions we ask booksellers to display prominently warn that this is an historic book with numerous typos or missing text; it is not indexed or illustrated.

The book was created using optical character recognition software. The software is 99 percent accurate if the book is in good condition. However, we do understand that even one percent can be an annoying number of typos! And sometimes all or part of a page may be missing from our copy of the book. Or the paper may be so discolored from age that it is difficult to read. We apologize and gratefully acknowledge Google's assistance.

After we re-typeset and design a book, the page numbers change so the old index and table of contents no longer work. Therefore, we often remove them; otherwise, please ignore them.

We carefully proof read any book that will sell enough copies to pay the proof reader; unfortunately, most don't. So instead we try to let customers download a free copy of the original typo-free book. Simply enter the barcode number from the back cover of the paperback in the Free Book form at www.RareBooksClub.com. You may also qualify for a free trial membership in our book club to download up to four books for free. Simply enter the barcode number from the back cover onto the membership form on our home page. The book club entitles you to select from more than a million books at no additional charge. Simply enter the title or subject onto the search form to find the books.

If you have any questions, could you please be so kind as to consult our Frequently Asked Questions page at www.RareBooksClub.com/faqs.cfm? You are also welcome to contact us there.

General Books LLC™, Memphis, USA, 2012.

BEING *A truthful Historie of the great and final Settlement of Ireland by Oliver Cromwell, and certain other noteworthy Events, from the Records of Ethne O'Connor and of Roger Standfast, Captain in the Army of the Commons of England.*

In lofts and Inmber-rooms of old Irish country-houses lie here and there boxes covered with the seldom-stirred dust of centuries. The papers within are moth-eaten, worm-eaten, mildewed; the ink is faded, the old-world handwriting close and fine. Once in a generation, perhaps, some curious eye falls upon these old papers; but their study demands much leisure, more patience; they are soon replaced, and left to their former slow decay.

Yet in some of these mildewed papers may be read one of the Romances of History, a story stranger than fiction, a drama more moving than any work of the playwright.

From that great scheme of Oliver Cromwell, the *transplanting* of a whole nation, arises the plot of the drama, and about it are woven all the elements of romance. All pasaions that stir the hearts of men were rife in that troubled time: love of country; love of home; the bitterness of enforced exile; the lust of conquest and the greed of gain; single-hearted devotion and fanatical zeal; and, above all, that strongest influence, upon which the framers of the scheme had scarcely reckoned, Love, the All-powerful!

Many a Puritan soldier, coming as conqueror, was himself conquered. Learning to know the country and the people, he learned to love both, so that the commanders declared in anger that some unholy and Circaean spells were surely at work.

The dramas of history have no end. On the world's stage the curtain falls only to rise again. The children of many a Standfast, of many an Ethne, stand now between the troubled past and the doubtful future, looking upon their fair country, whose strange destiny it is still, as ever, to be dearly loved, yet deeply unhappy. They may well ask, in old Biblical phrase, dear to their Puritan forefather—

"And what will ye do in the end thereof?" THE EDITOR CONTENTS.
CHAF. PA01
L FROM THE RECORD OF ROGER STANDFAST-ON-THE-ROCK. I
II. FROM THE DIARY OF ETHNE, DAUGHTER OF SIR GEEALD
O'CONNOR, KNIGHT OF LARA 14
III. FROM THE RECORD OF ROGER STANDFAST-ON-THE-ROCK. 28
IV. FROM THE DIARY OF ETHNE O'CONNOR.... 34
V. FROM THE RECORD OF ROGER STANDFAST-ON-THE-ROCK. 44
VI. FROM THE DIARY OF ETHNE O'CONNOR.... 54
VII. FROM THE SAME 60
VIII. FROM THE SAME 74
IX. FROM THE SAME 87
X. FROM THE SAME 93
XI. FROM THE SAME Ioo
XII. FROM THE SAME 107
XIII. FROM THE SAME.. 123
XIV. FROM THE SAME 135
XV. FROM THE SAME. 144
XVI. FROM THE RECORD OF ROGER STANDFAST-ON-THE ROCK 154
XVII. FROM THE DIARY OF ETHNE O'CONNOR....163
XVIII. FROM THE SAME. 173
Chai Pae
XIX. FROM THE RECORD OF ROGER STANDFAST... 190
XX. FROM THE SAME 4o2
XXI. FROM THE DIARY OF ETHNE O'CONNOR....211
XXII. FROM THE SAME 227
XXIII. FROM THE RECORD OF ROGER STANDFAST...234
XXIV. FROM THE SAME 250
XXV. FROM THE DIARY OF ETHNE, WIFE OF ROGER STAND-

FAST, OF OLDBURY-ON-SEVERN 256
XXVI. FROM THE SAME 265
XXVII. FROM THE SAME 282
XXVIII. FROM THE SAME 288
XXIX FROM THE SAME 3OO
XXX. FROM THE RECORD OF ROGER STANDFAST. 309
ROGER Standfast-on-the-rock do thank the
Lord.

Thus, with an ascription of praise to His holy name Who with His outstretched arm hath wrought for us a great deliverance,—thus do I begin my record of a time such as hath not been since the Lord Jehovah, under the hand of His servant Joshua, led His people into the promised land, and made them possess the gate of their enemies.

Even as Deborah the prophetess, and Barak the son of Ahinoam sang to the Lord of Hosts when He had trodden the wine-press of His wrath to the uttermost— in like manner do I Roger Standfast-on-the-Rock bless and praise His Holy Name.

Not unto us be the praise. Not unto me, a vile worm of the dust, be the praise and glory of aught that I have be»n permitted to do. For we are a stiff-necked people;

A and not because of our righteousness, but because of the sins of that people whose iniquity was full, has Jehovah cast them out before us, and given their land to us for an heritage to possess it.

Therefore with thanks to Him may I well begin my record of so wonderful a time, even I, Roger Standfast, who, according to the godly custom of His saints, have taken a name which shall betoken a true sense of the Lord's mercies, and am even now named among the elect "Roger Standfast-on-the-Rock."

Ay, stand there, Roger, not on the sandy foundation of thine own merits, but on the Rock of Ages, on the only foundation that shall never crumble away! There stand thou fast.

According to another of our pious customs, one which I could wish to see even more often followed, I have even now opened the sacred Book, and sought in the first verse upon which, after prayer, mine eye should fall, to find the message of the Lord to my own soul.

And these are the words upon which mine eye hath rested; surely never were words more fit and apt!

"Thou shalt remember all the way which the Lord thy God led thee these forty years in the wilderness, to humble thee, and to prove thee, to know what was in thine heart."

"Thou shalt remember all the way!"

Truly I do remember it, the marvellous way by which He hath led His Israel of England, going Himself before us; unseen, but as surely there as in the pillar of cloud and fire that went before His ancient people, and leading us like sheep by the hand of His servant Oliver, the Joshua of our later day.

"Thou shalt remember all the way!"

I, sitting here alone in the fading light, in a little house in the mean straggling town of Killegar, to which my regiment has repaired to receive the appointed lands in lieu of arrears of pay, I have time to remember it all. In the room below, my comrades are singing one of the songs of Zion; the sound comes up to me, and I long to join them. But I desire to write some record of all that has passed and is passing, so that when at last I cross this stormy Jordan, the Irish Sea, and meet my kinsfolk in peace, as I hope to do once again, before I finally take up my abode in this fair country, they may read ank know all, and may praise the Lord for His goodness, and declare the multitude of His mercies.

It may be that the blessed strains of their hymns will reach the ears and awaken the hearts of some of this idolatrous nation. May He grant it who formeth men as vessels of clay to election or to reprobation, according to His will and pleasure. May He suffer the word of life to come through our mouths to any whom He willeth to call as brands from the burning, and save from the idolatries of this land. Amen.

"Thou shalt remember all the way!"

Truly I remember all the way that Jehovah hath led His Israel of England, from the day when first His standard was lifted up against the mother of all abominations, and the sword went forth to devour in our land, even the sword of the Lord and of Gideon. But of this strife of ours, with all the particulars of our hopes, as well as fears, such as caused some at times to be despondent, as though He who had begun the good work would not perform it unto the end;—of these ups and downs of the strife I need not write here, since they are well known, even to the crowning mercy, as our noble Oliver rightly and piously calleth the great day of Worcester, and that earlier day when the tyrant gave up his life at Whitehall, slain justly, as was Agag before the Lord in Gilgal.

Since these things are well known, I need not here write them. My record shall be of the noble acts of Jehovah in this land, which we most truly call the land of Ire, or Ireland, though the people thereof love to use the name of Innisfallen, or Isle of Saints, or Eire, and Ierne, the ancient names of the land in their own tongue.

First, then, I will recall the beginning of all this strife and its cause, calling to mind the great and fearful horror of that day almost eleven years since, when tidings of a great rebellion and of the slaughter of many English came to our ears, first by doubtful report, and then with clearer certainty and just relation of the atrocities of the Irishry and Papists, and the sufferings of our kinsfolk and acquaintance who dwelt hitherto at peace, in safety, and with full assurance of mind, albeit among the tents of Kedar.

Then as these reports grew louder, and news arrived every day of murders and cruelties, which caused women to wail aloud and children to cling trembling to their mothers, strong men laid hands on their weapons, eagerly desiring to be within sword's length of these barbarous kerne. Still greater was the wrath, and truly it was righteous wrath, that filled the hearts of the faithful in England, when it came to be known that Sir Phelim O'Neill, the captain of this wild rebel host, would not have dared to rise but for the knowledge that the Man of Blood and his servant the traitor

Wentworth, whom men called my Lord Strafford, had purposed to make peace with the Irishry and then withdraw the army hence, to use it for their evil ends against the Commons of England. Since thus would this Phelim earn for himself great honour and favour with Charles Stuart; for by his zeal shown in slaying and conquering, and in making, it may be, slaves of the English, he trusted to gain his end.

But the Commons of England, remembering that it is written: "He shall thrust out the enemy from before thee, and shall say ' Destroy them!'" and calling upon God that He might remember His sure mercies, did offer 2,500,000 acres of Irish land to whosoever would raise and pay a private army for the service-of the Lord and of England in the rebellious country. And that the money might not fall into the hands of Charles Stuart and his evil counsellors, they caused it to be paid to a committee, composed half of the subscribers thereof and half of their own body, good men and true, on whom they could rely.

They were further to name the general and his officers; but since, in that year of 1642, the shadow of authority still remained with him who was called king, the commissions were to bear his signature, for in this at least he could do no harm.

My hand trembleth as I write of him who was even as Rehoboam, son of Solomon, to our Israel; but I will say no further of this matter, since now the tree lieth where it fell, and the guilty soul hath gone before the bar of the just and awful Judge whom no prejudice doth lead astray, or ignorance make blind. Moreover, it may be that that was fulfilled which is written—

"The fathers have eaten sour grapes, and the children's teeth are set on edge."

Therefore, because the heart of Charles Stuart was filled with anger and bitterness, and he sought how he might subdue to his wayward will the Commons of England, he delayed to sign the commissions whereof I have spoken, and five thousand footmen and five hundred horse tarried vainly day after day, ready harnessed, in the sea-port city of Bristol; so that when war was at last openly declared between Charles Stuart and the Commons, this host, under the Lord Wharton, was bidden to march against the tyrant. But here it would seem that the Lord was displeased because His good pleasure was not fulfilled, and the rebels and murderers of Ireland left unchastised, for, upon the very anniversary of the revolt of Sir Phelim O'Neill, the arms of the tyrant gained the victory, on the fatal field of Edge Hill, the 23rd of October of that year, 1643.

These tidings greatly displeased the Adventurers also, (as those were named who had given money for this good purpose), so that their purse-strings were closely drawn when the Commons desired further moneys, even though they offered to give the promised land in Irish acres, which are greater in measure than ours, or even to give twice the promised quantity in return for a fourth of the former sum. Thereafter, men's minds being sore troubled by the wars in England, none thought much of the Irish and their misdeeds for seven long years, till at length the head of the tyrant fell at Whitehall, by a true and righteous judgment.

Until then no just punishment had been awarded to the Irish murderers; only Sir Charles Coote, disregarding the ordinance of the dethroned king, had harried the country, reducing many places to desolation and scarcity, and keeping the Papists everywhere in awe of his very name.

Then at last our chief captain Oliver found leisure to cross the Irish Sea, a turbulent water leading to this turbulent land, and he needed a force to accompany him hither.

Here with shame and sorrow I must record the hanging back of many who were unwilling to be called upon to do service in Ireland, so that a part of the army was well-nigh in a state of mutiny, and our great leader thought it well to decide which regiments should go by means of lots drawn by a child.

And yet the special favour of the Lord had been signally manifested to our armies in Ireland. I have seen a printed record of a battle against some of the rebels ten years ago, who, in marching towards Dublin, were encountered by a Protestant army. Two glorious stars, so an eye-witness declares, were seen to hang over the Protestant army, and to move as they moved, thereby greatly encouraging them; and when the battle was over a dense cloud covered those stars, and they were seen no more, their purpose being accomplished.

We could not doubt of the Lord's will; the continued success of our arms under Oliver was surely enough to convince us that we went not in our own strength.

Moreover, the resistance with which we met was but feeble, and town and castle fell before us, and were utterly demolished and overthrown, since Cromwell prudently resolved to leave no defences fit for further resistance, but to breach every wall and every tower, and once and for ever to pacify this country.

The very sound of his name will blanch an Irishman's face for many years to come. Yea, by his hand the Lord has wrought a great work here, even as He wrought in England. Yet peace has not been won, either here or there, till after long strife, a strife of souls as well as of bodily strength, a searching of the heart and trying of the reins.

For some there are who have turned back in spirit to the old darkness whence we have been brought out. The fleshpots of the court and its favours have tempted some; others have halted between two opinions; others, again, have been but lukewarm.

Satan has sifted us as wheat, but our faith has not failed utterly, because He has prayed for us who did pray for Peter. May He ever continue to intercede for us, and especially for me, His unworthy servant, and for my kiustblk and friends, the people of Oldbury on Severn, in the county of Gloucester. Amen.

But my record moveth but slowly, as my heart overflows at the remembrance of our great deliverance. The kerne fell before us as the Amalekites before Israel; and, that we might remember that we fought with the sword of the Lord and not only that of Gideon, Bibles were served out to us, and every soldier was required to account for this Bible, as for every other equipment.

With the Bibles, scythes were likewise served out, and reaping hooks, and with these our men cut down the growing crops, so that desolation followed our steps, and much of the land became a howling wilderness, that land which was so green and fair that Oliver himself, looking down upon it from a hill top in Munster, cried aloud,

"Behold the land! Is it not worth fighting for?"

Thus he said, as Joshua may have spoken, or Moses, when from Pisgah he looked on the land that flowed with milk and honey, which the Lord had graciously granted to His Israel, even as He hath given to us this kingdom of Ireland.

—But of tho war I will speak no further, since it will be hereafter written in the chronicles of our nation. In truth, when men go forth to fight, when their blood is heated with the strife, and their heart joyful with hope of victory, war seemeth a fair and a glorious thing. But when the battle is past, and one doth take his way among the dead and the dying, then must the heart sink at the thought of so much trouble and anguish and woe, since, though a man were clothed in iron as a garment, yet would his human heart beat below, and grow sad at the misery of his fellows. Moreover, it is grievous that a man should behold the miseries of widows and orphans, of helpless children perishing of hunger, homeless, and without clothing. Although these be the children of the wicked, of whom it is written, "Let his children be fatherless, and his wife a widow," yet the sight of their sorrow must needs cause sorrow also in him that seeth. Of these I have beheld some who fought among themselves for a piece of leather, or for some carrion refused of the very dogs, being themselves in worse case than the starving animals who prowled about in great numbers. Some I have seen who tore up grass and sought eagerly for roots, and flocked to a plot of water-cresses with as much joy as if it had been a wholesome meal. Anything that might serve as food was welcome; and when looking upon these miserable creatures one might well doubt whether they were not spectres of the grave, or the creations of a sick man's fancy, rather than human beings. But woe is me! am I not yet in the gall of bitterness, even I Roger Standfast-on-the-rock, since I have pity for those whom the Lord pities not, and would spare those whom He wills not to spare? Was it not in yielding to weak human pity that Israel also sinned?

Already there be those of our army whose hearts have been turned away as the heart of the strong man in the valley of Sorek, for against the dangerous wiles of women neither strength nor courage avail, but only the grace of the Highest.

I, for my part, hold with a godly poet, who hath lately declared that he "rather than turne
From English principles would sooner burne,
And rather than marrie an Irish wife
Would batcheller remaine for terme of life.''

Oar excellent Ireton hath made just and wise provision against this folly, by forbidding any such marriage of a soldier on pain of dismissal, and as all hope of the acquirement of lands would with such dismissal be at an end, we may trust that the danger will not be great.

—Now, to this town of Killegar we have come, to receive by lot our appointed portions, lots drawn in Dublin having appointed our regiment to lands in this county.

For this is the great end, the victory of victories. This land is no longer to be Irish, but English only. The whole of the proprietors in the three provinces of Ulster, Leinster, and Connaught are to be dispossessed of their lands, except such Protestants as can show that they have borne a constant good affection towards the Parliament of England. All the bishops and clergy of the Episcopal Church are likewise dispossessed; and they being driven away and the Papists banished (if adjudged, for their share in the late rebellion, incapable of pardon) or transplanted into Connaught, their lands are to be divided among us for our arrears of pay, and among the Adventurers who bore the expenses of the wars. Thus a Protestant nation shall be established, and the pure worship of God at last be carried on in this country.

Yesterday we assembled in the Courthouse of this town, for the drawing of lots.

I, entering with my troop, was followed by my lieutenant, worthy Isaiah Heston, and we waited till all were gathered together, and our colonel, Fletcher Corbet, a valiant man and a man of God, took his place before a table, on which lay a great box.

"Are the lots written?" said he to a clerk who waited.

"They are written, sir."

"The names of the several officers and soldiers of each troop entered on the lot, the arrears due to each, and the number of acres due to the troop?"

"It is done, sir."

The colonel now lifted the lid. The box was filled with a number of folded papers of equal size, so fastened down that the writing within might not be seen. Then he turned to the chaplain—
"Let us seek the face of the Lord in prayer," he said, and we felt it right and fit that so important a matter should be blessed by prayer. For we would not be as worldlings, who, out of mere custom, pray before meat only. If food be a good gift, others are greater and better gifts of God; and it is meet and right that we should at all times and in all places remember this.

Master Jabez Allfrey therefore offered prayer, reminding the Lord of the lots which He had blessed in the choice of Matthias, and of all His covenant mercies. His prayer was long, and some of the soldiers grew impatient; for the carnal heart is thus minded, and wearies not soon of pleasure, but sadly soon of the things of eternity.

Then in the appointed way the lots were drawn, the baronies being laid out in a file, or string of contiguity. Each lot on being drawn out was read for the ears of all whom it might concern, and then filed on the file of each barony, till all the demands which the acres of that barony could satisfy were thus satisfied.

And to me and my troop the lot fell in the baronies of Iveragh and Cloyne.

The subdivision among the men was not yet to be made, but each man was bidden to deliver up his debenture, and in return was given a certificate setting forth that he had thus delivered it up, and that so many acres in such a barony were to be his.

After my troop had done this the colonel turned to me—

"Captain Standfast, in the barony of Iveragh, there are two houses of disaffected persons—Lara Castle, the seat of Sir Gerald O'Connor, who delights to be called the Knight of Lara; and Glendour Halls, the home of the Burke family. It is thought convenient that the captain and lieutenant respectively, alone, or with a few soldiers, should shortly occupy these, till the transplanting and disbandment be carried into effect, after which time these two houses may fitly be included in your respective portions."

The singing of a psalm closed the business; the colonel retired, and we marched our men out of the building, and gave the order for dispersal upon the market-place outside, a wide square, abutting upon the straggling main street, which consisted chiefly of thatched houses, and, with a few offshoots of mean lanes and alleys, made up all the town. Here officers and men scattered about in groups, and talked over the important matter in hand.

"And when it is all over," said one soldier, "I pray you, who wishes to live here? Not I."

"Not I; there is no beer here!" cried another.

"Nor cheese," said the first. "I had rather be among the Mounseers and live on thin red wine, and thinner soup of hot water and pepper."

"I have been a soldier since I was born almost."

"Ay, marry! thy nurse's nose was oft red and swollen," shouted his comrade, while several more gathered round.

"A pox of your folly," said the first speaker; and the men looked round to see if any officer heard, and hastily reminded the soldier that profane and blasphemous words are apt to be visited in our godly host by condign punishment. He said then dolefully—

"Truly I am nearer cursing than blessing, when I say that I know not how to turn my hand to ploughing. And I pray you, is it not hard when we have waited thus long for our pay to receive only land? My old mother is in dire straits, what shall I send her? A stone from my *own* land, in place of bread?"

"You can have money advanced on your debenture, Smith," said a sergeant who passed by, and heard the complaining voice.

"In truth I would gladly sell my piece of paper out and out. A bird in the hand would profit me better than the two in this schedule," said the soldier, pulling out his paper, and contemplating it sullenly. Several of the others did the same.

"They say that some of the officers will buy debentures," said Fulke Evans, an older man, who had enlisted by reason of bad trade and many losses; and he gave a sharp glance at me as I stood apart.

There was more said in lower tones, and a number of men of my troop assembled round these three. Later in the day some of them came to me, and asked if I would buy their proposed settlements, which in the case of two or three I did, for the sum of one hundred and thirty-six pounds each; a legal document conveying their rights to me being at once drawn up and signed, in such haste were they to have the matter settled. Not only Lara Castle will be mine, therefore, but much land adjoining it, for I think that I did well to relieve the necessities of the soldiers, especially of those who have kinsfolk to provide for, and who have truly been in considerable straits, because of the unsatisfied arrears.

This heritage, therefore, I will take as a portion and gift from the Lord. It may be that much of the land is not fertile or good, for the lands here are of strangely varying and uncertain value, some being fat plains and valleys, others low marshes or heathy mountain heights. But I know of a truth that the poorest spot of ground sown with the Blessing is better than the richest and fairest. Whatever be my portion, I am content; and inore—I am thankful.

CHAPTER II. JFrom tbe Diarg of GEtbnr, Ususbtrr of Sir cScralD 3'Connor, Knicbt of tiara. HIS morning's sun rose very brightly. There was not a cloud in all the sky, and I was very glad, for at all times I love sunshine, and on Sunday it seems only right to see it. I dressed quickly, and went down into the great hall, singing as I went. The great wolf dogs rose up from where they lay by the fire,—our turf fire that burns almost all the year round, for we love the cheerfulness of it—and came barking and fawning upon me. Dogs have a wonderful power of sympathy; if one is sad they see it, and are gentle in their demonstrations of affection, but when one is glad they are glad too, and show it with all their might, as these good beasts did now.

"Ah, Bran! ah, Rory!" I said. "But you must not forget your master! Pierce! where is Pierce, good dogs?"

At the mention of that name the dogs suddenly ceased their delighted capers, turned their eyes from corner to corner of the room, and whined piteously.

"He is not here, dear dogs," I said; "and I know not how we have the heart to be glad when he is in hiding, and Cromwell holds the land." But I think it is just because everything has been so dark that I have the heart to be glad now, because sad times always do give place to better in the end, and so I think it must be soon with us. The terrible avenger Cromwell has ravaged to his heart's content. It was 1649 when he landed; in 1650 our soldiers laid down their arms, and last year of 1652 the Parliament issued an act banishing those who had taken a leading part in Sir Phelim's revolt, and with them, strange companions in misfortune! all the Protestant hierarchy, and dividing their lands among soldiers and others at their pleasure.

My father bore no arms in that rising, because for many years he has been afflicted with partial numbness on one side of his body, making him incapable of warfare, strong man though he yet is.

We have little to fear I think, therefore, although indeed I think we have as little to hope.

Thus I mused this morning in the great hall until my mother came in, and my father followed her. After them came servants bringing breakfast; as many dishes and as heavy as in the days when the great hall was ever filled with guests and retainers, as I trust it may be again. But many a familiar face will never more be seen here; the King of Spain has a great army of Irish swordsmen now, and France and Poland too are rich in those brave and fearless hearts.

"What! up with the birds, my Ethne?" said my father. "The long day is never long enough for the child;" and, as I bent to kiss his hand, he kissed my forehead, and graciously gave me leave to sit down at once. So soon as the meal was finished, the servants brought mantles, and we went down together to the church, which we see from the windows of the great hall, Derraheen, our island church.

Outside the house is a broad terrace; beyond the terrace long slopes of emerald-green grass, descending to the lake that nestles among its wooded shores, and bears on its breast a wooded islet or two. On the right hand a long promontory juts out into the calm waters, and on this the church is built. Blue hills close the view; they might be the end of the world for all I care; nothing is so dear to me as the lake and the woods, and the fertile fields that stretch away left and right where the trees end.

The shore of the lake is a gay scene on Sunday morning, when the little bell rings for mass, and the people come from far and near afoot, or more commonly in their boats. They are amphibious like the beavers, and learn to swim as soon as they learn to run. Rowing, moreover, is very early learned; our flat-bottomed cots are not easily overturned; and even if a youngster should contrive to fall into the water he can swim like any fish, and his clothing of homespun can easily be wrung out and dried.

Up the lake came the boats as I stood watching. For oars the first thing that comes to hand will do—a fireshovel, a spade, a narrow log for cutting turf, a piece of board. Never were there such people as the Irish for contrivances. My father declares *something* is sure to be ready to hand, and *vogue la galere!*

I watched the crowd assembling— some of the men in the old quilted jerkin, which keeps the body warm at home and defends it in battle; others in the wide and long mantles which cover many deficiencies; some with bare feet; others with thick brogues, and in blue hose, made from beginning to end by their wives, who comb the wool and card it, spin it on their cheerful whirling wheels, and knit it afterwards into those comfortable garments.

For the women, their gowns were blue, or else scarlet, woven in the village loom. They mostly carried their brogues and stockings; if they came on foot they certainly did so, pausing before they turned the last corner to put them on, and so appear in full dress at the church door. The husbands of the married women carried the brogues for their wives as well as their own, being courteous at heart, though lowly born.

Some of the very well-to-do came on their cars, with the two solid wooden wheels and the flat planking nailed above the axles, the most elementary vehicle, I suppose, that ever was made. One here and there had a wicker creel affixed to it, for use on market days; another would have a rough wooden bench to form a seat for the passengers; a few had bits of wood nailed along to form low sides, a great convenience on week-days when sand or gravel forms the load.

The women who came by boat sat in easy dignity upon low wooden "creepies" set in the stern of the flatbottomed cots, while the men-folk rowed or punted with long poles. Some few solitary individuals came along in coracles of wicker-work covered with hide. From far and near they came as they might, none stayed away except those who by very grievous infirmity were compelled. Even old age was not a hindrance, for Terence MacSweeny, stout, sturdy, young fellow that he is, carried his old grandmother on his back—Judy MacSweeny, whose age no one accurately knows, but who had the great honour of being foster-mother to my father, which proud post gives great dignity to the MacSweeny family, and was bought by them as I believe for a great number of cows, fifty at the least, contributed by brothers and cousins, all the members of Judy's family, as was the custom of that day.

It was one of those strangely still days which come in early autumn, when nature seems to rest, exhausted like a new-made mother. All she could do has been done—her harvests are golden, her fruit is ripe, her roses

B have blown, her young birds are strong on the wing. In perfect silence, neither triumphant nor disappointed, she seems to rest awhile.

The first yellow leaves were dropping into the perfectly unruffled lake, like fairy gold thrown to the care of the water sprites. The sun was hot, but the air had a pleasant crisp freshness: commend me to happy September for a truly pleasant day!

Many a kindly greeting passed between us and our people, as my father sat on the chair that is always set for him outside the church door till the hour of nine strikes, and he enters the well-filled house of God.

In their melodious Gaelic the people wished us many more happy Sundays and saints' days, and all other good things in this world and the next. And ever a vein of poetry ran through their greetings.

"I am growing old, Teague; I cannot expect much more sunshine," said my father, to whom Teague Rafferty had wished that many years of such sun as was shining now might be his.

"But if the yellow sunbeams were gone from his lord's head," protested

Teague, " the moon of his silver hair had only begun to shine."

At which my father laughed, and said that it was strange that on *my* head there was no gold. What wish could Teague give to raven-haired Ethne?

"That every hair on her head may be a candle to light her to glory, the pulse of our hearts!" said Teague, and the hour of nine struck, and. we went into the chapel, where Father Ambrose stood at the altar and celebrated the mass. Our people's warm hearts were deeply moved by the sacred rites. They are eager alike in love and in hate; in devotion they are vehement. They sobbed oftentimes and beat their breasts, and tears flowed down many an old and wrinkled face. Not one word of the Latin is understood by them; it seemed to me almost strange that they should be so moved. But as the emotion rose, so it died away when the mass was ended. With the scent of the incense and the sound of the chanting it passed away; and a merry throng they were that streamed out into the sunshine again.

At the corner of the broad terrace in front of the castle windows is a great beech, whose branches spread very widely, and its top shoots far up into the sky. A splendid tree it is, and of great age, and under the shelter of its spreading branches my father's great oaken arm-chair was set after mass.

Then the people, repairing to their boats and cars, or fetching bundles which they had laid under the trees, brought the offerings due from them as tenants.

A basket of fat cackling geese from one; from another a tub of rich golden butter; from the poorest, eggs and honeycombs, hares and pigeons, or plump young ducks and chickens. From the better to do, a heifer or two, or a few sheep, which were driven up that the Knight of Lara might see that they were noble beasts and worthy of his acceptance.

Pigs there were too in plenty, the faithful friends of our cottagers, cheaply fed as they are, and easily tended.

"You have brought me a fair offering, friends," said my father, when all was spread before him. "Only Brian Lynch has nothing, how is that?"

Brian Lynch stood with downcast face in the background; ho now came forward sadly. Long illness had sorely hindered him, he said. Nevertheless, he had brought some honeycomb, if the Knight would be pleased to take so poor an offering. And he would gladly give labour over and above that which was required of him, if only his lord would be pleased to forgive his shortcomings this time.

"Take the honeycomb back to your children, Brian," said my father, "it may well be that they are hungry. And come daily to the castle for a loaf, Brian. Ethne," he added, turning to me, "it may be that you can help Brian Lynch's children with some of the work of your busy needle—is it so?"

I could, and I had promised to do so. Tears rushed to Brian Lynch's eyes; he threw himself on the ground and kissed the hem of my father's mantle, declaring that but for so good and patient a master he could not live, or survive his misfortunes; but now hope filled his heart again, like sunshine that comes back in spring.

"Murtough Fogarty," said my father, when Brian had gone away joyful, "you are hiding yourself in the crowd, and you also have brought me no offering. How is this?"

But when Murtough would have sheltered himself under the same excuse which had so well profited Brian Lynch, my father shook his head and frowned.

"That is not true in your case, and the excuse will not serve your turn, Murtough. Strong drink is the root of all your misfortunes—that, and idleness. Have I said truly?"

The man, hanging his head, confessed that nothing could ever be concealed from the master, so wise and discerning was he.

"I give you three months' grace, Murtough," said the Knight sternly. "If at the end of that time you bring me a due offering, well; if not, you and your family must come and serve me without any wage but your food, till all is worked for."

The sentence was meekly accepted, and the men came again one by one to ask what free labour they should give until Christmas. My father's harvest had been brought in, each man helping as he could; for our hired servants were but few, and this was customary. Now the turf for the great winter fires in the castle had to be drawn home, and each man was required to give the use of his car and of his own hands for a greater or less number of days, according to his ability. This matter also was settled for each one with due care.

"My friends," said then my father, "is all just and right?"

"It is all just and right," they answered; and again he asked, thinking of the changing times—

"Shall I do away with free labour and offerings in kind, and bid you pay me rent as they do in England? *r*

There was little doubt of the mind of the people, as with one voice they entreated that he would never change the old customs. Spend me, but defend me, has ever been their motto.

"Nor have I any mind to do so. But the times are changing, and the newly-come English ever demand their rent," my father answered sadly; and then he desired that all who had any case to bring before him should at once proceed. At this several men stepped forward, for the people will not, if they can help it,—that is unless summoned to appear,—go before any of the English courts. They come to my father with any dispute, and abide gladly and willingly by his decisions.

"Have you the roll?" my father asked; and a servant brought to him upon a velvet cushion the ancient roll of the Brehon law, which for so many and many a long year has been kept in our family, and was formerly expounded by the Chief's own Brehon in presence of as many of the sept as could gather upon a hill-top above our shining lake.

With much vehemence each side in the first cause argued before my father, the complainant accusing the other of a theft, which was eventually brought home to him; and lie was commanded to pay an eric of two pounds ten shillings in English money, or an ox, a fine beast being valued at that sum, to restore besides the valuables which he had taken, certain ancient jewels and ornaments of gold and silver, which had been preserved with almost religious care by the complainant. The sentence was the heavier because the theft had been committed on the Feast of Assumption, a serious aggravation, according to our ancient law, of the offence. In England, so I have heard, they take a man's life for stealing a sheep. Such a law seems horrible to our people, especially as the administering of it here has little comfort for them, since here, if the defendant be English, it is ever reckoned answer enough to say that the plaintiff is *a mere Irishman.*

On the next case there was conflict of evidence. That very morning, so the miller of Ardee declared, Lawrence Reilly had crept into his mill and had abstracted a sack of flour. In answer, Lawrence declared that he had not been there, but far away. Could he prove it?

Ay, that he could; he could call witnesses by the score to show that he had been in another place, or in several other places, if the Knight of Lara so desired.

Nor was he one whit abashed when it was pointed out by the laughter that arose that his last answer had not been for his advantage.

My father turned to the miller.

"You say you did not hear the thief?"

The miller had heard no sound. It was strange, for he was certainly in the mill.

My father beckoned to one standing by.

"Take off his brogues."

It was done. A pair of clean and neat blue hoso appeared.

"The hose next."

And Lawrence's bare feet showed unmistakable traces of the miller's white dusty floor. Strong evidence truly for the plaintiff.

Great was the triumph of the adversary; great was the respect paid to the wisdom of the Knight of Lara. Lawrence himself, though compelled to pay an eric, seemed as much pleased as anybody. It was a fine story to tell again, and to be sure *some one* must pay the piper.

"And now," said my father, having by a wave of the hand dismissed the attendant pleaders, and returned the roll to its cushion, on which it was at once carried into the Castle, "we have done a good day's work; let us have some play. Where is the cake, and Rory the piper?"

Rory, with his pipes under his arm, was to the fore in a moment. Girls in scarlet or blue skirts, with kerchiefs neatly tied over their shoulders, and perhaps another over their hair, or a gay ribbon to tie it, stepped forward readily enough, and the young men no less readily. Mantles were even thrown aside by many of the elders, and the piper's elbow was soon at work filling his pipes with a will. Meantime Larry Oge came forth from the Castle with a pike ten feet long in his hands, carrying high above his head on the point of it a round board, on which was the cake, a right good cake, as I know well, who helped to make it. Round the board was a thick wreath of Michaelmas daisies and red berries, and such field flowers as could still be found, while on pegs at the very edge the rosiest apples of the year were fixed, set close to each other in a bright circle, red cheek to red cheek.

Then, every lad choosing for himself a lass, they danced in a ring round about the cake, which Larry Oge held upright on its pike handle; and a merry scene it was, for llory piped, and those who stood round encouraged the dancers to do their best for the cake, seeing that the couple that held up longest would win it as a prize. So the mirth grew greater and greater, as one couple and another gave in with faces crimson as the apples, till at last no one was left but Teague O'Ruark, my brother Pierce's foster-brother, and pretty Nora ny Houlahan, who duly received the cake and the apples.

The cake they cut up, and it vanished wonderfully fast; then Nora threw the apples, and the young men scrambled for them, and each one who was fortunate enough to get an apple presented it to some girl and got in return a kiss *if he, could,* but as often as not he only received a clout, which was not an unmixed pleasure, I should imagine, as the arms of these fair ones were strengthened by hay-making and milking, and other tasks that make firm muscles.

Ah! it was a merry day! A comfortable meal was laid out upon the short grass in a green glade, and there the people rested, and ate, and were glad, and sang our old songs, that have mostly a wail in them, even if the words are gay. And last of all Teague O'Ruark sang a song of his own making, or more probably of Malachy our old harper's, which made a silence fall upon the merry gathering, as if a shadow passed over it.

For he sang of the Drinan Dhun, the sloe-tree, and by that name they call my brother Pierce, because his eyes are dark as the sloes, and his hair is raven black as it clusters over his forehead in the ancient Irish fashion of the Coolun, which we love, and which the English hate, and have long striven to abolish.

They were rude rhymes enough that Teague sang, but they went to our hearts as the finest melodies and most inspired words could hardly have done. And this was his song—

"My Drinan Dhun's fairer than a soft summer day!
My Drinan Dhun's breath is like the new-mown hay;
And his smile, *maghile1 m'hor!* like the ray of the sun;
And the name they call him is the Drinan Dhun.

"Cushla[2] machree! is the rain falling dreary
Where thou art keeping guard, toil-worn and weary?
Youth of the strong arm, oh! where art thou gone *1*
Dwelling in the shade of the Drinan Dhun.

' Curse upon the Sassenach! Joy bless them never!
The hearthstone of hell be their pillow for ever I
God's red wrath shall leave them no rest 'neath the sun,
For all our hearts are breaking for my Drinan Dhun.

"Teague!" cried my father, "I will not have that song sung. I have said it before. If you have a mind to sing, sing songs that will give ns the hearts of men, and not a Phillalu only fit for a woman. And you," he turned to the harper, "add at once a cheerful strain to the song, since I doubt not that it is of your making, and henceforth whoso sings it must sing the whole under pain of my anger. Ay, but he can sing the curses twice over if he list!" he added, under his breath.

Thus adjured, the old blind harper, who sat shrouded in his long mantle a little apart from the gay crowd, struck the chords of his harp and sang to the same melody, but in a major key—Teague having passed after his first verse into a wild minor strain—

"Hark how the blackbird sings Shule shule aroon 13
Slantha, mavourneen! My darling comes soon.
For the snow melts away, and the summer's begun
When we see the first blossoms of the Drinan Dhun!"

"There is hope here, but you might have promised him to us a little sooner than the Spring, Malachy," said my father, between sighing and smiling; and he called 1 My brightness (of my heart).
2 Vein of my heart.
3 Come, come, my dear. A health. upon any who were willing to come forth and dance again.

"And you, Ethne, my child, take part in the sport and lead the handkerchief dance. The Knight of Lara's daughter need bate no jot of her dignity, but will add to her empire over the hearts of her father's people by joining in pleasure as in worship with them."

I needed no such argument. To move to music is always a boundless pleasure to me. Do not all young and strong creatures find it so? Certainly a horse springs under the rider at the sound of cheerful music, as if to live and move had all at once became a doubled pleasure.

But I linger too long over the story of this day. We have lived through many a merrier after all—rent day, and patron day, and St. Patrick's happy feast; but this was the very last, and I think I shall never forget anything that happened from morning till the night of it. For as I was winding in and out with the best dancers present, holding a silken kerchief, and passing under it and back again in the various figures of the dance, there was suddenly a stir among the crowd and Rory stopped piping, for half-a-dozen young gentlemen of the neighbourhood rode up and dismounted, casting their reins to some of the lads standing by, and themselves at once approaching my parents.

"Who comes here?" asked my father. "O'Loghlen! you are welcome; and Fitzgerald! your father's son has always the Cead mille failthe here. And the rest of you" —those that remained were not of family equal to his own—" I am pleased to see you, be seated where you will on the grass beside me. Ho, Teague! cushions for The O'Loghlen, and the son of Hugh Fitzgerald."

Young Fitzgerald was evidently too much disturbed in mind to answer this welcome as readily as he ought. He - stood upright, holding a sheet of paper, and seemed uncertain how to utter what he had to say.

"What, bashful!" cried my father, whose patience, to say truth, is not so long as that of Job. "Why, man, thou hadst ever the gift of the gab like a true Irishman! What is there in that half-ounce of paper to turn thee as white as itself? Here, give me!"

There was silence while he read the paper which he had impatiently seized. It was a slow business that reading, or so it seemed to me, for the perturbed faces of the young men led me to fear that evil news was contained on that plain white sheet, a foot wide, perhaps, by two feet long, printed on in fair black type, with the official seal of Ireland drawn above. It was no wonder that my father rose without a word when he had finished, and went straight indoors, followed with eager anxiety by my mother—while we all stood and looked after them, dismayed. For the paper was a proclamation of Oliver Cromwell, declaring that from henceforth all estates and farms in the three provinces should belong to the English soldiers and Adventurers; and that the Irish nation must go bodily—children, cattle, and all—across the Shannon into the wilds of Connaught, before the first of March of the next year, under penalty of death if found out of that province or the county of Clare after that date.

Alas, alas! for us there is no blossoming of the Drinan Dhun to check our sadness; no spring following our long winter; no dawn to end our dark night; but only sorrow and sorrow, and yet again sorrow!

WAS glad to ride forth from the town of Killegar to see the inheritance that had fallen to me, and where, weary of war as I am, I may presently sit under mine own vine and fig-tree, or rather under the plentiful trees of pear and apple, and lesser fruit, and the mighty beeches of Ireland.
I was glad also of the company of my lieutenant, Isaiah Heston, one who from a turbulent son of Belial has become a saint of God, and is now as active in all good as formerly in the service of Satan. We set out at daybreak and rode on, beguiling the way with spiritual songs and godly talk, till near noon, when we came to a little town.

We had no fear of surprise or attack though we were but two, because the terror of our name goeth before us. Moreover, the wilder spirits among the Irishry have for the most part sought refuge in the hills, or in the islands among the wild swamps, which are named bogs.

Now, as we were about to enter the long street of this little town, or hamlet, as we in England should rather call it, thus said my companion Isaiah to me—

"And how purpose you to deal with these dogs who are to render up their lands and houses to you? Will you drive them forth on the instant, friend Roger? or will you rather for a short time use them as hewers-of-wood and draw ers-of-water in your stables and out-houses, as others have done?"

"Truly," I said, "I know not what to do. Sir Gerald O'Connor is a gentleman, and one accustomed to courteous usage, the master of many servants, and head of a great house. Surely with such a one some gentleness were best to be used."

"Thou wert always too soft-hearted," he replied. "Nay, in such cases as this, I should say *slack-heaxted.* Think you there was no Canaanite of gentle manners in the day of the first Joshua, used forsooth to courteous usage? Fie upon thee, comrade!"

And ere I had time for reply Isaiah Heston turned him to a peasant who was near, and cried out to him—

"Fellow, where is the house of Maurice Burke? Tell me speedily, and tell me the truth, lest I force thy tongue down thy throat on the point of my sword!"

Thus commanded, the trembling wretch replied that the demesne of Master Maurice Burke lay to the right, among some woods to which he pointed, and my comrade bade me a short farewell and rode swiftly towards his appointed estate.

For me, I kept on my way as I had been guided, communing the while with my own heart touching the present and the future of my lot, till I reached a lonely place where four ways met.

Here I was perplexed, and caused my horse to stand still that I might seek some guidance, and near to me I saw a young lad sitting listless and idle on a fallen tree. Methought that in his ragged clothing, his doleful idleness, and his abject look, I saw as it were a type of the nation to which he belonged, sitting hopeless and smitten upon their fallen land, so forlorn of aspect was he. But the face of the lad had in it something of the wit of his country, and he looked up at me with eyes that asked "Who art thou?"—half in anger, yet with a touch of mirth as he looked first at my clothing, sober and withal serviceable, and then at his own ragged jerkin. To him, therefore, I addressed myself courteously, praying him to direct me to the house of Sir Gerald O'Connor, which was called Lara Castle. The lad at first vouchsafed no reply, he only to himself muttered in his own tongue, and methought his words were unfriendly to me. I therefore drew forth some of our good English coins, and held them toward him.

"This shall be thine, friend," I said, "if thou wilt guide me."

The boy's eyes grew bright; he rose at once and gave me an answer lacking in godly gravity indeed, but quaint withal. In as little time as is needed to swallow an oyster I should be there, he said; and I judged that he meant to promise great speed.

By devious ways he began to lead me, among mud and stones, thorns and briars, till my good horse began to grow weary, and stumbled once and again. All this while his talk was of the mighty deeds of the O'Connors of Lara Castle, of their lineage from the days of the Flood, and of all their vain pomp and worldly power. Not one man of the race, it would seem, had ever peacefully yielded up his soul to his Maker from a sick bed; all had perished in the tumult of war, or by the hand of a foe, either secretly or openly. And in my heart I prayed that the Lord would quickly accomplish the number of His elect, and would hasten the coming of His millennium of peace.

My guide told me, moreover, and as with pride, that Sir Gerald O'Connor, though now old, was worthy of such ancestry, being not only a man of wrath and ready for bloodshed, but also one who took pleasure in vain hospitality, doubtless a mighty man to mingle wine and strong drink, and given to feasting and mirth.

In such idle talk the lad strove to beguile the time, but my thoughts turned ever from his tales, and from the weariness of the journey, to meditate on the journey of life, and that which lieth beyond. From such meditations I was roused by seeing that the Irish lad, at the sound of a far-off bell, let free my horse's rein, and, crossing himself in haste, muttered an Ave Maria.

At this sight my heart burned within me, so that I could not withhold myself, but at once laid before that darkened soul all the plan of salvation.

The boy gave heed, as it seemed, with great earnestness, asking at times a question which too well showed me the bonds of iniquity in which he lay, yet withal seemingly eager to hear the word of God. So that I heeded not whither we went, till on a sudden my wearied beast did stumble, and then began to sink into that dark and treacherous moist land which is here named a bog, and is at times deep as the bottomless abyss, and swalloweth men and horses, and whatso else is laid upon it. For all doth go down quick into the pit, which closeth her mouth over them, even as the earth over Korah and his fellows.

Now, therefore, I turned me in wrath to the lad, but he, with mockery and mirth, sprang with his naked feet from tutt to tuft of moss, and paused on a little hillock, from whence in his native tongue he mocked me, with peals of evil laughter adding further insult to the hurt he had done me.

Now the place where my good horse had by this time sunk to his knees was covered with grass of the most delicate and brilliant green; and this is, as I have painfully learned, the most perilous of all, and is called in the strange jargon of the English-Irish a *shaking scraw.*

I myself also, when I slid quickly from the saddle, sank therein, but by the mercy of the Lord and the strength of my good horse I was enabled after sore labour to attain to a small piece of firm ground in the midst of the mire.

Meantime the lad, whose willingness to guide me had been but an evil device, had fled yet further, and could neither by entreaty nor threat be induced to return. At the last, waxing very wroth, I drew forth my pistol, and would have slain him where he stood, but that I feared if he were dead to be utterly forsaken. And this indeed I was, for after some time the lad seemed to weary of his mirth and my distress, and fled from me with wild gestures and cries, leaving me helpless beside my good horse.

In truth, I knew not what to do, for in the zeal I had had to speak of the things of Zion I had not heeded whither we went. But now I saw that the evening shadows were falling on a great tract of this dismal swamp, which lay as it were in a basin of small low hills. Moreover, the clouds had drawn together, and a low mournful rain began to fall, adding to my danger and perplexity by shutting in my gaze with a wall of mist.

Bidding my good horse be still, I adventured a little way alone, but only to find myself in a yet worse plight, for I trod upon soft moss which seemed to be more than a foot in length, and hid the ground, or rather the marsh. So that finding no footing avail me, I could but lie down and so painfully creep and roll back to my horse again.

In this extremity there was nought left me but to call upon the Lord. And this, indeed, I should have done at the first. In this neglect I surely sinned, even as they do who commit their case to God only when there is nothing to look for from the physicians. Even as they I was altogether in error. The Lord pardon me in this thing.

I had prayed only a very brief space when the veil of mist and rain seemed to lift somewhat, and I could discern the form of a woman coming towards me.

The woman's face I could not see, for she was wrapped in a long hooded mantle, but from the slimness of her form and the lightness of her gait, I judged her to be a young maiden.

And in this I was right, for, as she came closer, I perceived beneath the hood a face so fair

Woe is me! Is it not enough that the first sight of this child of the idolaters held me as if bound by an evil spell? Let it suffice that she came to me in my peril, even as Rebekah came to Elimelech of old, for as surely as Elimelech had died from faintness and the want of water, so surely should I have perished from weariness and from too much water, even the black bog water that lay beneath the treacherous surface of emerald grass, treacherous as the unregenerate hearts of the people of this unhappy land.

CHAPTER IV. from tfje Oiarg of dEtJme 2D'£onttor. HE proclamation of the Usurper fell upon us like a thunderbolt. Since then we have lived in continual suspense, not knowing what any day might bring forth. Weary work it is to wait long for joy, but oh, a thousand times more weary it is to wait for impending sorrow!

In these days this diary has been a solace to me, my pen and ink kind friends with whom I could converse, and return with a lightened heart to the presence of my parents, to cheer my mother's heart with some mirthful tale of the wise doings of the dogs, or of the quaint sayings of Larry Oge, the odd child whom some think to be a fairy changeling, so sprite-like is he; or else I could sing with a steady voice to my father the old songs he loves.

I laugh in my heart—sometimes even loud—as my dear mother ofttimes says with a smile and a sigh—

"Light-hearted Ethne—happy child—nought troubles her!"

So be it, dear mother! and think of your Ethne as one who would fain play the sunbeam's part in this somewhat shadowed home of ours.

But I have forgotten—to-day there is indeed something to chronicle of greater note than the making of gooseberry cakes, or the birth of a foal to beautiful Noreena of the white-starred forehead. Something of great importance, whether for good or for evil I cannot as yet tell; still though fear has of late been the companion of our anxious days and wakeful nights, I am young—ah Heaven! I am yet young enough to hope!

Why not? I am not too young to have seen many a thundercloud hang heavily over our home, while the air grew so still and sultry that to speak or to look up cost an effort almost painful. And I have seen the same cloud drift slowly away to hurst over the hills and the great lake below. If thunderclouds pass, why not troubles?

Ah! but my heart is heavy to-night with the dread of coming evil that drives me to encourage myself, and thereby to encourage others! Let me forget this dread awhile in recording the event of to-day.

The sun had begun to decline when I went forth from my mother's chamber, where I had long sat embroidering fresh hangings, which I trust to give at the Feast of Trinity, to the glory of God for the adorning of the church wherein He is worshipped.

We had long sat silent, though happy in each other's company, in that silent companionship which is passing sweet with one we love, when at last she lifted her head from her spinning to look at me.

"Child, you are pale," she said. "These are sad days for young hearts, and they write their lines on young faces. I would I could shelter you now from the breath of care, my Ethne, as I was wont to shield you from the rough airs of the wintry sky seventeen years ago."

"Dear mother!" I said merrily, for her voice trembled and her eyes grew dim, "dear, dear mother! if wrinkles would but bring me wisdom, would I not climb to the Witch's Cave among our hills at midnight on a moonless Friday and buy from the hag who, they say, dwells there whatsoever potion or lotion might write such lines!"

At that she smiled, and drew me to her to kiss my forehead and call me "saucy child."

"But now I bethink me," she said, "Widow Meara is in sore need of food and physic for her sick boy." And she rose and fetched from her store a phial full of some remedy distilled from herbs by her own wise fingers.

"Take this, darling of my heart," she said, "and make what speed you may to the widow's house. Take food also, as much as you can carry, and bring me news of the child."

So I wrapped my mantle round me, knowing full well that I was sent this errand as much for my own good as for that of the Widow Meara.

Well, it was for the dogs' health too; my father has sat overmuch in his chair of late, and Pierce is absent.

Poor Bran the wolf-hound was wild with joy to run and spring, flying over bank or ditch and returning to challenge me to a race, till his high spirits roused me at last to run merrily down the first hill, followed by all the dogs, big and little, in an ecstasy of delight, down to the little puppy Brian, whose fat body must needs roll over as he ran, in his struggle to keep up with the rest.

So we went on merrily till we came

to the great bog under the hills, and hero we had to walk more circumspectly, for the path is at times formed only of sticks laid lightly upon the treacherous bog, which would swallow any weight laid suddenly upon it, and the dogs knew as well as I that care was needed in this part of our journey.

I had taken but a step or two on this pathway when I saw running along it, lightly and quickly as bare feet can go, Larry Oge, son of Magee the gardener. The boy's grey eyes were dancing with mirth and triumph, and at sight of me he flew to my feet and threw himself kneeling on the ground, claspirjg the hem of my dress.

"What is it, Lawrence?" I asked in his own native Irish.

"He will not trouble us!" cried the lad. "No, he will not trouble us, and I have done it, /. I, who am too young to carry arms and follow Sir Pierce to the wars!"

"Lawrence, what have you done?" I asked, trembling, for he pointed to the wild and dangerous bog, and a chill horror seized me.

"There! there!" he cried, "an enemy! a Saxon soldier; be asked the way to Lara Castle, and thought I would show him; /, who would be hacked to pieces before my mother's eyes sooner than help to wound Sir Gerald's little finger!"

"What have you done?" I repeated, "Done!" he cried; "left him where the bog will swallow him if he tries to move, or hunger will kill him if he stays. He is caught and held like a fly in stirabout, and I have done it, I!"

The boy sprang to his feet and waved his torn cap in delight. Then suddenly he grew quiet.

"What makes you so pale, lady?" he asked anxiously. "Am I pale? It is no wonder, Lawrence; how could you leave a man to die in this dreadful place? Go instantly and guide him back. Hark, is that a cry for help?"

I listened, but there was no sound. Only the oozing of the water beneath our feet, the heavy drone of a wild bee among the heather, the far off cry of a lamb, and the deeper reply of its mother. No human voice.

"Go instantly!" I said again, "and guide him out. Where is he?"

The child turned and pointed to a distance, where I could dimly see the figure of a horse, and a man standing beside him.

"Go instantly, instantly!" I repeated; "do you hear? Go and guide him safely to the Castle, or never come into my sight again."

The boy looked straight in my face with amazed, incredulous eyes. At last he said—

"I never refused before to do as you desired me, lady, and I never will. But now it is not your heart that bids me, it is only your lips, and I'll not obey them only."

"But I mean it! I mean it!" I cried. "Do you think Sir Gerald would let one who was on his way to Lara Castle perish miserably in the bog? I will go back and call for help unless you go at once."

Again the boy looked straight into my eyes. Alas! it may well be that he could read in them terror at the thought that an enemy was so near, for he turned away, saying: "You tell me to go, lady, and I *will* go," and therewith he fled by the way that I had come, never once looking behind or heeding my call, and vanished over the brow of the hill.

Enemy or no enemy, the man who was lost in this place was likely enough to die, if not by hunger then by the bog, and if not by the bog then by the hands of some of our nation, in whose eyes he would be an enemy only perhaps, and not a fellow creature in sore peril. One man only—that was strange, too.

The boy was gone; clearly there was but one duty for me, / must save the man. Quickly therefore I went on, for I knew the path too well to go astray, and it was not long before I came in sight of the unfortunate traveller. A tall man he seemed, and dressed in a strange guise, which however I knew well to be the garb of our foes; and for a moment, as my eye rested upon the buff jerkin, and long boots, and the closely shorn head, my heart grew sick. How could I tell that this very man might not have met in cruel fight, and perhaps have sorely wounded my brother, or maybe some friend of my childhood?— some kinsman of our house? As this thought filled my mind I paused for a moment, and hesitated whether to go on. For so long there has been no news from Pierce, no news from any friend. Day after day we have looked for a letter, or for a message, or for his return. Our enemies are victorious, our forces scattered; others have returned, sorrowful, but at least safe, to comfort their families, and wait to see what fresh hope might spring up. But Pierce is still absent. So for a moment I thought, and then I felt ashamed of such a thought. True, the man was an enemy, but he was in sore peril, and he had asked the way to Lara Castle. So that he was already, as it were, our guest, having claimed our hospitality, and what could be done for him must be done with all possible speed. No time was indeed to be lost As I came nearer I could see that he stood in the most dangerous part of the bog. Clearly he had lost the pathway; and that he had not perished already, was little less than a miracle. For a horse is no light weight, and it needed a strong beast to bear so brawny a rider as this man. Horse and man stood side by side upon a little hillock that stood, or rather floated, on the more perilous and soft ground. The treacherous emerald grass that grows often on this part of the bog had deceived him, and now this firmer island was slowly sinking under the pressure.

He saw me, and turned to me the stern and somewhat worn face of a man past his early youth. Conflicts had left their mark on brow and cheek, and firm resolve had drawn the lips closely together—again I was ashamed to feel a thrill of fear at my heart. In truth, I might well be ashamed to be so selfish and mean of soul.

There was still some little space between mo and the Englishman, the dangerous black mud lay between. A trunk of bog oak rested on the path. I stood on the old grey wood and called to him—
" You cannot stay there," I said, "the ground is sinking beneath you."

A grim smile came upon the rugged face.

"If you have no better tidings for me, maiden," he answered, "you do but waste time and breath,"

"I wasto neither in offering counsel and help," I said, somewhat angry at his speech.

"Counsel were well, but help were better," said the soldier. "Women are ever ready with the first"

"And unable, as you ungallantly would add, to give the last, sir," I said; but no time was to be spent in idle talk, so I addressed myself to the only task that could avail.

Tearing up the purple heather and thick moss, I made bundles of it, and laid them upon the quagmire, as our people do when they desire to make a path over it. He watched me with the same grim smile, and muttered only—

"A causeway of stones were better, but I thank thee, maiden."

At this somewhat ungracious speech I laughed. "Truly," I said, "it was a wise owl that blamed Jupiter for the small size of mice. A wise bird, sir, but not overburdened with courtesy."

And looking up, as I pulled another armful, I saw that he knit his brows in anger. It seemed to me that I had some cause for anger myself; but the ungracious behaviour of a man who stood in such peril provoked me to laughter instead.

"You are merry, lady," said the soldier. "I would I could laugh with you, but I feel rather minded to weep."

"And why, sir?" I asked, pausing a moment in my work, which indeed was not a light task.

"Because I am helpless in your hands—helpless as Sisera in the tent of Jael, as Samson in the hands of Delilah."

Was ever word so uncourteous spoken by a man to a woman who was doing all she could to save his life? I drew myself up; I know that my cheeks glowed more with anger than they were glowing already with toil.

"Pray you, sir," I said, "take heed lest by your unprovoked insults you cause me to feel that my time and strength might be better bestowed than in" and here, fool and weak of heart that I am, my voice broke in a sob. We in Ireland are haply too tender and gentle in speech one to another; we use harsh language neither to man nor beast, therefore hard words smite us in spirit more heavily than hard blows. The lines about the soldier's mouth softened; his tone was changed to a gentleness passing sweet, or so it seemed to me by contrast with his former speech.

"Lady," he said, "I ask your forgiveness."

And I felt, strange as it seems, abashed by his apology, and shamed as though I had complained without cause, or as though one far greater than myself deigned to humble himself before me.

Maurice Burke has often offended me—not by discourtesy, but as playfellows are apt to offend—by overmuch candour, it may be, or by forgetful and scatter-brained behaviour. Maurice has as often prayed my forgiveness, and I have given it, readily for the most part. But never, never have I felt as if Maurice honoured me in the request. He did what he should—no more.

It vexed me to feel thus towards this Englishman, and I worked the harder, till my heart beat fast and my limbs trembled, and I panted a little as I spoke, and asked the soldier to try if the causeway were yet firm enough. "With much caution and some peril he and his horse crossed it at last, and stood by my side on the firmer ground. Then, still holding his horse's bridle, the soldier fell upon his knees, bared his head, and lifted his stern features to the set sky above.

"I thank Thee, Lord," he said aloud, "that I am found worthy to fight Thy battles yet awhile. Enable me henceforth to live for nought but the preaching of Thy Word, and the utter overthrow and destruction of all Thine enemies."

The dull light of the grey sky fell upon his face. I trembled in spite of myself as, with fascinated eyes, I watched the man, who rose slowly and turned to me with the same gloomy look that he had lifted to heaven.

"Thee, too, I thank, maiden," he said, "for the gift of longer toil and suffering. From the sharpness of death to the greater sharpness of life thou hast been God's instrument to bring me back."

"Truly, sir," I said, "you have little reason to thank me, if death be to your mind so much sweeter than life."

"To depart is far better," he answered sternly. "They are reprobate who confess not that."

"But—but life is a good gift of God," I said; not seeking to argue, but feeling compelled to protest against the thought that life is not worth enjoying. For truly I have found it sweet. "God called the world ' very good;' are we not to love to be in it? Though we have troubles enough too," I said with a sigh, thinking of the near past and the anxious present.

"He hath set the world in their heart: ay, men will love it, and forget that it was only before sin had entered in—by the folly of a woman and the weakness of a man who listened to her voice—that the world was called good."

Again my cheeks burned to hear women spoken of with such scorn I remembered the teaching of the guide of my childhood, Father Ambrose. "Ay, sir," I said, somewhat hotly it may be, "and the Redemption of the world came by a woman too, even Mary, the mother of God, whom all generations shall call blessed. Now, I pray you, follow me to Lara Castle, and let me sustain the life I have been permitted to preserve."

The soldier's face was stern and impassive enough, as I have said; but for one moment, when he asked my pardon for his discourtesy, it softened strangely. And now again it changed to an expression I could not read, for a moment. Then, fixing upon me a keen glance from his brown eyes, that glowed under their dark brows with the fire of indomitable purpose and courage, he answered—

"I thank you, Mistress O'Connor, if such be your name."

"Such is my name," I said, "but one thing I have forgotten. Will it please you, sir, to wait a few moments while I carry some medicine to a sick child close at hand?"

Again he shot a keen glance at me, a glance which seemed to reach my very soul, and search there for treachery. I answered the look by words.

"You think I am going to gather enemies against you," I said. "You know not Irish hospitality, sir."

"An errand of death or life?" he muttered to himself. "As it is written and predestined, so it will be." Then to me—

"I will wait your pleasure here, lady, as you desire."

I turned, and went on my errand. And, having discharged it, I returned to find the soldier leaning against his horse in the place where I had left him, and bending his stern brow over a book which had the appearance of having been much used and worn, and which he put carefully into the breast of his jerkin as I came near. So it is that I have led him in safety back to Lara Castle, where he has been received as a guest should, and is resting now before the summons to supper. And I, as I write, am longing, yet fearing, to see him face to face with my father. He was on his way to Lara Castle, this Englishman. I have but enabled him to accomplish his mission, whatever it may be. All good angels be about us! for my heart is very heavy, and yet I know not why. Maybe I am but tired in body with the excitement and effort of this strange meeting. I will kneel to Mary Mother, the Star of the Sea, that her peace may be upon my troubled heart.

LAID down my pen a few hours since. Now in the silence of the moonlit night—sleep being far from me—after long wrestling in prayer, I take it up again. Truly I am tempted to think our task even harder than that of the chosen people, who fought with and destroyed nations hateful in the sight of God and man, being without natural affection, hardened, and utterly abominable.

But I, led by the fair maiden Ethne to her father's house —nay, to mine own house, though now I feel as if I were but a robber and spoiler, weak-hearted that I am—I, thus led to the dwelling of Gerald O'Connor, have found myself met by more than courtesy, by kindness and loving welcome, almost as though I had come to the house of some friend of my youth in mine own village of Oldbury-on-Severn. Folly and vanity I know it to be. Lord, let not their precious balms break mine head; I will pray yet against their wickedness, which clothes itself in fair hues, as Satan doth clothe himself in the garb of an angel of light. Let the righteous rather smite me friendly and reprove me, as Isaiah Heston, that faithful man of God, hath not failed to do.

Let my sin be forgiven, moreover, in that I was wroth at his coming, and wroth also at his reproving me. For my shame I must write the record of tins evening's doings, excusing not myself, but simply setting down in order all things as they happened.

The man Gerald O'Connor welcomed me, then, as though I had been his friend or his brother. The best room in his house was set apart for me, wine was brought, fire kindled, and fresh raiment offered in place of my travel-stained gear. And when the hour of supper was come, a page sought me and led me into the hall, where the master and the mistress, and Ethne their daughter, rose to greet me.

I am not a man to take delight in the vain pomp of silken raiment and hangings, of soft cushions and delicate food; I will but say that all these were here in decent order rather than wanton profusion. I learn that by reason of much intercourse with France, silken stuffs, and the wines, the dried fruits and the sweetmeats of that country abound in this land far more than in my own, where I trust all friendship between our people and the French, who gave a wife to Charles Stuart, and whose influence is all towards folly and vanity... all friendship, I trust, will shortly cease and be forgotten. But here the influence of France must needs be strong, when the priests, the teachers of the people, have for the most part been trained in her colleges to all those arts whereby they draw souls to destruction, learning all the vain wisdom of the world, and ignorant of that salvation which is wrought by the foolishness of preaching. Such a one sat with the family at supper, an old man with keen eyes, that left no word nor look of mine unnoticed.

For Master O'Connor, whom the vain world calls Sir Gerald, he too is aged and stately, and his wife a woman of a sweet and gracious countenance, and wise and grave of speech also.

Such a woman, methinks, must Deborah the wife of Lapidoth have been, one in whom increase of years hath wrought increase of wisdom, one meet to be called a mother in Israel. Alas, that such a one should be in the gall of bitterness and bond of iniquity! Alas, that the graciousness of speech and kindliness of deed of these idolaters should be but as the whitening of a sepulchre or the gilding of a false image!

Methought their greetings and welcomings of me their guest were harder to bear than stripes; methought their dainty food, which they pressed upon me, was harder to swallow than the most nauseous drugs of the apothecary. For I could not bring my mind to break to them the cause of my coming, at the moment when my life had been saved and again sustained by them.

"Not to-night; not to-night. It is a little time only till the morrow; let them once again rest in peace," I said in my heart, not considering the sin of Saul, who would spare Agag the Amalekite.

The old priest prayed a blessing upon the food, moreover, with the superstitious sign of the cross, which was imitated by all, the maiden Ethne glancing at me in wonder and reproach, as I stood erect and lifted up my heart to God without vain gesture, as is meet and right.

For the talk, it was hard to pursue, and oftentimes a painful silence fell. For of the things of Zion, of which we that fear the Lord would fain speak often one to another, I could not venture to talk with these darkened souls, without laying before them the whole plan of salvation, and showing to the priest his own dark and hopeless errors; and of the state of the land, or of the war, it was yet harder there and then to speak freely.

Of the nature of the dangerous soil, therefore, in which I had all but perished, we discoursed, and of the works of Master William Shakespeare, the great playwright of the day of our noble Queen Elizabeth, whose works I studied with much delight in my unregenerate youth, and do yet remember with some pleasure, and haply even some profit, though I must needs deem them now carnal and unfit to nourish the soul.

Every now and then, as I have said, a silence fell, and the women would look at me with eyes full of question and entreaty, as though they would fain ask something of the welfare of some they loved from me, the foeman in battle of those friends of theirs; or it may be they longed to know the purport of my coming.

Before the meal had ended there came a loud knocking at the outer door, loud and imperious. The two noble hounds, of a race that we in England know not, built for speed and strength, with sharp muzzle and smooth hair—these great dogs rose up, and growled with a low and deep growl, as though ready to make short work of any unwelcome intruder. In truth, he whom they thus encountered would surely repent himself, were he not well and fully armed.

A servant rose from the end of the hall, and looked to his lord for orders.

"Go, I pray you, good Terence," said the master of the house, and the menial obeyed.

It may be that Sir Gerald noted the look of wonder in my face, and truly I felt surprised, being unused to hear such courtesy towards a humble retainer from the lips of nobles, who in mine own country count themselves better than their fellow-worms, as though, forsooth, their Maker had taken another and better patch of the clay of Eden wherefrom to form their forefather.

"Go! and he goeth," is the rule among ourselves in the army. "Go, churl! Go, dog!" I have often enough heard said by the long-locked and foolishly apparelled followers of the man Charles Stuart, who fail to remember that they themselves came naked into the world, and naked must depart thence, and pride themselves on their fine feathers, as though, forsooth, these grow upon their backs.

"We have been accustomed to use courtesy towards those who serve us," said Sir Gerald. "We know nought here of your feudal system of serfs and villeins. Our retainers feel themselves to be of like flesh and blood with ourselves."

"Yet you disdain not to be addressed by them with vain and foolish titles of rank," I said sharply.

"Ay," he answered, "there are degrees of men, even as there are degrees among the holy angels. And was not one St. James called 'the Less'?"

"Of the angels some may be captains," I said, perceiving, as it were, the hem of her garment who is the Scarlet Woman, full of errors and deceits. "To *departed* believers alone we give not the name of saints; all they that are the elect are saints, there is none greater or less among the sheep of a flock."

Here Terence returned with a face flushed and wrathful.

"There is one outside," said he, "who had e'en best stay there;" and as he spoke a greater knocking and loud shouting without made the dogs spring np, and rush furiously barking from the room.

"You have dared to leave one outside who craves my hospitality!" cried Sir Gerald, starting up. "Now, by Mary, our Lady"

"In truth, it is as I say," repeated Terence, as his lord paused for fit words wherein to clothe his anger, "an unmannerly churl stands there without; shame forbid that I should repeat his foul words!" And Terence spat on the rushes that strewed the floor, as though he would rid himself of the evil taste of the words that had displeased him.

Whether his lord would have seen cause for reproof in so unseemly an act I cannot guess, for a wild storm of wind flung wide the door, extinguishing more than one of the lights, and scattering the rashes in every direction. And with the storm entered my friend and companion, Isaiah Heston, as if clothed in the whirlwind.

"I will not be stopped, I say!" he cried. "Dogs! churls! ye would shut me out! But I tell you I must and will enter. I will have access to the master of this house. Where is he?"

As he spoke, Isaiah strode into the centre of the room. His eyes seemed dazzled by the lighted room, for outside the wild wet night was dark as an unregenerate heart He looked rou d thus as if bewildered, and Sir Gerald O'Connor stepped forward.

"I am the master of this house—I, Gerald O'Connor. What would you?"

He spoke with no passion, but with a low deep tone, as of one who might be roused, and that to some purpose, if provoked too far, but who for the present was ruling his own spirit with a firm hand.

"Thou!" said Isaiah Heston, viewing the speaker from head to foot with scorn plainly written in his face. "Thou—thou Philistine!"

Now Isaiah Heston is short of stature and uncomely of face, and he stood before the man Gerald O'Connor, who is a mighty man and of noble bearing, even as David before the Philistine, Goliath of Gath. But to say the truth the comparison was not a happy one,—here the comeliness was all on the side of the Philistine, for Isaiah can boast of no beauty save that of holiness.

"Thou Philistine!" said Isaiah therefore; but scarcely had the words left his lips before he lay at the feet of Sir Gerald even as one dead, felled by a blow that might well have availed to strike down an ox.

I looked that the women would have shrieked aloud, as is the wont of these frail natures, but only the maidservants shrank back somewhat; the Lady O'Connor and

D

Etlme, her daughter, stood their ground, albeit pale of *face*. As for Sir Gerald—the man Gerald, I would say—he stood over his fallen foe and looked down upon him for a moment, then he turned him to me, and in a voice low and deep, as of distant thunder that will presently grow to a great storm, he asked, " Who, and what is this man?"

Now in my own heart I felt greatly reproved. For had I at once declared my purpose in coming, this proud spirit might have already been bowed to the Lord's decree, and so painful a scene have been averted. For I have often found it that if we do not the Lord's bidding at once, and gladly, we must yet do it in the end, and oftentimes with greater difficulty and much sorrow of heart. And thus it was now with me, as I opened my mouth and spake.

"Sir Gerald O'Connor, as men use to call you," I said, for it seemed but natural to render this title to so princely a man, vain as I knew such terms to be, "this man is my comrade-in-arms, Isaiah Heston, a lieutenant in the army of the Commons, as I am captain, to whom the lands of the family of Burke are appointed in the new plantation of this country."

There was silence—a silence so deep that the heavy breathing of Isaiah Heston, to whom consciousness was slowly returning, sounded painfully loud.

Then Sir Gerald spoke.

"Hitherto I have not asked your name, sir. Our manner of hospitality withheld me. But now I would hear it, and your purpose here."

And as I answered, mine own voice sounded in mine ears more rough and stern than is usual even to me.

"I am Roger Standfast-on-the-Rock, Captain in the army of the Commons of England. By the will of Jehovah, after solemn seeking of His face in prayer, Lara Castle and the lands thereof have been appointed as my portion."

Again there was silence. The women's faces waxed, it may be, even more pale. The Lady O'Connor looked straight before her, as one that looks and yet sees not. The maiden Ethne lifted her eyes and looked upon me with a sad and pleading gaze, which some might find hard to bear. But I set my face steadfastly, hardening my heart from aught that might oppose His will, who hath arisen to break this nation as a potter's vessel, saying as by the mouth of the prophet of old, "I will overturn, overturn, overturn it."

"Master Standfast-on-the-Kock, if that be indeed your name," said at last Sir Gerald, "this house and all my lands are yours, by law, which is the will of the strongest. Enter therefore upon your inheritance when it shall please you; but beware how you name the Most Holy Name as a sanction to robbery and violence."

He spoke with a lofty dignity as of a dethroned prince, and my heart burned with anger that had—alas for my frail heart!—a touch of compassion in it. So that these two feelings strove one with another, and caused me to answer yet more harshly—

"Because the sins of this nation have risen up before the Lord as the iniquity of Sodom, even idle and vain delights, mirth and strong drink, and the worship of her who is throned upon the seven hills—because of these, and of the evil and cruel slaughter of many of His saints in the rising of Sir Phelim O'Neill, He hath brought in this army, under His chief captain Oliver, that we may occupy it as a peculiar people, chosen for His glory."

"We are then Amalekites?" said Sir Gerald calmly. "And yet my neighbour Burke, whom this—this saint," said he, looking upon the yet prostrate Isaiah, " hath disinherited, his parentage is English, his forefathers were De Burgs, and came from France with the Conqueror to possess England, even as you come hither now. His lands here were a free gift from our gracious Elizabeth in consideration of his services to her. Well, well, it may be that our sins have been many, but it seems to us that we are as the bear, whose greatest crime is to have a hide that the merchant desires."

I would have answered again, being grieved at his hardness of heart, as also at this light consideration of the judgments of God. Also I would have said that we English must esteem of ourselves as the ancient Israel, to whom the promised land was not given because of their unrighteousness, for they were a stiShecked nation. From which reproach may the Lord save His Israel of England. But I had not time to answer, for Sir Gerald spoke again.

"With your leave, Master Standfast, I would give one more command in this house;" and to the servants he said — " Raise this man, lay him on the couch, and fetch wine."

His command was obeyed; but methought as Terence loosened Isaiah's jerkin, he looked as though he would more gladly have strangled him where he lay.

The ladies themselves brought perfumes, and paid what attention they could to the sufferer, who shortly came to himself and sat up. Whereupon Sir Gerald bade all retire, and himself went also, so that Isaiah Heston and I were left alone in the great hall, dimly lighted by the scented and glowing fire of turf, and by other such lights as had not been blown out in the rush of air that entered with Isaiah. Without, the wind howled dismally round the house, calling to my mind, as it rose now and then to a wild shriek, those Irish tales of Banshees, that wail through the darkness when death or some misfortune is about to fall upon the family.

Isaiah Heston, being now a little revived, told me of his journey, and how, having arrived at the house of Master Burke, he had been refused entrance, the inmates doubtless suspecting his purpose, and how he could only have forced an entrance at peril of his life, which he was not willing to do. For life is doubtless as a talent committed to our charge, and is neither to be heedlessly thrown away nor to be idly spent. He therefore retired, and sought me at Lara Castle, as I have related.

Thereafter did this man of God truly and faithfully deal with me for the good of my soul. Even as Paul, when Peter was come to Antioch, withstood him to the face, because he was to be blamed, so did Isaiah Heston upbraid me with the same sin as that of Peter, namely, want of uprightness in my way, because that I had suffered myself to appear other than I was in the eyes of the O'Connor family, and that out of a cowardice of spirit, as displeasing in the sight of the Lord as that cowardico of the body whereof even a heathen soldier is ashamed. Being conscious of error, I therefore accepted his rebuke in all meekness, as it is written, "Let the righteous smite me friendly and reprove me."

Lara Castle stands in a valley, as is usual with Irish houses of the better sort. But around it are gentle wooded hills, and fair lakes, in which these mirror themselves, and gardens full of flowers and herbs of many sorts, with fertile fields beyond. As I look from my sleeping chamber over the calm lake that lies under the great hill, like a little child asleep at the feet of a strong man, and the gardens and fair fields, I have cause to rejoice in my portion. If, as it seems to-night, my heart is not filled with thankfulness and holy joy, surely I only am to blame, and must own myself hard and cold of heart. For never in my sleep during the past years of continual war, while lying on the hard ground by our camp fire, have I dreamed of a fairer home than this, as the end and reward of all my labour and peril. The lot is fallen unto me in a fair ground, yea, I have a goodly heritage.

CHAPTER VL JFtom tfje ffiiatn of Ct&ne SD'Connor. OME of the days of our life pass quickly, for when we are happy we do not heed the waxing and waning of the shadows. I have often risen early, and gone to rest when the moon was shining, and yet have thought the day all too short, because some beautiful piece of tapestry was growing under my hand, or else because I was sailing on the lake, or wandering far afield with my brother and Maurice Burke. But lately we have spent sad days enough, and I have often lifted my eyes from my work and dropped them, and lifted them again, and once more looked sadly down upon my embroidery, because the shadow on the dial seemed scarcely to have moved, so heavily went the hours.

And yet on glad days and sad days alike falls the evening—they are, after all, of the same length; and God is gracious to us in this, that darkness and quiet return continually, so that we may be made strong to endure sorrow, and renewed also lest we might bo weary of joy.

In our present sad case, if at night we do not sleep, we may at least be still, and be freed from the effort of maintaining our cheerfulness for one another's sake through the hours of the day. For though, as I said, the days pass heavily, yet they pass but too quickly. The earth has put on her festal autumn dress, as in other years, as a proud captive who would appear in state before her conqueror King Winter, though only to be stripped of her gay apparel and bound with his frost-chains.

Her conqueror, I said; but I love winter too, and the stillness of the clear air and silent brooks. The white mantle which he lays over the earth is not a shroud, but only a coverlet She sleeps only—she will do well. And with returning spring our flowers and song-birds seem all the fairer and pleasanter to us because Nature, like a wise and kind nurse, has put them out of our sight for a while.

So autumn has come and is passing, and winter will come and will pass, as all things come to us and then pass away. And we wait, holding our breath almost, for the day that shall declare our doom and drive us across the Shannon to the wild and desolate region of Connaught, where we are henceforth to dwell with all who cannot prove that by overt acts during the late war they have showed " a constant good affection "—so runs the decree— to the cause of England. I am only a girl; these matters are beyond my understanding. But my father and the rest were faithful to Charles the King of England, whom his subjects have overthrown and put to death. Now we are held to be traitors to England; but are we not only against those who are themselves traitors?

It is said the King was a tyrant, and that his head fell justly; ot that I know little. But my father holds that all who have reigned in England have alike dealt hardly with Ireland, whether it were Sir Edward Poynings under Henry VUL, or Essex under Elizabeth, or"Wentworth, Earl of Strafford, under King Charles, whose plan of "Thorough," had it been carried out, boded little good to any save Protestants and English of his own planting, but to whom we owe the new and prosperous manufacture of linen in the northern parts, and therefore some gratitude. So that it would seem that we are as the earthen pot that swam the stream with the brazen kettle: whatever betide, Ireland must needs suffer for the good of the stronger.

Captain Roger Standfast says that our sins have provoked the anger of God, for that we—that is, our men-folk — have lived recklessly, feasting and hunting, and being always turbulent and unruly.

English colonies have settled over and over, and ever afresh in this country, since the first coming of Strongbow. They planted for themselves the Pale on the east coast, being a strip of land above and below Dublin, bounded by the Boyne and the Barrow, and strengthened between these rivers by four castles. But they spread continually into the country, married with Irish women, and learned to love the dear green island. Ah! how could they do otherwise? For myself I have never left it; but Mauriade Burke, who has travelled, says that nowhere has the sunshine so soft and sweet a light, as though a lovely face smiled through its tears. And I think she speaks truth. I hope so.

Those English who came hither—my mother's parents among them—became children of the country before many years had passed. Their young men spoke the soft flowing Irish, and delighted to wear the coolun in place of clipping the hair Nature had given them; and the saffron shirt, the badge of an Irishman. They loved our songs and dances, our games of hurling with a stick and ball, and of throwing the quoit, and heeded not the English command to follow rather the "gentlemanlike games" of war, as tourneys and such encounters. So that Giraldus, the Welshman, who, it is true, bore little love to the English, but held them to be men alike churlish and serfish, spoke of those who came to our Ireland as becoming degenerate like those who had drunk of Circe's cup, and as taking so entirely to our manner of life that they ceased to find pleasure in their own.

And this the English themselves seem to have understood, for they found that those who were established here threw off the feudal yoke, and would not, except under compulsion, render to their liege lord the King those moneys which were due as escheats, forfeitures, marriages, and what not, none of which were known among our freer customs. They, therefore, so early as when Edward III. was king, made it high treason to take any Irish woman to wife, and a horrible and lingering death was the appointed punishment of any who should do so.

Now at last, and once for all, it is to be done thoroughly and for ever. All Irish or English-Irish who are not driven into banishment are to be penned up behind the Shannon, and there shut in, being guarded on the side of the sea by a line, four miles wide, of English soldiery disbanded and settled.

And we among the rest must leave our home, our dear home. I think truly that in this world we can only have one home. We may have dwelling-places, few or many, but there will surely be only one little spot of earth dearer to us than any other—one *home.*

The graves of some of our dear ones are here; those of my grandparents are under the great beech beside the church, and my sweet baby-sister Devorgil sleeps beside them. I know that beech in sunshine and moonlight, in the fresh green of spring and the russet of antumn. I love every leaf of it. And I shall never see it again! And if even at seventeen I feel thus, what must the parting be to my father and mother, whose hearts have twined tendrils of love round every stick and stone of the old home, where he grew to manhood and she came as a happy bride, where their children were born, and they themselves have grown old?

My mother grieves in secret, I know it. But she sits with her Book of Hours open before her, and speaks no word of complaint. My father flashes at times into anger, and I am glad, for to bear his grief always in silence would be strange and unnatural.

As for Captain Standfast-on-the-Rock, the stern Puritan to whom all joy partakes of the nature of sin, as he himself says, he has certainly shown ua much consideration, I had almost Baid kindness, but that his stern and harsh utterances seem to exclude such a word from one's thoughts of him. After the purpose of his coming had been so rudely disclosed to us by Isaiah Heston, who, to our great thankfulness, departed early on the next day, Captain Standfast declared to my father his willingness that we should, if he so chose, inhabit the stables and offices of the house. I almost wonder now, as I think of it, that my father did not there and then fall upon Captain Standfast and do him grievous hurt. It must have been by a great effort, and in consideration of our helpless condition, that he restrained himself. The veins upon his forehead swelled, and his eyes flashed like a bright sword, as he answered in that low deep voice which is in him a sign of great anger, "I will not stoop to accept any, even the slightest, favour from you, sir," and strode from the room. My mother and I followed, and represented to him that neither home nor money was left us till land should be appointed us in Connaught, and that to cosher1 upon the tenantry, though they would gladly give us a share of their last oaten cake, would be as humbling to his pride, and yet more selfish, since we were justified in retaining some portion of our possessions till our final settlement should be made.

It was a hard matter to persuade him; and to induce him to speak himself to the Englishman and accept his offer would hardly have been possible, but we wrung from him at last permission that I should go to the officer 1 Cosher—to live upon the means of others. and declare our willingness to accept his kindness, which, with a heart that beat very fast, I did at once, clothing what I had to say in language as humble as I could bring myself to use. He did not for the moment reply, but stood looking at me from under his black brows, so that I felt the colour rise in my face, and I said hastily—

"That is if you have not yet repented of your offer, sir."

"It is written,' Let your yea be yea, and your nay, nay,' maiden," he answered, in his harshest tones, so that the words of thankfulness for his kindness died upon my lips, and I could but turn away with a formal courtesy, which he returned with yet colder formality.

Since then we have dwelt in the offices formerly used by grooms and servants, those who still cling to us having found holes and corners wherein to sleep, and serving us with a devotion and respect not diminished in the least particular by our misfortunes and our poverty, refusing to leave us, although we see little prospect of being able to repay them for their services.

"Pay us in love, then," said Terence, when my father, with faltering voice, reminded him of this. And indeed if love can profit them, the poor souls have all that our sad hearts can give, and perhaps that is not without value, for I remember a sacred verse which I once worked in some hanging for our church—" If a man would give all the substance of his house for love, it should utterly be despised." CHAPTER VII.

JFrom tjje Diarg of ®tfjnc ©'-Connor.

J HE days have passed, as I said, slowly, yet all too fast. We pined for news of my brother Pierce, but the weeks passed and no news came; nor had we any means of sending for tidings of his welfare, since we knew not where he was, but could only conjecture that, if alive and well, he, like many more, was biding in hopes of some turn in the tide of our misfortunes, which might enable him to take up arms again and strike even yet a blow for our dear country.

As for the Puritan captain, he returned to his duty, and through the winter days we dwelt in the offices of Lara Castle, the house itself being empty, but receiving now and again some officer of Cromwell's army who chanced to pass by. We ourselves have never entered it since the day we went forth—our servants have fetched for us such things as we required; and I could have wished that the time were come for us to transplant into Connaught, so heart-sickening has been our state.

Lately the captain returned, and came shortly afterwards to visit us. My father was sitting in his arm-chair by the glowing fire of turf which I always keep in these chill damp days. There is some art in the building of a turf fire too, and I pride myself on excelling in it. The sods must not merely be heaped together, but built up in such a way that the air shall have free course between them; then a little fanning, and one has a rich warm glow which I am sure the black English coal cannot rival, besides the pleasant scent that is peculiar to the turf, which to us seems delicious. The servants are vexed to see me do such menial work, but I tell them it is time I should set my hand to harder tasks than those light and pleasant duties of spinning, embroidering, distilling, and making of cakes and preserves. Therefore I let no one but myself tend our fire now, and on this chilly afternoon of early spring of which I write, I came to my father's side and made a brighter glow. Outside a soft slow rain was falling, as it had been for days past, as though the very heavens wept over poor Eire and her misfortunes. My mother sat by the window looking out into the paved courtyard where our gallant horses used to be led out, but where now the grass is springing green between the stones. Nature takes back so gladly to her own care any spot of ground that man has made his own, but ceases to tend. If our castle here were left empty, in a few years she would twine greenery about the mouldering ruin, doing all she could to hide it.

Our good horses have been sold to furnish us with the necessaries of life until our transplantation. My father cannot bear to look much into the courtyard; he was therefore sitting, when I went to tend the fire, with his eyes on the smouldering ashes. I think the hearts of Irishmen are like their own turf. They brood silently over their wrongs; and as in the turf one sees but cool grey ashes, while at the core is fire, so it is with them. But blow on the turf, or rouse the burning heart, and you have a flame so sudden and vehement that a stranger is amazed who judged from the outward appearance only.

I knelt by my father's side and laid my head against him. He stroked my hair lovingly, but spoke not, and only heaved an impatient sigh.

"Father," I said, "shall I fetch Malachy?"

"Ay, do, child," he answered, with another sigh, but he lifted his head and shook his shoulders as one who would shake off a heavy mood. And I went out and found the old blind harper Malachy, and brought him in to cheer my father by his music.

Malachy is a very old man. His beard is white and long; his sightless eyes have given to his face that strangely patient look which is peculiar to the faces of the blind—a look not merely sad, but patient, and, as it were, a waiting look, as though when sight should be at last given, the thing to be seen should surpass all human hope or dream. In his hand he held the old harp—

"Whose rusty metal Sounds like the patching of a kettle," as some English doggerel scribe has written—so Pierce, my brother, angrily says—certainly knowing nothing of the soft melody which hands as skilled as Malachy's can draw from it.

Malachy sat down and tuned his old harp thoughtfully, then swept his hand across the strings, as if consulting them what manner of music they were minded to give forth. But before he had fixed upon any tune, one of the servants entered, saying that Captain Standfast, as they use to call the English officer, was below, and asked leave to enter.

"Why should he waste breath in asking leave?" demanded my father over his shoulder, and I translated his answer into a courteous message—" Go bid him be welcome, good Terence;" and Terence went, making a wry face with that wide mouth of his, as though the word welcome were very hard to utter to the Englishman.

The Puritan soldier entered immediately. He has striven diligently to harden his lips against a smile; but I thought there was a kind look in his earnest eyes as he asked in his grave and formal way how we did. My father shook his shoulders and gave a blunt answer, as though to remind the Englishman that it was by reason of him and his comrades that none of us had at present much welfare in life. My mother hastily took up the word, and said that we were grateful for his kindness, which had in great measure tempered our sufferings, and that we all were well in a measure.

"Whatever be our lot in life, we must not look to be without suffering, lady," said the Captain, and his tone had reproof in it, as though she were a fractious child, whose rebellious spirit needed to be checked.

"I know it," my mother answered. "We must suffer till we are purged of our sins. I hope these sorrows of ours, which are indeed heavy, and, as it seems to us, undeserved, may avail to lessen the trial by fire through which we must pass after this life."

My mother sighed as she spoke, and I shuddered, for my spirit always quails before the thought that after the anguish of death this unknown but awful suffering awaits us, of which we know not the end nor the sharpness.

But over the pale stern face of the officer there came a light as of another world, and he spoke eagerly.

"There is therefore now no condemnation!" he cried. M Once, once for all, the Lamb of God took away the sins of the world! Look unto Him, and be ye saved, all the ends of the earth. Cast away that terrible superstition, lady, and believe on Him who died and rose again. Henceforth all your sin is forgiven; you are free, accepted."

I looked anxiously at my mother. This was not the doctrine I had learned at her knee. But I thought if the dread of that awful Purgatory were taken away, it would be as though a great stone were rolled off all our hearts. But she answered almost sharply—

"You Puritans call yourselves saiuts, sir. I confess myself a sinner, whose feet are daily stained by sin."

"Even so," said the Puritan; "he that is washed must yet wash his feet. You have spoken justly. But Christ is all in all. See, I will choose a most humble comparison from our daily life. We have the figure One, that is, as Christ. Bring nought to that One, you have ten; bring nought again, you have a hundred. So bring your nought, your vileness and wretchedness, to Christ, and He will multiply it a thousandfold. The more you bring, the more you will have!"

My mother looked up for a moment in surprise at the eager speech of one generally so reserved and silent. Then she bit her lips, and I saw that she repressed the answer that rose to them. As to my father, he frowned, and traced letters with his stick among the ashes, while old Malachy felt for the rosary at his girdle and began to tell the beads, as if to guard himself from the heresy which might endanger his soul.

Every word of this scene seems imprinted on my mind. I must ask Father Ambrose for counsel in my next confession, for my mind is strangely troubled by the thoughts the English captain's words have raised.

"Sing to us, Malachy," said my father abruptly; then, his native courtesy regaining its power, he added to our guest, " with your permission, sir."

The Puritan bowed, and looked expectantly towards Malachy, who made no pause, but vehemently struck his harp and broke out into the wail of the nurse of an ancient chieftain who was slain by English hands—a song full of bitter reproach and curses heaped upon the Sassenach.

My mother's face grew pale, my own, I know, was crimson, and we both looked anxiously towards the Englishman, who only looked steadfastly at the harper, though it may well be that his brow darkened.

"Malachy, be silent!" commanded my father; but it was not till the command was repeated, and more wrathfully, that Malachy would obey, and changed his song. Then he broke out again into the Drinan Dhun—

"Curse upon the Sassenach! joy bless them never,
The hearthstone of hell he their pillow for ever!"
he sang J and when he must at last and perforce be silent, he still played softly the wild passionate music which belongs to the words.

"I ask your pardon for my servant's offence, sir," said my father to Captain Standfast, who answered—

"Not for any ofience against me is there need of repentance, but such songs of wrath and strife are little fit for the house of a Christian man, where only the songs of Zion should be heard."

"I know no song of Zion, sir, wheresoever that land may be," answered Malachy, for the officer's face was turned towards him as he spoke. "But I will sing a song of Erin, which may chance to please you better." So tuning his harp again, he sang of the days that are now gone. He sang of the ancient Milesians wandering free upon their green hills, building their frail booths roofed with sods wherever their cattle found good pasture. He sang of the Brehons who kept the law, in which were no cruel deaths, lingering and full of nameless horrors as in England, but an eric paid in money to the families of the wronged. Of the meetings on a hill-top, where the tribes would gather from far and near under their chiefs, and the aged Brehons would draw forth the roll of the law and give true and just judgment. Of the records of the Four Masters also, and the old times when the fairies danced everywhere in the green fields, before the sound of war and the desolation following after drove them into a few quiet places, where they may still dwell, loved and

E yet feared by us, who are careful to call them the Good People always, for their anger is dangerous, and their favour uncertain. He sang of the ships that came from France and Spain to take our grain, our cattle and our high-spirited horses, and to bring us silk and wine; of the fair port of Galway, and the busy southern towns. He sang of Patricius the monk, whose heart became so fast bound to the island to which he had come as a slave, that all his desire was to return and preach the Gospel to the people whom he loved. How they received him gladly and obeyed his word, being convinced by the sacred emblem of the shamrock which he plucked, that the Divine Glory might be of Three and yet of One. How that Ireland was known as the Isle ot Saints, and sent forth apostles into other lands to carry the light in which her sons rejoiced— those men with hearts as bulls, to their foes as fierce, but to friend or woman tender as thrushes.

All this Malachy sang in English, and to a simple and flowing melody. Then his face suddenly kindled—he broke into his native tongue, which we knew well, but which our guest could not understand; and the tone of his harp changed too into a wild minor key, full of strange harmonies and clashing discords. And thus he sang of the English—how they came over as adventurers, and saw the island and found it fair; and how the hunger for land, which is sharp and strong in them, moved them to come again and yet again, and settle among the people, who welcomed them, and married with them. Till presently the newcomers looked darkly upon the old, and because there was not fresh land enough to possess, desired the land of those who had gone before. And so, because they would have semblance of right in their robberies, they goaded the others to madness, and wrote their unjust decrees in books, and called them laws, and called the revolt of those on whom they were thus imposed sedition and rebellion. Yes; and when they saw cause to change their faith, would have us change ours also; and when they were displeased with their king, cast him off, and called those of us who were true and faithful to him rebels and traitors. Always, always, they proclaimed loudly the crimes of those whom they thus goaded to madness, all the while cloaking their own cruelty and falsehood and tyranny. Until now at last

But at that word a harpstring snapped suddenly, the song ceased, and a shiver passed over me; for it was as though the singer's heart broke under the burden of the unspeakable sorrow.

Malachy set down his harp at once, buried his aged face in his wrinkled hands, and gave way to a passion of tears, so vehement that it seemed as though his worn frame could scarcely endure it. As for me, the tears coursed down my cheeks too, and I turned away to the window, for I would not willingly let the English officer see a weakness which he would surely despise.

Therefore I do not know how he

looked. But though he could not understand the Irish tongue, I think a word here and there, and the wild tone of lament, must have taught him something of its meaning. However, before any of us had spoken, there was a sound on the stairs, and before we well knew what was passing, my brother Pierce stood among us. It was as if he came from the dead, for we had had no tidings of him for all these weary months. But all joy in meeting us again seemed in him to be swallowed up by anger at the plight in which he found us, so that he stood silent and dismayed, looking from one to another.

"And you can calmly sit down here, and be content with this—*this*? Father, I would never have believed it!" he cried at last.

Pierce looked ten years older than when last we saw him. He was but a boy, too young to bear arms when Sir Phelim O'Neill rose, having, as it was supposed, received encouragement to do so by learning from the Duke of Buckingham of the King's design with regard to the Irish army. But he was with the garrison at Newry, three years ago, when Cromwell took that town, and we knew not even for certain that he was not languishing as a prisoner of war, or that he had not perished in the ensuing slaughter, when even the women and the innocent children perished in great numbers.

It seemed as if many years must have rolled over Pierce's head to make him look so careworn, so hollow in the cheeks, so sunken about the eyes. But a few days of misery will sometimes do the work of years; and besides, my brother's neglected locks, and stained and worn clothing, that had once been handsome, but was now fit only to give to the poorest beggar, showed but too well what he must have gone through.

They were a strange contrast—the victor and the vanquished—as they stood eyeing one another, for the English officer had risen, and stood tall and straight before Pierce, with his buff jerkin and jackboots, his plain collar replacing Pierce's costly but now tattered lace, and his hair smoothly cropped in that fashion which has earned for the party of Cromwell the name of Roundheads, and that stern set face of his, at which I look sometimes and wonder if it ever had the soft outlines and smiling mouth of a little child, or whether Captain Standfast must not have come like Adam, already a grown man, into this world.

"Who are you?" said Pierce, as my father made no audible answer, but only a murmur. He looked with burning eyes at the officer, but before he could answer my mother made haste to interpose.

"Pierce, this is the officer to whom our lands have been given. It is only by his kindness that we still dwell here."

"Here!" echoed Pierce. "By *his kindness* that you are allowed to be menials in your own outhouses, dogs in your own dog-kennels! You call that kindness! Why, it would have been better kindness to throw you all into the lake below—death is better than insult!" And as he ended he looked at the Englishman with utter scorn from head to foot, and from foot to head again, as though his eye took in every detail with increasing contempt. Then he bowed low.

"I thank you, sir. I thank you for insulting and degrading my father, who, in sooth, sir, is past his best years, or he would not be quite so meek. Lions whose teeth are broken, sir, may be tamed for watch-dogs, I have heard it said. And for other services, sir, will it please you that my sister should clean your boots? You have but to command."

"Pierce! for the love of God!" entreated my mother; and I went to him and caught his arm. But he shook me off with a roughness that I had never known Pierce use; for while we played as children together, and as wo grew up, he has ever treated me with the utmost kindness and thoughtfulness, and respectful courtesy even. So I stood trembling and looking towards the English officer, fearing lest he might strike Pierce to the ground, as my father struck down Isaiah Heston. But he stood still, and answered in his quietest, coldest tone. I think Pierce thought him quite unmoved. I should have thought so too, but that I saw how the veins upon his forehead swelled suddenly, as if his blood boiled at Pierce's insults.

"Young man," he said, and the words fell like icicles from his lips, "I counsel you to weigh your words, for the tongue is a fire that kindles much strife."

His coolness angered Pierce the more, as a little water thrown on fire only makes it blaze up more furiously.

"Words are too good to waste on a dog like you, canting, psalm-singing hypocrite, who, forsooth, turn up your eyes and despise the world, but enter gladly into possession of other men's goods."

Still Captain Standfast answered calmly, but this time I saw that his hand went towards the breast of his jerkin, and his fingers closed firmly upon the Book that he ever keeps there.

"Young man, for your own sake and that of your family, I counsel self-control."

Pierce saw the movement too, and his eyes followed the soldier's hand. He thought, doubtless, that some hidden weapon was there, and his hand sprang to his own sword.

"Draw," he said—"draw and defend yourself, *I* at least can make you answer these insults."

"Pierce! Pierce! for God's sake!—for our sakes too!" entreated my mother again. But my father spoke not, nor did I, for matters had now gone too far for peacemaking.

"To what end?" asked the English officer. "You may strike me as I stand, if you will; my sword is laid aside."

This was true. Of late, and as I would willingly have thought, out of consideration for us, the Englishman has unbuckled his sword before entering; but my father holds mere bravado to be the reason, and a desire to show that he fears not to go unarmed.

"I strike no unarmed man. *I* am a gentleman," said Pierce, and I looked to see the Englishman blaze into anger. But it seemed that his cold phlegmatic nature was not to be roused, though Pierce's words might well have seemed an insult that only blood could wipe out. Or was it perfect self-control?

"Fetch your sword and meet me on the green below, there to answer to me the degradation to which you have reduced my kinsfolk!" cried Pierce, and his grey eyes gleamed like bright steel under their dark lashes. He turned to the door, and waited for the English officer to follow. But he stood still.

"I will not fight you, sir," he said; and there was a dead silence, and we all looked at him in utter amazement and almost dismay. For whatever reason to hate him we might have, at least we should hitherto have held him to be a brave man

Pierce stood for a moment and gazed at his antagonist, who calmly turned his forbidding face to him. Then in a voice choking with rage and disgust he cried, " Coward! coward! and yet again coward! What! will no taunt sting you into manhood? Or will you wait till more of your sort are gathered here to fall upon me? Robbery and murder mostly go together, but it is easier, ay, and wiser too, to kill a man first and take his goods thereafter."

"Have you done?" asked the Captain, as he paused for breath.

"For the present I have done. But so long as the breath is in me I will never cease to call you coward, sir, coward, coward, coward!"

He shouted the words after the English officer, who had already, after bowing formally to us, left the room, and was now crossing the courtyard, walking with that steady step of his—the step of a man who knows whither he means to go, and will go thither straightway. For us, divided between anxiety lest Pierce's words should move the officer to take vengeance on us, and the mingled gladness and pain of our meeting, we gathered closely together, and we sat long in converse.

Of all that he told us I have little heart to write, for it was only sorrow, and sorrow, and yet again sorrow, so that my mother at last clasped her hands and lifted her streaming eyes to the great crucifix hanging on the wall above us.

"Lord, by the memory of Thy sufferings, pity us. Make us thankful that we too are permitted to suffer!"

My father and Pierce have not such patience as hers. I have known her in illness thrust away reliefs, gladly enduring all that might be borne, in the hope of growing worthy of a place at the feet of the Saints, who suffered so much. I have ever thought it terrible, feeling that we ought to welcome and be thankful for all merciful alleviation of pain. My father endures proudly. Pierce feels only bitter anger against the English, always our tormentors and betrayers, as he says. One thing gives him real pleasure, it seems, if pleasure it can be called—the woe that has fallen upon the poet Edmund Spenser, the writer of "The Faerie Queene," and other poems held in high esteem.

This Edmund Spenser was secretary to Lord Grey de Wilton in the days of Elizabeth. He wrote much to urge the utter destruction of all the native Irish, and it was with the utmost joy that he recorded the doings of his master, who so devastated the province of Munster that from Cashel to Dunquin in Kerry there was heard neither lowing of cattle nor herdsman's voice. Lord Grey set garrisons in a circle in various places. This was Mb mode of warfare. He cut down the crops, drove off the cattle, and left the Irish to starve, so that they scraped at last the very corpses from the graves to eat, and crawled forth upon the road on their hands and knees, for their legs could not carry them. Children were killed and eaten, and Lord Grey had those hanged whom he had driven to such horrors. This was in the year 1580; and Spenser, dwelling in the castle of Kilcolman, given to him by the Queen, and taken from the Fitzgeralds, joyfully recom mended the plan to my Lord Essex, after whose disgrace it was in truth carried out by Lord Mountjoy.

This gentle poet lived to see his castle burned before his eyes, and one of his children within it, and died himself in poverty and neglect in London. Among us his memory is hated with a bitter hate, however highly the world may esteem him as a poet.

Now Pierce, with pleasure, as I have said, has declared to us that his grandson William is to be treated as the poet desired all Irishmen should be treated, and must march straightway into Connaught, leaving his lands by Fermoy to some soldier of Cromwell's army. Such is the irony of Fate!

CHAPTER VIII.

JFrom *tie* Diarg of ffit&ne D'donnor.

UE nearest neighbour, Lady Burke, is surely to be pitied. A widow and forlorn, her only son is in Spain, and has not yet returned, though she looks for his coming. How, indeed, could he remain absent now! Pierce would fain hear if there were tidings of him; so, since he needed rest and refreshment very sorely, I yesterday undertook to walk the three miles that lie between our house and hers. I went alone, for the dogs fawned upon Pierce, and were not willing to leave him. I had scarcely gone a few steps when I met the English officer pacing to and fro upon the western terrace—*his* terrace now—where we used to love to walk and sit in the golden summer afternoons.

He paused when I came near, and greeted me in that grave and formal way of his, as if he feared to be courteous, and yet he was courteous, almost in spite of himself. He would have spoken, but I only saluted him, and passed hastily on. I could not bring myself to talk with the man who had so little spirit that he could coldly refuse a knightly challenge, although I could not but be glad too that Pierce was free of the peril of such an encounter.

So I went hastily on by the path that leads from the terrace down to the lake, and so round its shore to Glendour Halls, the home of the Burkes. But when I reached the little gate that shuts the garden from the wilder part of the demesne, to my great surprise and greater vexation I found it locked. *We* had never locked it. The poor could pass freely in with their petitions; our friends could enter and be welcome. Locks and bolts were truly fit to use by the English, whose thoughts are always on trespassers and the troublesomeness of beggars. I was angry as I turned back, and still more angry when the English officer came down the path to meet me with a key in his hand. His unsmiling face seemed hateful to me. I would have given much at that moment to have chosen the other and longer way to the Halls of Glendour.

"I will open the gate, Mistress Ethne," he said; "and if it please you soon to return, I shall still be here, and will open it again."

"I thank you, sir," I said, and I scarcely knew my own voice, it was so cold; "I shall not return soon, nor shall I need to give you so much trouble."

"You go far, then?" he said, looking earnestly at me.

"I go far."

"And alone?"

There was grave surprise, displeasure even, in his tone, and I was much offended. For what was it to him if I chose to roam all day, or to do anything else that might or might not please him?

"It has been said, and it has always been true, of our countrymen, Captain Standfast," I said, and I drew myself up to meet his pride with mine, "that they feared no foe but a woman. You have, perhaps, heard of the maiden who walked from end to end of Ireland, dressed out in the richest jewels, and had no cause to fear."

"That which may be safe may yet not be seemly," said the officer; and the blood rushed to my cheeks, and I know that my eyes flashed.

"I will answer you in the motto of your own kings, sir," I said; "' Honi soit qui mal y pense.'"

"And I will answer you again from a higher authority, Mistress Ethne. It is written that women should be sober, discreet, *keepers at home*. When Dinah, the daughter of Jacob, went forth to see the daughters of the land, grievous harm befell her. Her fate should be an example."

That little book which this man carries about with him, and in which he for ever reads diligently, seems to supply him at every moment with counsel and example. At this moment I hated him the more for his readiness to strengthen his own words with divine authority; and, not arguing this point further, I asked with a vehemence which, now to remember, makes me a little ashamed—

"Captain Standfast, have *none* of the joys of life any charm for you? Do you think it right to look with suspicion on the good things God gives? Does He not mean us to enjoy them? Is there not sorrow enough in life already?"

"Surely God made the world very good," said the soldier slowly, as if thinking how to answer. "But our sins are too many. It is written,' The joy of the Lord is your strength;' and yet we never read that the Saviour smiled, though we know that He wept."

"I think," I said softly, "that He must have smiled when He took that little child in His arms."

Captain Standfast lifted his downcast eyes and looked at me with a face so strangely changed that I was filled with wonder. His look was so kind, and his eyes smiled, though his mouth kept its stern lines. It was as when the soft evening sunshine suddenly lights up some rugged mountain peak, and shows that among the hard rocks spring sweet flowers and mosses.

"I think you speak truly, Mistress Ethne," he said; "and in that quiet family gathering at Bethany He may have been glad, as also at the marriage-feast. But these things are a snare to us, and it is written,'Blessed are the pure in heart. '"

He lifted his eyes to the changeable sky, and I saw that they were full of a great longing, as though he would pierce the blue vault and see what lay beyond.

"Mistress Ethne," he said, and his voice was not harsh, but full of the yearning of which his eyes spoke, "we are taught that the blessing of the pure in heart is this—that they shall see God. Does not His servant John truly say that every man that hath this hope—so wonderful a hope!—will purify himself, even as He is pure? If I might—at last— see God!"

He seemed almost to have forgotten my presence as he spoke. The tears had sprung to my eyes; it seemed that in such a hope as this lay consolation for all things earthly. I would willingly have asked some further question, but the sight of my brother Pierce, whom I suddenly saw standing among the great trees at the end of the terrace, recalled my thoughts. I made a movement towards the gate, and the Englishman in silence unlocked it.

"I thank you, but I shall not return this way," I said, and his face and voice had recovered their wonted sternness as he answered—

"As you will, lady," and again turned the key.

I looked back once before I quite lost sight of the house. Pierce was no longer there; only the Englishman was still pacing to and fro on the terrace, reading in his Bible.

Father Ambrose says that the Bible is no book for the laity, being hard to understand, and easy to interpret wrongly, so that it is better for us to listen to the voice of the Church, which is the voice of God. It may be that this Puritan darkens his own life thus, being overburdened by his sins. When we Catholics sin, we carry our load to the priest and lay it down in confession. Absolution and penance set us free. Only for that of which we have failed to repent we shall suffer hereafter those dreadful fires of Purgatory. Much penance and fasting and ill-treating of our body makes us holy; but if we do not aspire to such sanctity, we can enjoy what we may, and be purified from any stains. Such is our creed, the only true creed, as we know. But this Puritan seems to long to keep his soul unstained. He fears joy because it holds temptation. He cares not for Church or priest; he will have nothing between God and his own soul.

So I thought, as I went along the woodland path, and as I went I passed our little church. It came upon me with a pang that this lofty and beautiful religion, as it seemed to me, was that of a heretic, and I turned from the path and entered the church.

"' Blessed are the pure in heart, for they shall see God!'" I said, half aloud.

If the Bible holds many such lovely words, I should like well to read it. I dipped my fingers in the holy water, and made the sign of the cross. That was the symbol of purity; it should help me to be pure. One or two poor people were kneeling in different places, as is mostly the case when one enters. They were telling their rosaries, or fulfilling vows or penances, as Father Ambrose had bidden them, to do away their various sins. I drew near to the high altar and knelt, and looked up at the great picture over the altar. The anguish of the Cross was painted there. I looked steadfastly at the face of the Crucified, as I have often looked before. Anguish, even to death, was painted there; but the painter was no great master of his art. I gazed earnestly at the face; there was only anguish in it; the glory of God did not shine through. I closed my eyes and tried to think how that face should have looked; then I opened them again. The Saviour throned in glory was figured in the window above, but neither had that Face the glory for which I looked. And yet until to-day I had loved those paintings. I said a Paternoster and turned away. An old woman was sobbing before a figure of Mary, the mother of God, who held in her hands the burning Heart, transfixed by a sword.

I too had often prayed there, but now I could not.

"They shall see *God!*" I went out of the chapel, and as I went I met Father Ambrose.

"You are disturbed in mind, my daughter," he said, looking attentively at me.

"Father," I said, " what is it that makes us pure in heart?"

"Confession, penance, absolution. Have you not learned it from your infancy, my child?"

"Yes, father," I said humbly, and I went on my way, and made haste, for I had delayed much already.

But it seemed that many delays were to be mine today. The path after a while leaves the shore of the lake, and goes out into the more open fields. And here before me, crouching beside a low stone wall that edges the field, I saw the little ragged figure of Larry Oge.

He put his finger to his lips as I came near, and fixed his wild black eyes upon me with such earnest entreaty that I could not but do as he seemed to wish, and therefore I came near as softly as possible.

"What are you doing, Larry?" I whispered.

The child caught my hand and drew me down behind tiie wall. There was a small hole in it, where it seemed that a stone had fallen out.

"Look there, Lady Ethne," whispered Larry excitedly. "Look through that hole, and tell me do you not see his red coat there among the springing corn? It is a Leprechaun, I do believe!"

I looked, and certainly I saw something red far off and hidden among the blossoms of a blackthorn bush. Hitherto I had been glad to see the blackthorn, the first flower of the spring; this year I have been sorry to see it blossom, for when May comes and the earth is beautiful we must go, and everything that tells of spring tells of our departure.

Larry sprang up, and stole with his bare feet along the field by the side of the springing crop, holding his breath and treading with the utmost care till he reached the flowering bush and peeped cautiously over. Then with a cry of disappointment he turned and came back.

"0 Lady Ethne! I have tried so hard! Every day I go to look for the Leprechaun, the little red-coated fairycobbler. I have hunted every hill, and at last I thought I had found him, for I was sure I heard the tick-tack of his tools, and I *could* have caught him! But it was only a wisp of red rag thrown away there!"

"But why do you want so much to catch the Leprechaun, Larry?" I asked, half sorry for the child's grief, and half amused too.

"It was all for you!" said Larry, almost in reproach. "*We* are used to being poor; it is very well for us. But ever since the day when I wanted the Englishman to drown, and you saved him, I have tried to find a Leprechaun. For you know, Lady Ethne, if one holds him fast, he will give great heaps of gold for his freedom."

"I know they say so, Larry," I said. "But I never knew any one who found a fortune that way."

"Oh, but they do!" cried Larry; "my grandmother knows it, and many people have heard the Leprechaun hammering among the hills. It was all for you, Lady; how will you bear to have everything taken away? I wish I were a man to fight for you! It *should* not be!"

The boy clenched his fist as he spoke, and my eyes swam in tears, for love is precious in one's prosperity, but doubly precious in adversity.

"Foolish Larry!" I said. "*You* will not have to transplant. You had better forget us, and serve Captain Standfast. He will be a just master, I know well."

"I will never serve him! I will follow you to the end of this world, and so will we all, if you will but let us," said Larry Oge, and as I went on I saw him wander further up the hillside, as if he still sought his cobblerfairy. At the gate of Glendour Halls I stood a moment and hesitated. I knew that this place had been given to Isaiah Heston; but Lady Burke had closed the doors in his face when he attempted to enter, and had gathered her armed servants about her. For the present she had been left untroubled, but every day during the autumn and winter she had expected that he would return, and would use force to put himself in possession.

Any day this might have happened, so I determined to enter by the garden way, and I went a little further to the small gate in the wall, by which Lady Burke's only most familiar friends are permitted to go in and out. For she has always loved state and ceremony: nothing would persuade her to leave her house except outriders went before her, and the countryfolk must draw their carts to the side of the way and stand bareheaded till she is gone by. So it was in the past, but now

Now, as I took the little gate in my hand to open it, I started back in dismay, scarcely able to believe my own senses. For with a heavy load of hay bound upon her back, and a great knife such as is used to cut hay from the stack in her hand, Lady Burke herself came towards me.

Seeing me, she stood still, and the blood rose in her

F cheeks and brow. Her white hair was disordered under the black veil of her widowhood; her eyes flashed under her eyebrows that were still raven black

"Ay, you may well stand there amazed, Ethne," she said. "Do you know what I am doing—I, the daughter of an English earl, the widow of an Irish baron. Come and see."

I went to her, and tried to take the load from her shoulders, but she repulsed me.

"No; the back must bend to the burden, and your young shoulders will have their own, my poor child," she said, and she turned away and walked with steady step beyond the gate and into the ruins of a deserted cabin, which had been roughly roofed over and divided into two tiny rooms. Into one of these Lady Burke went, and I followed. It was dark, and I only slowly distinguished the shape of a cow, to which the lady went, and spread her bundle of hay for the creature with her delicate white fingers, on which, as a sunbeam filtered in through the hole that did duty for a window, the diamonds burned and sparkled with a lustre that seemed, indeed, a cruel mockery. Then she turned to me.

"I have fed my cow, you see, Ethne. I must fancy myself to be Eve in Paradise, who was not ashamed of such tasks, I suppose. Now, if you will come into my home, I will bring you what food I have, if you are hungry, and set a seat for you, if you are tired, for I am mistress and servants all in one, as you see—a very Eden-like state of things, is it not?"

"0 Lady Burke!" I faltered.

"Ay, I am still Lady Burke, after all," she said; and she drew me out of the shed and hasped the rough wooden door with those fine fingers of hers, whose hardest work hitherto had been the mending of cobweb lace, so daintily done by her that it seemed as though there had been no rent.

I followed lier into the other room of the miserable cabin. Here there was a small window of glass, but the walls and floor were of clay, and there were spaces in the rotten roof through which the sky could be seen. But an embroidery frame stood there, and a costly mantle lined with fur was laid over some cushions on the ground that seemed to form a bed, or at least a resting-place. A rough wooden bench was strewn with the dainty adjuncts of a great lady's toilet, and a book or two, handsomely bound and with jewelled clasps, lay there also.

"Welcome to my home, Ethne," said Lady Burke, pushing and lifting the door by its iron hasp. "This is all I have to make you welcome with; you must pardon all shortcomings, for they are not my fault."

"I am so sorry, so sorry, Lady Burke!" I said, scarcely knowing what to say. "But your servants, how comes it?"

The lady drew her heavy black brows together.

"' The hireling fleeth because he is an hireling,' " she said. "You remember, Ethne, that when this robber, whose very name I scorn to take upon my tongue, came to see his heritage, as he dares to call my house, I shut the doors in his face?"

"I do indeed."

"And would have shut them! Ay, if there had been but three men of my mind, I would have fired the house, and myself have perished in the flames. But they prayed me for their sakes, since resistance was useless. Ay, that was two days ago, when the man—the reptile—came again." Her voice trembled as she spoke.

"I bade them open. I stood and faced him when he entered—the worm! what would I have given to have trodden him under my feet. '1 trust, madam,' he said, looking at me with evident apprehension, the coward! 11 trust, madam, that you mean to render me peaceable possession?'

"' Oh, very peaceable, sir,' I said. '1 mean to render up my house as willingly as your anointed King rendered up his throne, and afterwards his life, at your holy and righteous request, sir.'

"' It is well,' said the wretch; '1 rejoice to see that the Lord hath bowed your stubborn will to the acceptance of His dispensations' But I broke in—

"' Do not dare to take that Holy Name in vain, sir, and add to the wrath that hangs over you. Though the mills of God grind slowly, yet they grind exceeding small, as you will find to your cost.' My servants had gathered in the room. I turned to them.

"' Men and women,' I said, 'your master served his King. He was a Papist, as you are; but I, as you know, am an Englishwoman and a Protestant.'

"' A Protestant!' said the soldier, under his breath.

"' Yes, sir,' I said. 'A Protestant of the Church of England, who, in taking off from the robe of her faith the additions and fripperies of Rome, has not thought fit to rend that seamless garment and disfigure it as you have done.'

"' Soh! an idolator under another name,' muttered the soldier; but I heeded him not, and spoke to the servants.

"' He joined Sir Phelim O'Neill. He would have men's bodies ruled by the King, men's souls by the Pope, to which lawful authorities he had been taught from a child to be subject. The same authority which beheaded the King—*your* King, hanged your master. They called both justice.'"

Lady Burke had told her story hitherto in a steady voice, flashing into angry scorn only as she spoke of Isaiah Heston. But now, as she spoke of her husband's death, hanged for his share in Sir Phelim's rising and the disorders that followed, her voice broke, and she covered her face with her hands.

How future ages will judge that time of 1641 I know not, since even now it is hard to know the truth. The English proclaim loudly that there was a great and terrible massacre, which could scarcely be adequately punished, so horrible was it; while, on our part, it is utterly denied, except that some blood was certainly shed in the taking of the garrisons. The cruelties of the English are but too well known among us; in their own country they are, doubtless, smoothed over, and justified even.

Lord Burke of Glendour was hanged. His lady might well weep. But she looked up again with eyes that flamed, and went on with her story.

"'Your lord was an Englishman in spirit,' I said. 'He called himself Burke, but he had still the pride of the De Burgos. He was a hard master to you, and you did not love him!'"

"There was a low murmur among the servants.

"'None of you loved him, nor did you love me. Which among you all loves me well enough to be willing at this moment to follow me into Connaught?'

"I did not look at them as I asked the question, but I knew that they were looking into each other's faces. The only voice that answered was that of Honora, my son's old nurse.

"' I will go, my lady,' she said.

"' You shall not go, Honora,' I said. 'See, all of you, I am English, of the English, and a Protestant, but for my husband's sake and my son's I must go into Connaught. English as I am, I cannot bid you love England. I have said enough and too much, sir,' I said to the soldier, whose face had shown evident satisfaction when my people conld profess no love for me. 'I go now.'

"Did I tell you, Ethne, that several of the tenants had gathered among my servants? Some of them came to me now and offered me house and home with them. But I would none of their welcome. What I have to bear I can bear alone till Maurice comes, if he be yet alive. But, indeed, I would rather hear that he is in his coffin, at rest like his father. I would I were there also, but death flies from the wretched."

"0 Lady Burke!" I cried, shocked and grieved, " take some comfort! Surely the love of God is over all."

"Is it?" she asked, in a hard and bitter tone. "There was a God in the old times, for He swallowed up a whole army of oppressors in the sea. These regicides cross the waters safely now. Ah, you think I am a terrible woman, Ethne; I can see your thoughts. Fly from me, child, like all the rest. I am not fit for the society of kind hearts—I, in whom every drop of blood is turned to gall."

I prayed her to return with me and live with us, at least until Maurice should return, but she refused with vehemence.

"To live by the sufferance of another regicide! Never!" she cried. "That your father, and, still more, your brother, shoald endure to do so, almost passes belief."

I told her of Pierce's challenge, and her eyes sparkled.

"Was not that what I said? Cowards they all are! Cowards and hypocrites both! Mark my words, Ethne, if your brother and that man have words again, Pierce will kill him where he stands; and he will do well," she added, in a tone that made my blood run cold.

I had done my errand, and I went away. I had always from a child feared the Lady Burke, but now it seemed that trouble had exasperated her hard proud spirit to a fierceness which was certainly not womanly— was hardly even human.

KSTSl WAS glad to breathe the fresh air and feel K$9 Ksa t'ie sunshine when I left Lady Burke. I Ggbbbk took a longer round to avoid all chance of meeting Isaiah Heston. But these very efforts brought me face to face with the object of my aversion, who came upon me suddenly as I went through the fields. Lieutenant Heston is not a comely man, and a great sword wound that crosses one cheek, and reaches almost to the temple, gives his face a strangely repulsive expression. As he came towards me now I could see that he was much flushed, and walked unsteadily; and I must own that my heart beat a little faster, though I went on, for I could not show fear, or swerve an inch from the path, or even quicken my steps. I saluted as courtesy required, and went on past the officer, thinking myself fortunate to have no need of speech. But in another moment I found him by my side.

"Ha! pretty Mistress Ethne!" he said; "how comes it that I meet you here? These are *my* lands, fair maiden, and I have a right to demand toll from all who pass over them."

"This is a public pathway, sir," I said, continuing still to walk on, "and has been from time immemorial. I pray you accept my farewell."

I stood still and courtesied, then I turned and went on, but Master Heston was again by my side.

"I am loth to see so fair a lady without escort," he said. "I pray you, since you have dismissed your retainers, let me attend you."

"I thank yon, sir," I said. "We women in this country walk abroad freely if we so desire. If we desire attendance, we ask for it."

He laughed loudly.

"Well spoken, gracious daughter of the land; pretty Amalekite! We that are now masters in your country do what we will freely also, and it pleases me to serve you in this matter."

I stood still again, and now indeed my heart beat fast.

"Master Heston," I said, "I do not desire your company. Since I cannot command, I would at least pray you to leave me."

"Ah!" said the soldier, looking at me with an evil smile, "it is pleasant to be so humbly entreated. But now I bethink me, your face is set the wrong way. I pray you turn. There will be rain, and you are leaving the friendly shelter of my poor house behind. I pray you return and stay till the storm shall have passed."

There was no need to answer in words. The look which I gave the wretch, as Lady Burke had well called this man, seemed for a moment to be enough. He stood still while I went on, thanking Heaven to be free of him. But I had not reached the edge of the woods that skirt the lake when he ran after me, and this time made no pretence of courtesy, but caught my mantle in his hand.

"We are the conquerors, and you are the prey," he cried. "Listen to me, maiden, and it will be well for you. These lands are mine, and you are a beggar, but I will make you my wife, for you please me. You are too handsome for Connaught,"

"Let me go, sir!" I said, and I drew my mantle from his grasp, and turned to run. But he caught my wrist in an iron grasp, and I felt myself helpless against his strength, so that in my despair I cried out aloud, though he would have stopped my mouth.

And there all at once stood Captain Standfast!

The miserable coward loosed me, and cast his eyes upward, as if absorbed in thought. Captain Standfast looked at him, and then at me, and I cast down my eyes in anger and shame, for that which he foretold had come true, and I felt that in his heart he would triumph over me. Then he looked at Isaiah Heston, who brought down his eyes a little, and spoke with tipsy solemnity.

"Yea, friend Roger," said he, " there be yet Delilahs who would lead us back to earthly vanities. But we will put them from us as I have put this woman from me, who sought to entice me to a feast that her father holds, and cried aloud because I over-roughly pushed her from me."

I spoke not. The red that burned on my forehead might answer Captain Standfast, if he chose to look on me. And if he chose he might believe his comrade; what was his belief to me?

"Friend Isaiah," he said slowly, "I fear you have been enticed, and have mingled strong drink. It is written on your face but too plainly."

"Drunk, but not with wine," began Isaiah; but the other sternly interrupted—

"*This* is no pious fervour. Confess your fault, my brother. It may well be that you have been led astray through the weakness of the flesh, that you may understand the temptations of others."

"The flesh is weak," said this wretch, with a pious snuffle. "And there are those of whom the prophet teaches who put their bottle to our lips and say, 'Let us entice him, peradventure he will be enticed.'" Then in a humble, frightened tone he said, "I pray thee, good Roger, keep thine own counsel; let not this matter come to the ears of our superiors, but rather shield me. For thou mightest thyself also have erred."

I looked up quickly at Captain Standfast, and said in my heart that such gross evil would have no hold on him. I thought he would answer indignantly. But he only said, "You speak truth, Isaiah. I also might fall, but for the sufficient grace."

I could not fail to see the look of relief that passed over Isaiah Heston's evil face.

"Aha, brother Roger, the temptation is strong," he said, leering up into the other's face. "Ah, those days of going into Bristol market and the old Half-Moon in the eve."—But Isaiah Heston seemed suddenly to remember what he was saying, and his face grew long, and he cast up his eyes: "Those were our unregenerate days," he said, "alas! Bat as you truly say, good Roger, the flesh is weak, and sinners entice us"

But Captain Standfast interrupted in his sternest tone. "Friend Isaiah, I pray you forget not that it is written, 'My son, if sinners entice thee, consent thou NOT.'"

The emphasis which he laid upon the word made me start, but Captain Standfast turned quickly to me—

"I pray you, lady, since it would seem that the ways are not quite free from peril, let me offer you my protection on your way home."

I was angry that he should taunt me in this fashion, and I fear that my answer had little of maiden meekness in it.

"I ask your pardon, sir," I said; "I forgot when I spoke of our perfect safety that the times were changed, and that some of those who walk our ways now are not *Irishmen.*"

Here Isaiah Heston broke in. "Good Roger, I had hoped, in coming this way, to find you at liberty for some sweet converse touching spiritual things; but since you are—not altogether free—I will e'en commune with my spirit alone."

And he turned and went back with unsteady gait along the path, droning out some hymn of most dismal sound.

"Captain Standfast," I said hastily, " I pray you, follow your friend. He desires your company"

"And you do not. But I hold it unseemly that Christian women should expose themselves to any possibility of hearing overbold words. I will therefore go with you, if you will suffer me so to do."

It seemed to me that there was little room for denial on my part, and I walked by his side as meekly as a chidden child, but inwardly chafing. Little was spoken between us till we reached the gate below the castle terrace, and there I looked up to see my brother Pierce standing again at the corner of the terrace from whence the way to the stables branches off, and where the great lime tree stands, under whose buzzing scented shade our favourite place—his and mine—in summer days has ever been. "Meet me under the lime," was ever our tryst. Alas, for the happy careless days.

The officer drew forth that hateful key to open the gate.

"I thank you, sir, for the trouble you *would* take," I said, "and for the courage which you would doubtless have shown. I am sorry we have met no dragon, but I greatly fear Saint Patrick banished such creatures also when he preached the great sermon that drove all serpents and toads out of Ireland."

Something like a smile flitted across the man's grave face.

"I fear, lady," he said, " that your wish had been rather to see the dragon devour me, than to see me overcome the dragon."

"Ethne!" called Pierce from the terrace, and at the sound of his voice the question which I had been pondering all the way as we walked leaped to my lips.

"Captain Standfast, why would you not meet my brother? You are not" "afraid to go to battle," I had almost added, but I could not bring out the word *afraid.*

"Because," he answered at once, "life is a precious gift of God, not to be risked in satisfying carnal pride and vengeance, but to be readily given, if need be, for His glory. The reproach of men is better to bear than God's displeasure."

"Then it *was* hard for you to refuse," I said eagerly. "At least, it would be for most men harder than to fight all the battles that ever were."

And as Pierce called again from the terrace, I turned away and hastened up the hill. He met me with a scowl, and that he had never done in his life before.

"Ethne," he said, "how is it that you

have so much to say to that—that coward?"

"I have not *so much* to say to him," I said. "And besides, Pierce, you wrong him in thinking him a coward. He"

"What! you take his part? Ethne, I am amazed!" "I would only be just," I said. "We owe that to our worst enemy."

"We owe nothing to a coward."

"Then we owe it to ourselves," I said, and the anger disappeared from Pierce's face.

"You are right, little sister, and that speech is worthy of a daughter of our house."

We went in together.

CHAPTER X. JFrom tlje Dlarg of ffitjme SD'ffionnot. HAVE been trying to train myself to household tasks. There will he need for me, when this transplanting is finally carried out, to be able to turn my hand to anything and everything necessary for the daily comfort of my parents. Hewers of wood and drawers of water we must be; and as I can hardly hope to be able to hew wood, I have at least tried to accustom my arms to the carrying of water. I trust they will soon grow strong; I am ashamed of the stiffness and aching I feel in them when my load has been at all heavy. Every morning of late I have risen early and gone down through the fields to the clear well, which we call the Wishing Well, because it is believed whoever comes to the spot before sunrise, and sprinkles the water north, south, east, and west, and for the rest of the day speaks no word except when spoken to, and then no word beyond what is necessary, will have whatever he has wished for. So they say; and indeed I have often tried it in my childish days, but I never had my wish. Perhaps I said some unnecessary words.

The sun was shining brightly, and the air was fresh with that wonderful freshness of early morning which it seems a shame and pity to waste in slumber, but which mankind strangely neglect, deeming it a painful duty if by cbance they do rise with the sun.

Perhaps it is as well; the birds and the shy, wild things have at least that peaceful time to themselves; through the livelong day man scares and affrights them, till they must often feel as though the world were not their appointed place, and they may as well get out of it as soon as may be.

I was np early, but the birds were earlier still; and the rabbits were playing in the meadow, washing their faces in the dew, and looking saucily at me as if I had no business to be out at that hour. At any other time they would have run away; as it was, they waited till I came quite near, and then made a great fuss about escape, as if they would have said, "Dear, dear! this mortal; what needless trouble she is giving us!"

A hedgehog, taking a morning ramble, was crossing the lawn. One of our peacocks suddenly became aware of this curious apparition, and went closer to look. The hedgehog took no notice, but leisurely went on his way, and the peacock walked after him, nodding his head as if longing to peck, but distrusting those serried spikes— a comical picture of unsated curiosity.

There was a great stir in the rookery. The rooks were all talking at once, and none were listening. Presently they got into order again, and flew down in a black cloud upon the grass, where they held a very serious council. I watched till they came to a satisfactory conclusion, which they presently did, and flew back to their village. Evidently their solemn conclave had been a court of justice, for they flew straight to a tree in which was a half-finished nest, and tore it to pieces. Doubtless the nest-makers had stolen from the houses of others, and were justly punished. The pair flew round and round the tree, cawing indignantly; and at last made for another tree at some distance, where they sat down to think it over. So robbery and spoliation among the birds, and retribution falling upon the offenders!

I hardly knew whether to laugh or cry aa I went on my way. Ah! there was murder too! A thrush had pounced upon a plump snail, who doubtless repented that he at least had risen so early, for the bird held him tightly in his sharp beak, and beat him against a flat stone to break his shell.

What parables were here! I was sad, as I thought that the world, which had always seemed so bright and happy to me, was full of sorrow and suffering, and had been so while I rejoiced in its beauty, for I find it hard to realise that the world is the same as it used to be. Every time that I look upon one of the old familiar scenes attentively, I find myself foolishly wondering that it still looks the same.

I stopped thus as I reached the brow of the little hill on the side of which is the Wishing Well. The lakes shone like jewels set in the green shores, fringed with grey woods, over which the artist Nature was laying her first wash of pale soft green. Westward the more open country lay spread out like a piece of patchwork; our little, odd-shaped, variegated fields fit thus quaintly into one another, edged with green hedge or grey wall. I looked at the landscape for a moment, then I quickly filled my pail, thinking that it is not well for me to look too long on these loved scenes.

The sun was just coming; there was still time to wish. I know not what impulse possessed me at that moment that I took water and threw it according to the charm, and wished that Maurice Burke were at home again.

"My wishes have never been fulfilled," I said.

I shall never dare to doubt that legend again, for as I turned to take up my pail a horseman was at my side, riding noiselessly over the soft grass. I looked at him in some alarm, fearing to see the face of Isaiah Heston, but I saw a far more attractive form and figure than hia

The horseman wore a fawn-coloured Cavalier hat, with a long plume of the same colour, a green surcoat slashed about the sleeves and laced with gold. Gold buttons fastened back the ample skirts. Long hose of fleshcoloured silk reached above the knee, and met the green trunk hose, which, like the upper dress, were slashed. A short mantle hung over one shoulder, ruffles of costly lace edged throat and wrist. Long scented love-locks hung upon the shoulders, and the whole dress was perfectly trim and fresh, although from the look of his horse the gallant must have ridden for several hours, if not all night.

He dismounted, and stood bareheaded before me.

"Pray you, pretty maiden, is there still a way by this hill to Glendour Halls? The country is so changed, I scarcely know what to expect."

"There is no way now," I said. "No way, and no welcome—Maurice Burke!"

"And who are you that are so free with my name? But I entreat your forgiveness, madam. May I know to whom I speak?"

"To a working woman," I said, as gravely as I could, and I took up my pail. But it was heavy.

"Working women don't do that," said he, for I spilled half the bucketful in my effort to lift it easily and carelessly; "and you are no working woman—you are Ethne O'Connor, my playmate of old days, grown into a beautiful woman, and as good as she is lovely, unless her looks belie her."

"Maurice, you have learned to flatter," I said, looking at his handsome face. It was indeed a very handsome face—every feature might have been cut with a chisel; and on the smooth boyish lips rested a smile, a proud smile, but gracious too.

"I have learned to do that. You are right, Ethne. But I only do it when there is need, which is not now."

"True, sir. I think it was flattering to take me for a serving-maiden."

"But 'I serve' is a royal motto," said Maurice, with laughter in his eyes; "and my greatest pride will be to be serving-man to the serving-woman, and carry your pail, since it is your freak to play the Arcadian shepherdess."

He looked at me all over, and I blushed, for I had put on a short blue skirt of my maid Nora's, and had bunched my silken skirt over it in haste, and over my head I had but tied a scarf; and he was dressed as if for a Court pageant!

There was laughter in his eyes as he scanned my dress, but he looked in my face, and I felt that I coloured rosy red, for the mirth gave place to an admiration which I could not pretend to misunderstand. I know God has given me a fair face; the mirror would tell me so if no one else did. What of that? I did not make it for myself. I have no more need for pride than the rose on its stem.

"Maurice," I said hastily, "I am glad you are come, and yet I am sorry. I think you do not know what sorb of homecoming you have to expect."

"Oh yes, sweet Ethne, I do. The place is full of these Canaille! I know not what to call them. Do not sully your rosebud lips by speaking of them."

"But I must. Maurice, do you know that your mother" Oh, how could I tell him!" Do you know that we are living in our stable-rooms by the kindness of the officer who lives in Lara Castle?"

"The monster! How dares he face the arrows of your glances! What triply armoured braggart can he be? Nay, I think you and he can never have met face to face, else he would not be alive to tell the tale."

"Maurice, I am not used to the language of the Court," I said, a little vexed.

"But you shall learn it, fairest Ethne. I have been in o

Spain; I will teach you all the alphabet of the fan, which can say all that a lady desires without troubling her to open her lips. I will sing you canzonets, and read you the songs of Herrick and of Sir John Suckling, which are fit for ladies' ears, and we will forget these horse-boys and beer-drinking troopers."

"Maurice, are you mad? How can we forget them when we are turned out of our houses and sent into banishment into that place forsaken of Heaven beyond the Shannon?"

"Even there we can gild the sordid surroundings by courtesy and grace, by music and song. You will be Ethne still, I think."

"Shall I? I am not the same Ethne I think that I was till—till now."

"Ethne," said Maurice, suddenly taking a grave tone, "do not think, because I speak lightly, that my heart is light. But I hold it unworthy to turn any but a composed face to the world. Our misfortunes are heavy; we need the more courage to endure them. At least for very pride's sake, do not let us show ourselves crushed or broken in spirit before these despicable miscreants, the murderers of their king, the scum of the earth!"

"The scum of the earth!" Captain Standfast's face passed before my mind as he spoke, with the look that it had worn as he spoke of the pure in heart.

"Your mother has shown herself proud, Maurice," I said.

"The Lady Burke would not fail to do that," said Maurice. "I must hasten to her; but you will let me carry your pail first, Ethne."

"No, I will not. I may be wanting in that pride of which you speak, Maurice, but I intend to learn all menial duties."

"Like Psyche in the house of Aphrodite?" said Maurice, smiling. "Nay, then, I must aspire to the dignity of the Pope himself, and call myself servant of servants. You cannot go higher than that."

And he laughed as he lifted the poor tin pail, filled it again, and carried it. His hands were white and longfingered like a woman's; but I knew that the martyrking would have had no braver soldier in all his ranks on the bitter day of Wakefield fight than Maurice Burke, had he been there. Maurice, serving his king at the Spanish court, heard the news of that sad day, and as we heard afterwards, sat down and wept that he was not there. That was the only battle in which he did not strike a blow for his king. In all the rest he fought with a quiet, cool courage, till the heavy blow of Worcester fell, and he with difficulty escaped to France, where he had wandered for a while, and then had taken service under the King of Spain, being only drawn back to his native land by anxiety about his mother's fate, coupled, as he owned, with a wish to see the old home and the green hills again.

This much of his life since the fatal day of Worcester Maurice told me, as he carried my can in one hand and led his horse with the other, till we were met by two of the maids, who had wondered at my long delay. Maurice expressed himself willing to carry the load for them, but yielded when I represented to him that there would be an end of serving-maidens altogether if men must needs interfere with their duties. Whereupon he mounted and rode away, looking back many and many a time before he was out of sight, waving his hat with as cheerful an air as if all were well, and we might make merry like other people.

I trust his gaiety may cheer Pierce a little, for he goes about all day with a look either heavy and woeful, or fierce and wrathful; and of the two, bad as the choice is, I think I would rather see him fierce—his wan, despairing look is so hard to bear, so impossible to cheer.

CHAPTER XI.

Jrtom tfje jDiatg of *Bttne* 2D'«Sonnor.

0 Maurice Burke came home, and went to the miserable hovel where his mother had taken refuge. To his surprise, she absolutely refused to leave it. The people on the estate implored her to come and cosher upon them in turn, but she would not. When her husband was executed, she had by great favour obtained his remains. They were buried close to his own house, in the little graveyard occupied only by Burkes, with the little chapel in it, which had been closed since that calamity, as Lady Burke was a Protestant; and although her son was brought up as a Papist, he showed little care for the worship of his church. Now Lady Burke shut herself up in her grief. Maurice was welcome to come if he chose; he might go away again when he pleased, she said; this was no place for him. One faithful servant came, as it were, by stealth, brought food to the miserable hut, and waited on the lady, who seemed scarcely to notice her services; but if she did so, only said—

"Are you not gone yet, Honora? Why do you not go too, like all the rest?"

"I would love her if she would let me," said Maurice, but his mother would not let him. She closed her heart against all affection.

"It is not well to love any one or anything," she said. "All love is Dead Sea fruit, and ends in bitterness."

If she were proud of her handsome son, she would not allow it, but spoke ever of what the young men used to be when she was at court as maid-of-honour to the Queen of James the First.

It was when we went to visit her that she uttered these things, for no inducement that we could offer would bring Lady Burke to visit us. But Maurice came away gladly from his sad home— if home it could be called, and spent much of his time with us. In truth, he was a pleasant companion, and shed not a little light and sunshine on our lives; and Pierce's face brightened again when he came, and my mother smiled oftener when Maurice was there than through all the other hours of the day.

To me Maurice paid a devotion which provoked me often to mirth. I was the only queen of his heart, he would say, and I, laughing, would answer, "Ay, indeed, one of the only queens." At which Maurice was or seemed grievously offended, and swore that though the sky be thickly sown with stars, yet there is but one moon. And he would tune his Spanish guitar, and sing all manner of foolish ditties, praising my eyes, and my mouth, and my hair, as though never maiden lived before with two grey eyes and a straight nose.

My father calls me his cluster of nuts, and laughs because my skin is brown; but Maurice calls me Samela, because of a ditty which he specially loves, and thus he continually sings—

"Her cheeks, like rose and lily, yield forth gleams,
Her brow's bright arches framed of ebony;
Thus fair Samela
Passeth fair Venus in her bravest hue,
And Juno in the show of majesty—
For she's Samela:
Pallas in wit,—all three, if you will view,
For beauty, wit, and matchless dignity,
  Yield to Samela!"

I laugh at Maurice and his songs, but I am glad he is here. They are pleasant to hear, foolish though they be. And we should miss him sorely if he went.

So the days have gone on. Of late they have been days of interminable rain, as if poor Ierne wept and would not be comforted. At times, when we sit round the glowing turf fire in the closing evenings, and Maurice sings, or tells us of the gay doings of the Spanish Court, or that of France, or Captain Standfast comes in, and the talk has to be kept to those subjects which will not provoke my father to anger, such as the manner in which coal is dug in his own county of Gloucester, and the great salmon in the Severn, and the brave adventurous merchants of Bristol, we could sometimes almost forget how hollow is the ground beneath our feet, how dreary the future must at best be for us.

So that it was with another shock, as though the blow had been quite unexpected, that we learned on the 28th of February that another proclamation had gone forth under the hand of Fleetwood, Lord-Deputy, and his Council.

It was well that Captain Standfast was not there when Pierce brought in the printed sheet of which he had obtained a copy. How odious to us those neatly printed sheets have become, with the likeness of the official seal above, and the signature of Thomas Herbert, Clerk of the Council, below. No good thing for us is ever to be looked for from them! And yet this one seemed to have some kindness in it. I said it was well Captain Standfast was not present, for my father's wrath boiled over, and he flung his crutch from one end of the room to the other, fairly beside himself with indignation.

"The pious hypocrites, who rob us and turn up their eyes to give God thanks for that which they have received of His bounty, forsooth! The holy men who will be merciful, who will strangle us with a silken kerchief, drown us in Malvoisie, burn us in sandal-wood!"

So he stormed, drowning my mother's voice, who counselled moderation and self-control, and holding the sheet in his trembling hands, he read it aloud—

"'Whereas by an order of the 30th November last it is declared that all persons in Ireland who, having right to Articles or to any favour or mercy held forth by the qualifications of the Act of Parliament, intituled *An Act for the Settling of Ireland,* are Proprietors'—"

Are! I was once! Good gentles and merciful, I pray you give the dog whose bone you have snatched your merciful permission to eat his own tail!"— 'The Lord-Deputie and Council' (he continued reading),' taking into their serious consideration the immoderate and unusual fall of raine at this season of the year, and how much the deepness of the waies and weakness of cattle occasioned thereby may make their journeys more difficult and hazardous, especially to their wives and young children'— "So that they might unfortunately die and escape too soon from their troubles," commented my father, and read further—' It was ordered that the masters of the house do transplant themselves before the first day of March the next ensuing into the province of Connaught and county of Clare, according to former declarations, and address themselves to such as are empowered for that purpose to take out their respective assignments of land and proceed to build and settle for themselves there. And it is further ordered that such persons so transplanting themselves as aforesaid, their Wives, Children, and necessary Servants, with their Cattle, or such persons so transplanting themselves respectively, shall be permitted to continue at their dwellings and holdings for such time as the Commander-in-Chief, with two Justices of the Peace of each precinct, shall think fit to give licence for under their hands and seals respectively. Provided the said persons themselves so to transplant, as aforesaid, do procure a certificate under the hands and seals of two or more of the Commissioners in Connaught appointed to set out their land in Connaught and County Clare, that such persons have personally appeared before them there and are preparing for their families in Connaught or County Clare, for want of which certificate aforesaid their Wives, Children, and Servants remaining in the Provinces of Leinster, Ulster, and Munster after the last day of March now next ensuing are hereby declared to be out of protection, and to incur the penalties mentioned in the above said declarations.

'Dated at Dublin the 27th of February 1654.

'thomas Herbert, *Clerk of the Council.'"*

So much of the proclamation my father read. Then he crumpled the paper again and again, and would have flung it into the embers, had not my mother stayed his hand.

"Dear husband," she said, "some say Heaven is not a place so much as a state. I am sure *home* is not so many walls and floors, but the presence of our loved ones. We will have a *home,* even in Connaught."

My father's mood softened, as it ever does, at her touch. He groaned as he looked at his crutch, which I had picked up and had set ready to his hand again.

"I think I could bear it better if they would not call their vile deeds by the name of law," he said. "Truly said Master Shakespeare that— 'Man, proud man,

Dress'd in a little brief authority...

Plays such fantastic tricks before high Heaven

As make the angels weep!'

But you are right, wife, as you always are. In Connaught even you will still be Madam O'Connor; for even if they pass an edict that your very name is not to belong to you, but to some English scullion, you will still be my own brave and noble lady." And he took her white hand and kissed it with the respectful courtesy which he ever shows her, being, I think, as truly her lover as he was when she was young and fair.

Then, having vented his wrath, he regained composure, and prepared himself to go at once to Athlone and obtain a hearing before the commissioners there. For which purpose a paper was hastily made out, describing, as was required, the proprietor himself and all who would accompany him. In this latter category every tenant, and all the promiscuous tribe of servants, horse-boys, cow-boys, pensioners, and hangers-on who had ever been fed from our table, insisted on being reckoned, those who might be of use refusing to desert us, and those who were useless entreating with tears that we would not cast

them off. So that the list was indeed a strange one when made out, numbering one hundred eighty and five persons, each having his personal description and his property set after his name, which " We the said Commissioners" certified to be true, and set their hands and seals unto.

My father headed the list as "Gerald O'Connor, Knight of Lara, adged sixty-five, tall, grey-haired; numb of part of his body; twenty cows, five garrans, ten yearlings; thirty acres of wheat, ten of flax, ten of oats, five of pease and beans. " Next followed my mother, and Pierce, and I, " Ethne, daughter to the said Gerald, adged eighteen yeares, tall, dark." Then came the tenants—" 14. Morish Ffallon of Killdagan, fortie, graye, low, tenant; four cows, fifteene sheepe, eleven garrans, seven acres of wheate and beane." And so down to Honora ny Houlahan, adged twenty, brown, spinster; and Larry O'Hulterie, adged twelve, lowe, flaxen, horse-boy.

I could borrow a simile from Captain Standfast, and say that the paper might well have told the family of an Israelite journeying into Canaan. But, ah me! behind our Jordan, the Shannon, there lies no Promised Land; only the heathy hills, and low bogs, and rock-strewn valleys of Connaught.

CHAPTER m jfrom *(tt* Diari' of (Stfme SD'£onnor. jE have always kept the seventeenth of March, the Feast of St. Patrick, with laughter and merriment.

Mass is said early, and the rest of the day is spent in every sort of play and diversion. It seems strange this year to think of merry-making, but Father Ambrose encouraged it. Doubtless the blessed saint would still have poor Ireland in his keeping, he said; and surely if we desired that he should remember us we should remember him, and not be as these English, who blot out every remembrance of the Stars of the Church, and deny even that they worked miracles for the conversion of unbelievers and the glory of Holy Church.

So says Father Ambrose; and I was therefore quite willing to take proper interest in the announcement which my pretty maid Nora ny Houlahan made me a day or two since. "The 'boys' were going to hurl for her," she said; and the honour was a great one, for the young men of two whole baronies meant to compete, having, according to their custom, decided amongst themselves that pretty Nora had stayed long enough unwedded, and she must not be allowed to remain so any longer.

So they had sent to notify to Nora that she must be the prize in the coming encounter, which was to begin after mass on St. Patrick's Day, and, if not finished then, to be continued on the following Sundays. And Nora blushing rosy red, begged that I would grace the proceedings with my presence, which accordingly I promised to do.

"You will go with me, Pierce," I said, as we sat at breakfast.

"I may as well," said Pierce; and Maurice, who had walked over thus early, dressed in blue velvet, and smiling as usual, laughed and said, "In truth, if that request were made to me, I would answer eagerly enough." And Pierce laughed too, and told him he would give but the same answer if the request had come from his sister. From the sister of another man—the matter was different altogether. At that Maurice put on as serious a face as he could, and sighing deeply, said he would there were such a custom in our rank of life. *Some* maidens would then not be allowed to live at liberty and tread down the hearts of men at their pleasure. So I handed him an oaten bannock, and bade him take and eat it. He would not want for butter, that was certain, nor vinegar for a relish, I said; and Maurice broke out into his verses, that come ever as readily to point his sayings, as Captain Standfast's sacred texts to sharpen his severer words— "Go, lovely Rose!
Tell her that wastes her time and me,
That now she knows"

"The full extent of Master Maurice Burke's love," I said.

"Nay, that cannot be known till you know the stars of the sky, the pearls of the sea, fair Ethne."

"Oh yes, I know it well," I answered; "the lore is not so hard as you would have us think. Maurice Burke loves to be in love; his own sighs are delightful as music, his woes are a never-failing source of interest. What would he do if all women were suddenly withdrawn from the world? Poor Maurice! no object for his rambles, no listener for his music, no subject for his songs! What a pitiable case!"

"Ah, you may laugh, my Samela," said Maurice; and Pierce laughed, and even my mother smiled, and did not reprove my saucy tongue, as I feared she would do. "You may laugh, but I shall win your favour yet. For—
'You may train the eagle
To stoop to your fist,
Or you may inveigle
The phoenix of the east;
The lioness, you may move her
To give o'er her prey,
But you'll ne'er stop a lover,
He will find out the way.'"

And Maurice insisted that he must ride with us to the hurling.

"Two are company," I said.

"Pierce, my friend," said Maurice, gazing from the window, "the sky is growing dark. I am pretty sure it will rain to-morrow. Besides, the wind is in the east; and as I came up just now the sun was over-hot. Your health is a little delicate; I fear it would not be well for you to ride forth to-morrow."

"Maurice, Maurice!" remonstrated my mother, "Ethne must have her brother's escort."

"With all my heart, so I may go too," declared Maurice.

"I am sorry for you, Maurice," I said, "for I fear you will have to discourse to the hedgerows, and sing to the wandering sparrow, and court the shy rabbit, while Pierce and I hold important converse. But I have it! We will not be three! Captain Standfast will grace our company, and enliven the assemblage. *I* will invite him, I myself."

"Ethne, Ethne, foolish child!" said my mother, while Maurice made a grimace, which he declared to be the proper face to wear in the Puritan's company—a very long and solemn one.

It happened that at that very moment Captain Standfast himself crossed the courtyard, and Pierce dared me to go and invite him as I had said. At that challenge I went quickly downstairs, and met the officer half-way across the court.

"I have a petition, sir," I said; and I told him what we intended, expecting in truth a curt refusal. But to my surprise, his brown face actually reddened, and he said in an embarrassed tone that was strangely unlike his usual sternness: "I—am hardly like to be a—welcome guest at such a gathering."

"But if I assure you of a welcome?" I said.

"I think you are truthful," he answered, in a tone that seemed more natural, scanning my face as he spoke.

"Besides," I said, trying not to feel angry at a certain implied doubt, "for the sake of the kindness you have shown us the people who love us are grateful."

"They should not so think," he answered, and now the harsh tone had quite returned. "It is written, 'Be ye merciful.' It is duty, not favour!"

"At all events we are all grateful," I said, with an effort, "if you will allow us to be. And if you will ride with us we shall be glad. You said I was truthful"

"I will ride with you," Captain Standfast said; and I went back to the assembled party, who received my tidings with incredulity at first, and afterwards with a dismay which would hardly have seemed flattering to the Englishman.

"I hope you are satisfied with yourself, Ethne," said Pierce. "*You* may talk to the Puritan if you will; I shall give him just a good-morrow—if the words do not stick in my throat."

"0 Pierce! be courteous to him," pleaded my mother. "Think where we should have been but for him."

"There's not much choosing in degrees of misery," muttered Pierce; and Maurice broke out into singing—

"' Come carol us a carol, oh!
The Soundheads to the devil go!'"

"For shame, Maurice!" said my mother, who, for all her gentleness, could flash out into anger sometimes, as she did now.

But no one could long be angry with Maurice. The apology he made was so graceful that my mother's sweet smile returned at once—sweeter than ever, as Maurice the flatterer told her, like the moon emerging from a cloud.

St. Patrick's Day broke in sunshine, and Maurice came over early, yet not so early as to go with us to mass. He wore a whole suit of saffron satin, in honour of the occasion, relieved by the colour of the shamrock,1 and by a great bunch of the dainty leaves and sweet pale blossoms fastening into his beaver hat a great plume of a pale and delicate green. And the lace that he wore was a marvel. Alas for the eyes of the poor Flemish women who worked it in their underground cellars with but a *point* of light upon their needles, and the knowledge that blindness must come sooner or later! My mother's tender heart will not allow her to wear this hardly-won treasure, or to let me do so. But I *did* think it a very lovely ornament, as Maurice greeted me and offered a posy of shamrocks newly gathered, and tied with a silver string, to match the silver fringes which my riding-dress bears, as he l The original shamrock was probably the wood-sorrel, as appears by various mentions of the eating of "shamrocks." *Saffron* was the ancient national Irish colour.

seemed to remember. I had not donned it yet, but in honour of the occasion I had put on my fairest brocade, of satin thick enough to stand alone, and of a blue ground covered with roses—mighty fine! Maurice viewed me with satisfaction, and praised my gown, declaring that it was exactly like the favourite dress of a certain Spanish Infanta, who, however, did not grace it so well. But I had not time to answer, for Captain Standfast stood there in his sober grey and his leather boots and plain linen, with his cropped hair and set face. I looked from him to Maurice and back again, and I think he saw the look, for he scanned Maurice's figure searchingly from head to foot, and then glanced at Pierce, who also was bravely dressed, and who greeted him with a cordiality such as I hardly had dared to expect.

We were soon in the saddle and away. The dogs raced and jumped and barked, in utter unreasoning joy that they were alive. And I felt light of heart too as my horse—Maurice's horse—bounded under me. Pierce rode a horse belonging to one of our tenants, who was proud to lend it. He had no stirrups, for our nation have ever despised these helpers of the bad horseman, and the sliding reins were fastened to a brass-bit of old Irish pattern, which pleased my brother greatly. He was very cheerful, and told all manner of strange tales to amuse the Englishman; and in truth that is not a hard matter, since every brook and lake and hill and rock in our country has its story of saint or fairy.

Lough Divreagh, by the shore of which we were riding, is called by that name, which signifies " The Lake of the Severe Judgment," because a man who had stolen a cow strove to drive her home across the ice upon it. But the cow, hastily driven, fell and broke her leg, and the man, not knowing what to do, killed her there and then, and carried off so much of the carcass as he could.

However, he missed his knife, and on going back to find it, behold the ice had become rotten where the warm carcass lay. He fell through, and the ice closed about his neck and beheaded him. And as he fell he cried in Irish, with a cry that was heard far and wide, "Wirasthru, this is a Severe Judgment!"

"This lake has the strange property of turning wood into stone," added Pierce; "the reason being that a certain saint once asked leave of the king of the country to build a stone church on its shore, as wood, which was plentiful enough there, rotted so fast. To which the king, mocking, replied in a jingle which may run in English—

'Take stones from the wood,
Get cement from the flood,
Your church will be good,
When long years it has stood.'"

"' Bad scran to you,' said the saint, for he was a courteous gentleman, explained Pierce, ' I never thought of that. ' And he cut down every tree in the royal forest, soaked the planks in the water, and built a splendid *stone* church, of which the ruins yet remain, the walls being composed of curiously long and neatly hewn stones."

"Such a story, if true, would not tend to glorify your saint," said the Puritan. "But it may well be that the water has some property which gives a stony look to substances soaked in it. I myself have seen wells in England"

"I daresay," said Pierce. "However, our people always invoke St Earvain's help when they build a house."

He did not hear, but I did, that Captain Standfast said softly to himself, " Except *the Lord* build the house, their labour is but lost that build it."

We had left the lake shores and were climbing up the sides of a lonely glen, wooded to the top of its steep sides.

H

Far below, as we rode, a river brawled over stones or fell in a white sheet into a black pool. The Devil's Glen, they call it, and there are strange stories about the place, but the Puritan would not hear them.

"It is not well," he said, "to make the prince of this world the hero of a fairy tale. He is too real and terrible, as we know who have wrestled with him, and have come out of the conflict sorely wounded, if victors also."

And as Pierce bit his lip, not liking to be thus schooled, the Englishman told us of a wonderful thing within his own knowledge, that might indeed well be called a miracle.

"One Master Colston," he said, " a merchant of Bristol, was well nigh lost with all his sailors and his costly cargo. When, just as hope seemed at an end, the leak suddenly stopped. And it was presently found that, doubtless in answer to prayer, a dolphin had firmly fixed herself into the hole, and the ship came safely into port. In remembrance of which signal mercy Master Colston had taken a dolphin for his own arms, and had founded various charities, honouring the Lord with his substance."

So he, too, believed in miracles after all.

As he finished his narrative the rain rushed suddenly and violently down, and we who had trusted too much to the bright promise of the morning bethought us of the nearest shelter. Most happily for us St. Earvain's cave was close at hand, and in a moment more we had reached it, and by dismounting were able also to lead our horses in. Maurice looked ruefully at sundry drops that had fallen on his delicate satin. Then, for want of a better occupation, and after an unusually long silence, he burst out into a song, a wild cavalier war song, that made the hollow place ring again. Pierce meantime was telling Captain Standfast that the saint having built his church built also a mill, and being much absorbed in devotion, forgot that there was no water to turn it. But that troubled him little; he prayed, and the river changed its course, and burst this hole through the hill.

"It is a childish story," said the grave captain, "more fit to move laughter than reverence. Pray you, friend Pierce, do *you* believe in these acts of your saint?"

Pierce shrugged his shoulders.

"The common people do devoutly, and in time of flood they come and fetch a pebble from this spot and throw it into the flood with a prayer that St. Earvain would turn back the waters."

"From which base superstition and idolatry may the Lord deliver them," returned the other, with a fervour which seemed much to surprise Pierce, who looked at him as though he would say, " Pray, what affair of yours is it?"

The roof rang with Maurice's merry song while they spoke:—

"A steed, a steed, of matchless speed!
A sword of metal keen!
All else to nohle hearts is dross,
All else on earth is mean.
The neighing of the 'war-horse proud,
The rolling of the drum,
The clangour of the trumpet loud,
Be sounds from heaven that come.
And oh! the thundering press of knights,
When as their war-cries swell,
May toll from heaven an angel bright,
And rouse a fiend from helL"

"If war be so pleasant a game, I marvel that you can dally here so long, Master Maurice," I said.

"So long! Are you weary of the sight of me, Mistress Ethne? Then I will rid you of that sorrow." And he sang again:—

"For I must go where lazy peace
Will hide her drowsy head,
And for the sport of kings increase
The number of the dead.
But first 111 chide thy cruel theft Can I in war delight,
Who, being of my heart bereft,
 Can have no heart to fight "
"Can I, Ethne?"

And as I did not answer at once, he turned to Captain Standfast.

"Have you no songs now in England, friend? You have forsaken these merry poets from whom I have sung— the poets of the golden age of Elizabeth, a Protestant like yourself for that matter. Have you nothing to replace these vanities?"

"They are indeed vanity of vanities," said Captain Standfast; "but," he added with some hesitation, "there *are* poets. One Master Baxter, and others, have written godly songs. And now I bethink me of one that might well be worth your consideration For thus he says, Master Baxter to wit—

'The silly lambs to-day
Pleasantly skip and play,
Whom butchers mean to slay
 Perhaps to-morrow;
In a more brutish sort
Do careless sinners sport,
Or in dead sleep still snort
 As near to sorrow;
Till life not well begun
Be sadly ended,
And the web they have spun
 Can ne'er be ended."'

At this Pierce was so overcome that he went farther into the cavern, and there, as I could see, though the soldier could not, shook his shoulders, choking with restrained mirth. I also coloured, and knew not what to say. But Maurice, enjoying the situation, went on with a grave and demure tone and look—

"It is indeed a godly song, sir, and, as you say, well calculated to edify. For indeed we do frisk and say baa most heedlessly, even now when we are about to be made mutton. I pray you repeat to us another poem of the same melodious sort?"

I shot an angry glance at Maurice, but Captain Standfast paid no heed to his flippancy, and looked only at me as he spoke. I had not thought it possible that his voice could take such a softened tone of love and longing as it did while he repeated these fair lines—

"Jerusalem, my happy home!
When shall I come to thee?
When shall my sorrows have an end,
Thy joys when shall I see?
Oh happy harbour of the saints!
Oh Bweet and pleasant soil!
In thee no sorrow may be found,
No grief, no care, no toil.

In thee no sickness may be seen, Nor hurt, nor ache, nor sore;
There is no death nor ugly dole,
 But life for evermore.

There lust and lucre cannot dwell,
There envy bears no sway;
There is no hunger, heat, nor cold,
 But pleasure every way.
Thy walls are made of precious stones, Thy bulwarks diamonds square,
Thy gates are of right orient pearl
 Exceeding rich and rare!
Thy turrets and thy pinnacles With carhunclea do shine;
Thy very streets are paved with gold
 Surpassing clear and fine.
Thy houses are of ivory, Thy windows crystal clear;
Thy tiles are made of beaten gold—
0 God that I were there!

At that he broke off abruptly, and said hastily, and in some confusion, "But I have wearied your patience. I ask your pardon. Has not the rain stopped? Will you ride on?"

"Pierce!" called Maurice; and as Pierce's voice answered from the further end of the cave, or rather tunnel, for such it was, Maurice went to meet him, first tying his horse's bridle to a trunk that lay by the stream.

"0 Maurice!" I said, "if you go to meet Pierce, do me a favour. The willows at the other end must be covered with catkins, and I need some to copy in my embroidery."

Maurice declared my lightest wish to be a command to my humble servant, and went. I was glad he did, for tears had come to my eyes, and I would not have had him see them. Nor would I that Captain Standfast should perceive a weakness which he would surely despise. So I said, half laughingly—

"I am afraid your home *lure,* must in some ways be uncongenial, Captain Standfast. You must be lonely."

"It is true that my spirit is often solitary," he said, a little sadly. "When I pass through a village the people shrink away into their houses. Yesterday a child flung back a rosy apple I had given it, and cursed me in its own tongue. I was sorry, for I love children."

He loved children—was it possible? In women the love of children seems but natural; she who has it not seems hardly a true woman. But in a man it means ever a certain gentleness of soul and tenderness of heart. But to be repulsed by the children when one loves them, that must be hard indeed! "I am so sorry," I said.

"It is better so," he answered. "How evil is my heart that dares complain! Lonely, forsooth! It is enough— far too much—for the servant that he be as his Master. And *He* was lonely!"

"Do you mean the Saviour?" I asked. "But we always see Him in pictures surrounded by saints and angels. Even on the Cross He had Saint Mary and Saint John."

"I think, perhaps, when men were round Him, He may have been most lonely," said the Puritan slowly, " because there is a loneliness of the spirit into which our brother man cannot enter. *We* can never be so utterly lonely, for we have always the Friend that sticketh closer than a brother."

"Is He a *friend?"* I asked, wondering at his happy look as he spoke the last words. "He is God, and He will come to judge us, and we cannot see Him till the fire has burned every stain from our souls. He is terrible, but Mary our Mother has pity, for she is human; she will plead with Him."

"Oh, Mistress Ethne!" cried the Puritan, and he clasped his hands together as if to entreat me, "do not think thus of Him. It is now as it was then. He comes to His own —His own! and they receive Him not. You do not know Him, the chief among ten thousand, the altogether lovely, the Sinless who ate with sinners!"

"I know that He died to save us from God's anger," I said slowly.

"But you hardly know that He lived! And His life is as precious, if possible, as His death." He looked round to see if Pierce or Maurice were near, and then drew out the little worn Book in which he continually reads. "Here is the story of His life and of His death. Your Church keeps it from you. Have you courage to read it? Yon will never repent of so doing, Mistress Ethne," he added earnestly.

And I, trembling a little, took the Book and hid it in my dress, thanking him, and promising safely to restore it; for I think neither gold nor jewels have to him half the value of this little dingy volume.

Maurice and Pierce came along the rough way, Maurice bemoaning sundry splashes on his costly dress, and Pierce extolling his own suit of fine blue cloth, that cost half the price, and would outlast two of such suits as Maurice's.

"My catkins, Maurice?" said I.

"*Your* catkins, Ethne? Nay, but the catkins of whosoever will adventure a whole bucketful of water from the soaking trees," said Maurice.

"So you have not brought them?" I cried, affecting great indignation. "O Maurice! you who have so often declared death for my sake a positive pleasure!"

"Certainly," answered Maurice unabashed; "death by fire or water, or any other mode. Most joyfully would I be drowned for your sake, Ethne; but as to getting wet— No; such thing as that you would never command your slave!"

"So I must do without my catkins," said I; "and small profit is it to me to have a *slave."* "You shall have plenty to-morrow. I will send my boy Brian for them."

"To-morrow I shall not care to have them," I said; and Maurice laughed, and appealed to Captain Standfast whether this was not reprehensible fickleness.

"It is ever thus with the fancies of women," he answered gravely, and I felt angry with him, and with myself, and Maurice too. Which was natural, I think, if not quite dignified.

The rain had really ceased now, and we mounted and hastened on, for we had already delayed too long. The game had already begun when we reached the ground, a flat, smooth meadow, where the friends of the players were gathered in a wide circle, or oval rather, having at its ends the two goals formed of withes bent and fixed hoop-fashion into the ground. Through these goals the players had to try to drive the ball with their flat wooden hurlies, the attempts of any one player being, of course, vigorously opposed by all the others.

Active and well-built young men they all were, but among them all none was so fine a lad or so skilful a player as Teague O'Ruark, Pierce's foster-brother. At one end of the ring, beside comfortable seats kept for us, was a deal table, on which was set a creepy, and here Nora ny Houlahan sat enthroned, watching with intense interest the efforts of this formidable array of lovers. She might well feel anxious, though too high-spirited to show it, for I knew well that Teague was the true choice of her heart, and this hurling match had been proposed by the young men in the hope of ousting the favoured suitor. The game ceased when we appeared, and the players joined with the rest to bid us welcome, and invite us to our seats near the Queen of the day, whose cheeks glowed as brightly as her red skirt, or the scarlet kerchief pinned about the neck of her blue bodice, when Maurice paid her some of his compliments, a *little* less high-flown perhaps than those he offers me. Then we sat down and watched the game, and talked with the people, and Captain Standfast presently gave utterance to his surprise.

"They are as humble friends to you," he said. "They speak to you freely, but never presume. The puffed-up nobility of England treat the poor as scarce fit to wipe their shoes on."

"Neither they nor their fathers were ever serfs and villains," said Pierce eagerly. "For their sakes I entreat you to treat them as we have treated them; they will soon be your friends as they have become the friends of each new colony of settlers, if you will but do this."

It was a strange speech to come from Pierce, but I think his love for the people drew it from him. And the people, seeing the English officer to be in our company as a friend, made him welcome too, and brought him cakes and ale, as they brought to us; and the children to whom he spoke looked up into the stern face that softened to them, and smiled, and were not afraid. So the pleasant day passed, and it seemed to me a wonderful thing, as we rode homeward in the lengthening shadows, that our enemy and the spoiler of our goods had sat with us as a friend and companion, and rejoiced in the issue of the game. For Teague won at last, after many hairbreadth 'scapes, and pretty Nora, blushing and smiling, was hailed as his bride by general acclamation.

CHAPTER XIII. JFrom t&e iDiarg of ffitjjne 2D'eTonnor.

N leaving my room next morning I found on the sill of the door a great bunch of yellow catkins. And downstairs I found Maurice; cause and effect were evidently close together. "I am grateful for the catkins, Sir Puss in Boots," said I. "The title becomes a knight who is so timid of water, you must confess."

"Honour to whom honour is due, I will confess," said Maurice.

"What, did you not bring them?"

"I did not say that, impatient Ethne."

"Let be, Maurice," chimed in Pierce. "She thinks the Puritan brought them."

At which I coloured hotly, and cried—" And if I had asked Captain Standfast I hardly doubt but that he would have fetched them for me, rain or no rain."

"Ay, the bear is growing tame," said Pierce; " he will dance presently to Malachy's harp."

"He did that once, or nearly, with rage," said Maurice. "But certainly the animal's ferocious ways do seem mollified. I have heard an old wife's tale that wolves fed on honey and fresh butter forsake their wild nature. See what wonders your sweet conversation is working, Ethne."

"I would I had some magic to control your too sweet language," I said, as coldly as I could.

"Nay, that is easily done," laughed Maurice; "that thunder-cloud obscuring the heaven of your eyes will turn my talk, which is the cream of courtesy, to sourness."

"In truth, I might as well try to get sweet from sour, as sense from you, Maurice," I said; but Pierce bade me hold my peace, for that Maurice had certainly given me a good answer, and one that I should not easily match.

The two young men went out, and I spent most of the day at my embroidery frame, longing for the night to come, that I might light my little lamp and read again in the wonderful Book the English officer had lent me. So night after night I read till a glimmer began to appear in the east, and then I put out my lamp, and lay quietly with closed eyes, thinking over the subject of my reading.

Father Ambrose never forbade me to read the Bible. He only spoke of it as an undesirable study for the laity, as requiring much training before it could be duly understood, and as without such training tending only to confuse the mind, and lead, through the abuse of private interpretation, to heresy and schism; whereas the Spirit of God, speaking through the Church, expounds rightly that which many theologians might expound in as many different ways, and we, having this infallible guide, do best to follow it with unperplexed minds. So he has ever taught me. It was therefore with some tremor that I took up the dangerous volume and read the New Testament from end to end, having taken that firstt

The short portions appointed for Gospels at the Holy Mass I had often heard read, but the rest of the book I supposed to be taken up with expoundings of the subtleties of theology, and other things hard to be known. So that it was with surprise and delight that I studied the four first books, which, like four paintings of the same person, show the various features in different lights, and thereby make the person represented more living and familiar to us.

And what a Person is here painted! *The Word was made flesh, and dwelt among vs.* I have seen Him in pictures as the Babe on Mary's knee, as the agonised Sufferer, as the just and severe Judge. But here I learned to know Him as the Carpenter's Son, as the Teacher who spake as never man spake, as the Redeemer whose invitation to the weary-hearted was ever " Come unto Me." "Come unto Me!" and I had fled trembling at the thought of His anger to Mary His Mother, the Star of the Sea, the hope

Ah, how grieved that loving heart would have been, if, when He walked on earth, and said, " Come unto Me," we had turned from Him to Mary. Truly, I think she too would have been grieved.

Captain Standfast said well that I had never known Him truly, who knew Him only as Lord and Judge, or as the Babe on Mary's knee. I learned to know Him now! I saw Him at the wedding of one friend, at the burial of another—adding to the happiness of the one, weeping at the other.

I saw Him pitying the sick and healing them; I saw Him bearing with the faults and follies of the few who followed Him, and sorely tried by their unbelief and hardness of heart. How *could* they have forsaken Him and fled?

What would it have been to me to have been able to steal to His feet like the poor Magdalen, and pour out all my love and sorrow! And then four times over, and the last time most touchingly told of all, I have read the story of the bitter cup He drank.

I have hardly borne to read it. I suppose those who from childhood have read and re-read it, till every detail is familiar, may read that story unmoved. But I know that I cast myself on the floor of my room in a passion of tears long before I had finished the first of those four accounts of it, and again and again I wept afresh. No wonder that a sword pierced through Mary's heart! What must it have been to *see* that which I have found so terrible to read?

No wonder that darkness covered all the earth. What mercy was God's that lifted that darkness again! I know that if

I had sat in God's seat that day I would assuredly have plunged the whole earth and all that was on it into the bottomless abyss, and shut the door of hope upon it for ever and ever. Perhaps God would have done so, but that *He* interceded, He who died with mockery added to the bitterness of His death. We do not mock even our worst criminal—his death is a solemn and awful thing. But He was mocked; the scourging was as nothing beside the horror of the purple robe and the reed.

Surely, surely the whole earth must have been cast into hell but for His death! And yet we live and move, and are glad or sad, and spring comes, and autumn, and the sun still shines, while men think and speak of anything and everything else, morning and noon and night, except that awful deed, the one thing of any real importance in all the world's history. But Captain Standfast reads and re-reads this Book. I can understand why— now.

The story of the Resurrection calmed my mind again, and that of the Ascension, with the strange mystical promise of the Lord's continued presence. And when I had read and re-read the four Gospels by night, pondering them in my heart all day for many days, I found leisure at last to read further.

Then I found that when the Sun had gone to rest, the stars came forth. Those weak, fallible men who quarrelled about precedence, and slept in their Master's hour of anguish, and only half understood even His simplest teachings— these men in all their human weakness became suddenly strong.

Councils and tyrants, the stress of public opinion, or the perils of torture and death, had no effect upon their determination to preach their Christ and Him crucified.

Some of their doings were here recorded; how with the symbol of a degrading death for their glory and pride they went forth, telling their scarcely credible story, and inviting men to embrace humility and poverty, to face ridicule and persecution—for His sake.

That seemed natural enough to me now. I could well understand how, when they heard that which I had read, the learned and the ignorant, the rich and the poor, the Jew and the Gentile fell at those pierced feet, and all else became utterly worthless then, and thenceforward —all else but Christ.

The letters of these men to their believers filled a great space. These are they whom we call greatest among the Saints—St. Peter, St. John, and the rest. But never, never once do they call to the people, "Come unto me!" One and all they stand like Moses holding his serpent before the despairing eyes of the dying, holding up Christ alone. Nay, once when worship was offered them they were driven almost wild with grief, and rushed into the throng of their intending adorers with entreaties and protests.

These letters held many good counsels, each letter reflecting the mind of him who wrote it. Paul, with his rugged and broken style, now arguing with the Jew, now entreating the foolish and backsliding Galatian, now joyfully communing with the faithful Philippian, or with Timothy, his friend and pupil, and ever and anon rising to an outburst of splendid eloquence, as he spoke of the hope of the Resurrection, or the perfectness of the One offering. John with his keynote of Love, and Love, and yet again Love; James with his grave and sober exhortation—how I learned to know them all, and to reverence them more, ay, far more than I had done in the old days of blind and ignorant worship.

And how noble and beautiful was the life they set forth! To be a Christian such as they described, how lovely a hope was that! To go on to perfection, guided by that promised Spirit—how I longed to tread that path!

One more book there was—a strange, mystical vision of the last days, and the home of the Redeemed. And here I found the last pages much worn. That place which Bays, "His servants shall serve Him: they shall see His face," was deeply marked. Evidently the owner of the Book loved to study this part of it; this mystical, poetical Revelation has clearly a great charm for the stern, grave soldier, strange as it seems. I read it eagerly. There was much that was strange and hard to understand, but it was almost with dismay that I reached the last page, and read of the crowning glories of Heaven. For in all those descriptions of the Holy City I found no mention of the Mother of God, and of her throne beside her Son. How is it that we know that she died, and that her body, taken all undecayed from its tomb, was borne heavenward by angels? That she reigns there now, Star of the Sea of this troubled Ufa?

The night that I read that book I had no sleep, with such anguish did this discovery come home to me. It was anguish enough, that in all the letters of the sainted apostles I had found no directions for penance, and only a general recommendation to fast when we pray in times of need, and never a word of saintly intercession. But this I found— that if any man sin, we have an Advocate with the Father. And oh, since His compassion was so infinite that even after the Cross and the Rejection He could intercede, who could fail to take advantage of such a hope! On my knees from midnight till the sua was high in the sky, I lay prostrate, beseeching Him whom I might now dare to *love,* that among the songs of His redeemed He would bend to hear me, while I owned myself a sinner, and offered to Him my whole self and all that I have, or ever should have. For He needs us, that is the wonder of all wonders! In the Psalms of David, for these also I have read, I found the Father speaking to Him and saying, "Desire of Me, and I will give Thee the heathen for Thine inheritance." And as I read I remembered that His answer to the Father was none other than this: "Father, *I will* that they also whom Thou hast given Me be with Me where I am."

I see now why Captain Standfast longs to be pure in heart, that he may attain to that reward.

"Ethne, Ethne, who are you that He should have need of you?" cried my heart. But I answered to myself, He had need once even of an ass's colt. He may need me, and here am I His, soul and body, to do what He will—if He will. In this thought there came to me a radiant happiness, in which for the whole day that followed I seemed to tread upon air.

I sang as I went about the house— what did I say? about the stables! As I write that word, for the first time I have a delight in remembering our condition. For *He* lay in a stable once. I think the mean place has a glory about it ever since then. At least that thought makes me more than content to live in a stable now,

All the day I went about in perfect happiness, my own thoughts being a heaven.

Maurice came while I sat at my work, and praised me that I could be so cheerful under adverse circumstances.

I

I think Maurice's praise never made me very vain. But this day it seemed hateful to me, and I cried—

"Maurice, do not talk so. You little know what a poor creature your Samela is at heart."

"My lady wears her humility like a crown," said Maurice.

"Nonsense, Maurice; it is too true— only too true, if you could but know."

"But, fair Ethne, I cannot allow you thus to wrong the Ethne whom I adore. I tell you she is absolutely perfect, else I should not adore her."

"But I tell you she is highly imperfect, and therefore you had best at once leave off adoring her, since it is the condition."

"But if you bring calumnies against my Ethne—the Ethne whom I love—I shall stand up as advocate for the defence, and the other Ethne, the calumniator of my lady, will have to pay a heavy fine," said Maurice; and I knew that I should never hear a reasonable word from him, so it was little use to be serious. But I did feel a great longing to open my lips, and tell him all this wonderful new thing, and try what effect the story would have on him. Oh, surely he could not hear it unmoved! Light-minded as he is, there must be *something* serious at bottom; the wildest tangle of flowers springs out of solid earth.

We went to rest as usual that night. I wanted to be alone and think, and I put out my lamp and lay down, striving to compose myself and arrange my thoughts.

These thoughts had burned closely locked in my bosom. I had uttered no word to any one. But now and then my mother's calm thoughtful gaze had rested upon my face. She saw that I was not quite as usual, though I strove to do and be exactly as I had ever done and been.

But to-iiiglit as I lay alone I thought of her. How much of all this did she know? I asked myself. As much as I knew a week ago? Little more than that. But a week ago I was another Ethne almost.

Heaven! what a distance I had travelled in spirit. I realised it with affright. I was not the same, but something different. "What was I then? And as if the words had been written upon the darkness in letters of fire the answer stood out before my recoiling spirit—

A Protestant.

Could it be? No longer a Catholic like my father and mother, but a Protestant like Captain Standfast. A Protestant, a heretic!

At the sudden terror of the thought I shrieked aloud, and in another moment a light came to the door, and my mother entered softly.

I was sitting up in bed, and with my black hair falling about my shoulders, my face doubtless pale, and with wide frightened eyes, I may well have caused an anxious look to cloud her dear face.

"What ails you, Ethne, my darling?" she asked; and as I did not at once answer she laid her hand on my hot forehead.

"An evil dream, my darling; you are overwrought, dear child." She laid me down, and held water to my lips, then from the little fount beneath my crucifix she took water and sprinkled the bed and me, saying an Ave and a Paternoster to drive away evil and disturbing spirits.

Then she went softly away, leaving a kiss on my brow, and bidding me sleep. But I, ashamed and grieved, and longing to throw myself on her loving heart and tell her all, I buried my face when she was gone in the pillows and shed tears,

the bitterest indeed that ever I have shed since those baby days when we give way to utter despair over a broken toy, or feel as though the world must immediately come to an end because the snow-man has irrecoverably melted, or the callow nestlings which we took to bring up tenderly are discovered cold, and with vainly gaping beaks. I think we never shed more bitter tears than those of childhood, although these are so soon forgotten.

Through long hours I fought blindly with my terror, now crying passionately to God to save me from this— only from this. Whatever else He might will to lay upon me, I could bear gladly— only not this. Again I tried to reassure myself. My father and mother were Catholics, and how good they were I knew. Many and many good people I had known were Catholics too— every one almost, except Lady Burke, of whom Father Ambrose used to say, with a smile and a shrug, that she stood with one foot within the fold.

A few other Protestant gentlefolks I had known. They heeded neither fast nor feast, but on Sundays put on their religion with their best clothes, and went to the Episcopal Church, a good many miles away, in our county town. Whether they were better or worse than my own family, I could not tell. They drank as much good French wine and kept as many horses and dogs as their neighbours; and sometimes they went over to London and brought back new fashions from the Court. We met them on the usual terms of friendship, though I used now and then to think with dismay that they were heretics, and in grievous spiritual danger.

The Lady Burke's children, Maurice and Mauriade, were brought up as Catholics, as was right and fit. To be a Protestant by parentage was a terrible misfortune for any child; but to become one! Did not Father Ambrose often point to the dreadful Civil War in England as the natural result of the national apostasy, the judgment falling most heavily on the royal family, the children of those who had headed the evil movement?

And I—was it towards Protestantism that I was drifting? Then if reading the Bible made men Protestants, no wonder the Church discouraged the reading. But if the Bible was God's message to man, should not man hear it? And if that message made him a Protestant, was he not right? But every teaching of my youth cried out against the supposition that there could be any right in heresy.

Thus I lay, my soul tossed by such a storm as I had never before experienced. But I think, even in all that agony, if one had come and had offered to wipe out the whole memory of what I had read, I should have said, "No; any suffering rather than that!"

At last, in utter inability to remain still any longer, I sprang from my bed, and in the chilly, grey light of a rainy dawn, utterly cheerless and disconsolate, I took the little book from under my pillow and opened it again, turning the pages and reading a line here and there, mostly those marked by Captain Standfast. At last my eye rested on one very heavily marked in black, and again in red, as though not once only, but again he had found help there—" If any man will do His will, he shall know of the doctrine."

I lifted my eyes to the leaden sky. How dreary it was! But into my soul, as though the dawn had broken there, there stole a ray of hope and comfort.

"If any man will do His will."

That meant the nearest duty, for me at least, since there was nothing great that I could do. There stood the promise of the Compassionate One, that knowledge should come to the obedient.

I closed the Book and folded my hands. "I will not 134 exercise myself in great matters which are too hard for me. I will refrain my soul and keep it low, like a child that is weaned. I will wait to be taught."

And in the peace which that thought brought, I lay down and fell asleep.
JFtom   t&e   Diarg   of   GEtjme 2D'2Tonnor. HEN I awoke my mother was standing by my bedside. The sun was high in the sky, and I was ashamed to have slept so late. But she was more tender to me than ever, if that could be.

"Sleep is Nature's medicine," she said. "Try to sleep again, my Ethne."

But I had no mind to sleep now; and when she was gone, after I had kissed her and confessed myself a troublesome child to have made her anxious, I got up and dressed myself at once. The rain was falling steadily and dismally. My head ached, and at my heart there was a dull aching too. The peace that I had found last night was gone again, and though I said the words of comfort over and over, and tried to anchor my weary soul upon them, they failed to still the inward trouble.

I have seen the great sea, when a storm was over and gone, troubled to its depths as my soul was then, heaving and moaning in a weary unrest, for which there was no present cause.

Pale and heavy-eyed I went down. I could not spin, I could not sew, I ate a morsel for my mother's sake, and then I sat down on a low stool at her feet, and leaned against her knee, as I used to do when I was a child and was tired or sad.

And as she ever used to do, she took my face in her hands, and lifted it to look at and kiss.

"My Ethne is troubled, and has been troubled for many days," she said, in that low sweet voice which always soothes and comforts, like a cool hand on the hot brow.

"Oh, mother, you knew it?" I cried, and my voice broke in a sob.

"A mother's eyes have marvellous clearness of sight, my Ethne," she answered.

"But they cannot read a child's heart," I said, with a deep longing that the loving eyes could read all my soul. For words could never tell all the thoughts that lay there, much less those strange embryo ideas of which one has but a dim consciousness, which have not developed yet into thoughts, and therefore cannot be translated into language, but which influence one's own mind so strongly.

"No, my Ethne, they cannot do that," and she sighed. "If that were possible, a mother's power would be more than human. But my Ethne has ever told her mother all her griefs. And I think she has not often gone away uncomforted."

"*Never*, dearest of mothers—oh, never!"

"But she fears it will not be so now!"

"Oh, mother, mother!" I cried, in tearless anguish, "not now; not yet! The bitterest part of my trouble is that I cannot tell you now; not yet, if ever. Oh, do not be angry with me," for she had turned her face from my beseeching gaze, and was looking out at the weary rain. There were tears on her worn cheek as she turned back to me, but her own smile was there too.

"I was thinking, my child, my own child," she said, in a voice that faltered a little, "how once, when you were a very little child, you lay in a fever, a fierce dreadful fever, that seemed to have taken a hold upon your baby framo that only death could relax. All that medicine could do for you was done, and I sat by your cradle and watched the awful fight of life with death, and felt so utterly powerless to help that I could but wring my hands in agony, and pray with all the strength of my soul. At last the crisis came; it passed, and you fell asleep. And I, sitting through the dead midnight and the chill hour before the dawn, said to myself, 'Even a mother's love has limits.' All my love could not help in this struggle of the frail body. What if one day I have to watch a struggle of the child's soul, and feel as powerless—except in prayer?"

"Dear, dearest mother," I sobbed, "I would tell you all; but I feel I cannot."

"Nor do I desire it, my darling. The mother who forces her child's confidences risks doing more of harm than she can hope to do ot good. This battle you feel you must fight out alone; but as I sat by your cradle seventeen years ago, my darling, and my heart was with you, so it is now."

"Oh, mother, mother, saint upon earth, if you knew how deeply I love you!" I said in my heart, and I kissed her and sat silently down to my wheel, and all that day and the next I worked with might and main at whatever task lay nearest, till Pierce good-humouredly relieved me, and then said kindly that I must not work so hard—he was too idle, and must help me. And I set him to card wool, which amused him an idle hour, and helped forward my spinning.

The third day I woke in much perturbation; for it was my day to go to confession; and how should I meet Father Ambrose? I had some thought of feigning illness; but that would only be to defer the evil day, and besides, strange as it may seem, I felt an intense longing to speak of what was in my heart. I was thankful that Captain Standfast was away; to meet him would have been an additional trial during these days.

Whatever I might say to Father Ambrose would be said under the seal of confession, and in this was great comfort. So on a calm sunny afternoon, when the birds were singing, and all green things were breaking out into leaf, I went down to our little church by the lake, where other penitents were sure to be gathered. There were not many in the building. An old woman was kneeling at the grated confessional, half shrouded in the curtain. I knelt and closed my eyes, and tried to remember the category of sins accumulated since my last confession, and noted them down in order as I could think of them.

My mind was in such a tumult that to remember was not very easy. But the priest would help me out with questions; and last of all, I would tell that I had read the Bible, and speak of my doubts and fears.

The old woman came back with a happy look from her absolution. The other penitents looked up at me. If I wished to take my turn now, I was welcome. I was glad to face the matter at once, and I rose and went to the dark wooden box, and with my lips at the grating began my Confiteor.

"I confess"—in the presence of the Blessed Trinity and of the Virgin, and of certain saints mentioned by name, and of the angels—" and to you, my father, that I have sinned exceedingly;" and at the end of the formula I paused a moment, and almost against my will the words came out—" that I have read the Bible!"

There was a movement inside the confessional—a start, perhaps, of surprise.

My voice had failed utterly; I could not say another word.

"You have read the Bible, my daughter," said the priest's low voice from within. "You have disobeyed the admonitions of Holy Church? Some sins bring their own penance with them. Has this given you peace of mind?"

"Oh no, no, father."

"No, my child, of course not. Your mind has been tossed incessantly on a sea of doubt and perplexity. You have never known an easy moment. Is this true?"

"Quite true," I said, in a choking voice.

"You have done some penance, then. But I must withhold absolution for the present. You are not in a fit state of mind for it. I recommend that you do penance for a week at Lough Arbella, after which you will return and finish your confession, and if you are truly penitent, I will grant absolution then."

There was silence. I waited meekly, hoping at least for a benediction. Never had absolution been withheld from me before.

"As a first proof of your penitence, my daughter," said Father Ambrose, after a pause, "you will give me that dangerous book. In my hands it will be safe, and do no further harm."

"But I cannot, father!" I gasped; "it is not mine."

"Not yours, my daughter? I pray you, whose is it, then?"

"It was—lent to me."

"There is only one person who could thus have led you astray," said Father Ambrose, in the sternest tone I had ever heard him use. "Ethne, my daughter, you have tampered with temptation; you are greatly and grievously to blame. I charge you, on your obedience as a daughter of the Church, give me that book."

"Father," I said, though I trembled so that I could scarcely shape the words with my dry lips, "I promised to give back the Book to its owner. May I not keep my promise?"

The priest was silent for a moment.

"Yes, I think you may, provided that you do so on the earliest opportunity, and that you tell him what suffering it has caused you."

I promised readily to do both, and Father Ambrose blessed and dismissed me, in the confidence, as he said, that he should soon have the happiness of absolving me, by the power committed to him, from that and all my other sins.

I went away and out into the sunshine, my knees trembling under me. I was disappointed, too; there were so many questions I had longed to ask the father. But out of the confessional I could not venture to ask him anything, even if I should have the chance of speaking with him alone, for he would not be bound to silence.

He came up to our dwelling next day and saw my mother. I was not anxious about the interview, for I knew he would utter no word of my confession. He came to propose a pilgrimage for me, he said; he counselled it, and his counsel in these matters was always welcome. Assuredly I should go, my mother said, and asked me if I were willing. I assented gladly, for to be away for a week would be an intense relief.

The reason Father Ambrose gave for proposing a pilgrimage was that prayer and penance were much needed to gain the favour of Heaven for our unhappy country. Who could tell how much of her misfortunes were owing to her children's neglect of holy things? My brother Pierce was in the room, and took up the plan with an energy which surprised me.

"Ay," he said, "nothing could be better. And indeed, there seems no reason why Ethne should not stay longer."

"What! do you not want me at home, Pierce?" I Baid, a little hurt, and Pierce muttered something I did not quite understand.

It chanced that I saw Father Ambrose alone for a moment that very day, and he came up to me. "Ethne, my daughter," he said, "forget not to ask of Mary our Lady, the grace of closed ears."

"Of closed ears, father?" I asked.

"Ay, of ears closed to all voices but that of the Church. What think you would become of a soldier in battle, Ethne, if he obeyed every voice that shouted round him. Utter confusion and overthrow. But you are not fighting as a soldier; you are rather like Noah's dove that wandered once over the waste of waters and found no rest. Come back to the true Ark, my child; how gladly will I open the little window and take you in!"

My father grumbled a little at the thought of my departure; but he yielded, to my great relief. So the matter was settled.

The day before my departure Captain Standfast returned. Now I must fulfil my promise, but how?

I would send the book by one of the servants, but that I did not wish to do. Moreover, I had promised to tell him of the trouble it had caused me. I must try and see him myself. He came over to our rooms, and sat for an hour talking to my mother and Pierce, not seeming to notice me, except by a greeting as I sat apart. When he was gone I went to my own chamber and watched to see if he would come out and walk on the terrace in the dusk, as he was fond of doing.

I waited long. At last he came out and paced to and fro with hands behind his back. Then, with trembling fingers, I wrapped my mantle about me, and stole downstairs, feeling like a criminal who fears to be detected. As I went out, I heard the door of our sitting-room open, and Pierce's voice called "Ethne;" but I wrapped the cloak closely round me and round the book I held, and went on to the terrace.

"Captain Standfast," I said, in a low and breathless voice, following the officer as he walked. He turned quickly.

"I have brought back your book," I said, in the same smothered tone. "Did you guess when you lent it what trouble it would cause me?"

"I *knew* it," he answered, looking keenly at me from under his dark brows. "The Word of God is sharper than a two-edged sword; it must pierce soul and spirit."

"That was strange friendship," I said scarcely knowing what I said, " to cause me pain deliberately."

"Better friendship than you think as yet. But friendship cannot be from me to you," he said, in a low hurried tone.

I had done my errand in excited haste, and I turned and hurried away, wondering as I went what those last strange words might mean.

Then suddenly I felt a strong hand grasp my wrist, and Pierce stood above me, his face black with anger.

"Ethne! what are you doing?"

"Nothing that I have cause to be ashamed of," I answered haughtily.

"What book was that you gave to that man? Answer me."

"I do not know what right you have to ask."

"I have a right. I insist on knowing."

"It was an order-book for soldiers," I said sturdily; and Pierce loosed my wrist, and bade me have nothing to do with the man and his books.

I went in slowly. It was a lie I had told Pierce—not a *real* lie; but one of those doubtful sayings which are white lies, told for convenience, for peace' sake. I should naturally have remembered it to confess next time to Father Ambrose.

But to-day it struck me in a light that was wholly new and strange. Was any lie *white?* Would not all untruthfulness grieve Him whom I longed to please? I ought to strive to be like Him, that I might at last see His face. Would He have stooped to the smallest deceit? Never, never! Then neither will I, Ethne, so long as I live, He being my helper.

Jftom t&e Diarg of ffitjme JD'Connor.

TMY mother has been glad of my intended pilgrimage. "Ethne," she said that evening, in a hesitating tone, that was not nsual to her, "Pierce thinks—that is, we all think—that the religious life had once some charm for you. I do not know if it is so now?"

"I think it must be wonderfully beautiful to give up one's whole heart to God without any reservation, dear mother," I said. "When Mauriade Burke went into the convent at Arbella, I thought her happy."

"You will see her now, my child."

"I shall see her. I trust she is happy."

"I am sure she is. And, Ethne, my child, I would not willingly part with you; but if that holy life should seem— if you should desire it"

"But the convent is to be closed, mother."

"But the Brides of Christ will re-assemble in some Catholic country. Inside their quiet walls there will be peace. The breath of heresy"

"Dear mother, did Father Ambrose give yon this counsel?" I said; and she avoided a direct answer, so that I asked her again. Then she said—

"Father Ambrose thought that we know not what a day may bring forth. So that a safe shelter under the wing of the Church— But indeed, my Ethne, it is not what I would have desired for you. I hoped to see you wooed and won as other maidens, as I myself"

"But we will not talk about that, dearest mother. To be with you and cheer you is enough for me."

"It is enough now; but we must go the way of all flesh; and what of our Ethne then? The contemplative life is higher than the active, so Father Ambrose says; but to us mothers our own path seems a fit and safe one for the feet of our daughters—betrothal, marriage, the bringing up of children, building in our strength the props for our old age."

My faithful handmaid, Nora ny Houlahan, was to go with me. She also went gladly on pilgrimage, to pray for blessings on her coming marriage with Teaguo 0'B.uark. A garran from the farming work was the best horse I could have—good enough, in sooth. Nora would go a-foot. I covered my silken dress with my cloth riding-skirt, put on my silver-fringed riding-jerkin and plumed hat, and bade my parents farewell.

At the very door as I went down I met Captain Standfast.

"What, you travel, lady?" he asked.

"I do, sir. I go on pilgrimage."

"On pilgrimage?" he repeated.

"On pilgrimage, sir, to the Seven Holy Graves at Arbella, to ask the blessing of the saints and of Mary our Lady on poor Ierne."

"But will they hear you?" he asked,

looking in my face, then saluted me, and went away. Now I stood thoughtful and vexed. I had not meant to say what I said. But a cheerful voice cried to me—

"What, you travel, fair Ethne?"

The voice, of course, was Maurice's, and I answered his question as I had answered the Englishman's.

K

"I do, sir. I go on pilgrimage."

"Nay then, fair pilgrim, you do wrong. There are candles enough at yonder shrine, I warrant; and we cannot afford to lose those two bright lamps which you carry under the shadow of your brows."

"In truth, Master Maurice, if you need a lamp, your tongue can spare you oil," I said; and Maurice laughed. But as my pony was led out, he grew grave again, and said—

"Why must you go? It is cruel of you, Ethne. Do you not feel that you are selfish?"

"No; for I go to pray for all whom I love."

"Will you pray for me, then, Ethne?"

Maurice's voice was low and pleading. Perhaps he longed after something better, I said to myself; and to him I said—

"What, then, Bhall I ask for you, Maurice?"

"Sweet Ethne, the present is real, the future is— possible. Why should your delicate feet tread the sharp stones of Arbella? Let us eat and drink, for tomorrow we die."

"But after that, Maurice?"

"But after that—*quien lo sdbe?* as we say in Spain. These trees will soon be covered with leaves, but they are not last year's leaves. Those have had their day and are gone."

"0 Maurice, Maurice!" I cried, and I could say no more. Maurice was trained in the faith of our fathers, like his sister; Lady Burke was allowed no control over this sacred matter. But this was worse even than heresy.

"Do not look at me like that, Ethne! I will say or unsay anything sooner than meet such eyes. Let me give you a poet's advice—

'Gather ye roses while ye may, Old Time is still a-flying;
And that same flower that blooms to-day,
To-morrow may be dying.'

Enjoy the present, in fact, and do not embitter it with self-imposed sufferings. That is a poet's advice, and the poets are always right."

So, half pleading, half teasing, Maurice tried to withhold me. I could not be withheld, of course, and I mounted my pony and rode away, Nora trudging beside me.

Pierce walked beside me as far as the great gates. As he was parting from me there was a shout behind us, and Larry Oge came at the top of his speed, his hands full of flowers.

"The bodagh Sassenach," he cried, breathless, "sent me with these for Lady Ethne to take with her."

Such a strange nosegay! Evidently the flowers were from some of mine own cherished plants which I had left behind in the castle, there being room where we were for but a few. A number of the choice blossoms the soldier had taken, and with his clumsy man's fingers had crammed their heads together into a pitifully crushed mass, tied with stout strings. I fear I smiled, as I looked at his offering. I stretched my hand for it, but Pierce took the posy from the child.

"In truth, Larry," said he, " the flowers are not very well chosen, and they are very ill grouped. Altogether, the nosegay is hardly one to offer to a lady. I detect, also, a certain odour of heresy about it. Faugh!" And Pierce sent the flowers spinning through the air, and into the wet ditch close at hand.

"0 Pierce!" I cried indignantly, while the boy Larry grinned from ear to ear. "How could you do so? I wanted them, and you have no thought for the poor man's feelings." Saxon churl.

"His feelings, forsooth! The feelings of a hog in armour. Go back to him who sent you, Larry, and report what I—no, what Mistress Ethne did with his offering."

"Pierce! No, Larry, tell him I thanked him."

"Tell him what I say, Larry," commanded Pierce; and the child looked from him to me, and then sped away like the wind, leaving me with a heart hot and burning with vexation.

"I think it is well yon go to Arbella, Ethne," said Pierce; and I shook my rein and rode away without another word.

In a basin of hills, high above the sea-level, lies a deepblue lake. None knows how deep it is—no line would measure it. You can look far, far down and see no bottom, so clear is the water—only the fishes darting by through the crystal deeps.

In old, old days, when the fairies had power, they say that this was a lonely valley, with a fair spring filling a well which the good people loved, and about which they danced at night, and till cockcrow. Whoever would draw water there must draw it just after sunrise, for if the stone that covered the well's mouth were not put back, and the sun should fall upon the water, it would certainly rise and overflow the whole valley. There was, so runs the story, a wicked king at that time who sent to one Aodh O'Donnell and demanded his seven daughters, threatening, when refused, to come and take them by force. So the maidens bethought them of the fairy well, and they rolled away the stone after sunrise, expecting to be carried away by the rising water. The water rose indeed and filled the whole valley up to the crests of the mountains round, but the spot of ground on which the maidens stood rose with them, and spread into a fair island. And the fairies cast a spell about it, and it made shelter and food for the maidens upon it, and the spell made it invisible to all men who came to the shore. However, at last Saint Patrick came, and his eyes were clear, and saw through fairy spells, and he rowed over to the island, and said to the maidens, " Let us praise God together, since out of love for Him you did this thing."

But they said, " We never heard His name."

And Patrick answered—" You know Him, though you know not His name, for the choice of death before dishonour came only by His grace."

And there he taught the maidens, and they prayed to be baptized. So Patrick went to the lake to fetch water, but the wicked king had power enough to turn the water to blood. Then Patrick prayed, and a fair spring sprang up in the centre of the island, and he baptized the maidens, and he laid a curse on the king that he should die of thirst, and so he did, for whatever water he put to his lips dried up before they touched it.

As for the maidens being baptized they made a petition to Patrick, and said, " Pray for us that we may die before we commit sin and soil the white robes of our baptism." So he prayed, and that night they all died, and were buried in seven graves on the island in Lough Arbella.

On this island the convent stands now, and all round are the heathery hills. Perfect peace reigns in that lonely place; holy singing and the sound of the convent bell fall sometimes upon the still air, else only the wind and the lark overhead are to bo heard.

It was with a real feeling of happiness that I entered the convent. To live all day in that calm, to sing holy hymns, to hear no echo of the troublous world, and every day to offer the prescribed prayers at the graves, and endure the appointed penance, what could be happier?

Round each grave is a wide path of sharp stones. Round each grave, after bathing face and hands in the holy well, and repeating certain prayers, the pilgrim travels on bare feet or bare knees, praying afterwards at the shrine of Our Lady of Arbella beside the spring.

For women especially this pilgrimage is intended, and hither they come in great numbers, for great gifts and the pardon of many sins may be bought by the prayers and penances. And who would heed torn and bleeding feet, and a body faint with fasting and long vigil, if thereby the soul were made fit to enter the Light of God?

"Blessed are the pure in heart," said the Puritan soldier; and he shrouds himself in grim reserve and gravity, lest laughter or song might stain the soul. Does he do penance thus, as I on the sharp stones of Lough Arbella?

Day by day I have fulfilled the appointed rites and penances, in the hope that I might yet find consolation in them, and might within the fold of the Church of my fathers find balm for the sharp pain in my soul.

"But are you sure they will hear you?" said Captain Standfast, and his words echo in my ears every time I kneel before the image of Our Lady. The duty is to go on bare foot or bare knee thrice round each grave, then to say nine aves and nine paternosters, with other appointed prayers. But I have risen early, and have done three times all that was required to be done once, so that the sisters wonder at me, and foretell that I shall attain to great holiness.

"Are you happy, Mauriade?" I asked of Sister Mary Francis, who used to be Mauriade Burke; and she from the depths of her heart answered that she was as happy as was possible out of heaven.

Her day, every day, and all day, seems spent in meditation and prayer. Of the world she will know nothing.

"Tell me not of them," she said, when I would have spoken of her mother and brother. "They are strangers to me now. I have done with the world."

"Have yon no love left for them?" I cried, thinking that to me it would be impossible to feel thus.

"My whole heart is given to Heaven; I have no love left for earth," she said. "The sanctification of the soul— for that and that alone I live."

My parents erred in sending me here, if they truly desired the convent life for me. There are sisters who care for the aged, and teach the children—among them I might have learned to desire the religious life. I might have been—alas! what am I now? My mind is in a whirl. I cannot pray. Kneeling on the chapel floor through long hours, now that the course of my penances is over, I cover my face; but I cannot pray. My soul is like a little boat cut loose from its moorings, and tossing alone on the wide sea.

Through the perplexity, one thing at least has grown clear to me. The example of the Lord's life is given us to follow. He never shut Himself away from those who needed Him, though to give Himself over to communion with the Father must have been the one joy of His human life. Else He could never have uttered those glad words, "I have finished the work that Thou gavest Me to do."

I will go home and do whatever work He will vouchsafe to give me. "If any will do His will." Indeed, I will do it, so far as I may. It is not likely that He should will great things from a girl like me. Yet in my few things I can at least be faithful.

I will go home and do my duty by my own peopla If great men, learned men and wise, have disagreed about the faith, what shall I do, a girl, young and ignorant?

Mauriade's peace of mind could never be peace to me; it seems so utterly selfish. Peace there is none for me, in this place of peace, where prayer and song rise up continually, and scarcely an echo of the outer world enters, except when pilgrims are entertained, and then only the lay sisters usually attend them. I will go home, and that at once. There is enough to think of there besides the doubts and troubles of one human soul.

So I set my face to go home, and Nora trudged sturdily beside me, singing as she went the ballad of the Drimin dhu dheelish.

"Drimin dhu dheelish! och, why did you die?" sang Nora; but her voice was so much more merry than her song that I could not help saying—

"You seem light-hearted, Nora I wish I felt as merry."

"You, lady!" Nora opened her grey eyes wide in amazement. "You that have always been merry as a bird, though indeed the birds cannot sing through a thunderstorm."

"Why, then, are you so happy, Nora?"

"Because I have done my pilgrimage. Is not that good reason, lady? The sharp stones hurt my bare knees, and every pain made me happy, for it brought good to me and to Teague."

"I hope it did, Nora," I said; and my voice sounded sadly, I thought.

"Why, you do not doubt it, lady?" Nora's eyes had a frightened and wistful look as she lifted them to mine, and I said hastily—

"Oh no, no; why should *I?*" "We shall begin our married life so happily," prattled Nora. "Do you know, Lady Ethne, I have brought away a sprig of thorn that grows close to one of the blessed Black cow, our darlir.g.

graves? I mean to plant it by our cabin door. I have heard it said that where that is done husband and wife never quarrel, and I am sure it is true, for my grandmother knew a couple who tried it. And I hung a strip of my dress and a bit of Teague's old coat on the thorn, so the holy women, the blessed saints that they are, should not forget us."

I remembered the thorn; it was covered over with such rags. Poor saints! that could need such reminders. And oh, poor worshippers! I longed to open my lips and tell poor Nora that God is a Spirit, and must be worshipped in spirit and in truth.

But all utterance failed me. For to what would the revelation tend? How dared I set her simple soul afloat on the sea of doubt on which mine own was tossed, and found no haven in sight?

At least her faith, however erring, was better than the tide of unbelief in *everything* that threatened at times to overwhelm me. For where such difference of opinion was, *some one* must needs be wrong, and to decide between two bodies of learned men seemed hardly a task for a girl. And since the decision was so hopeless, how comfortable it would be to take life as Maurice Burke did, and make up one's mind that nothing particularly mattered. How comfortable, and how easy!

CHAPTER XVI.

Jrtom tijr KecorD of Eooer $tanBfa0t»on=tJe=l£loc&.

HEN darkness reigned over the land of Egypt, the children of Israel still had light. I suppose, therefore, that each of them must have carried with him, when he moved among the idolaters, his own daylight, that shone for himself alone, through that darkness that might be felt. Even so we move now among these blinded souls, having light where they have darkness, even that thickest darkness of which we are told, the very light of the inward eye is darkness, so that the soul cannot so much as perceive the light and apprehend it.

The order for the transplanting of the nation permits the common people to remain in the country places, on condition that they embrace the Protestant faith. Truly, sometimes I think they are as much of Pagans as Papists. On St. John's Day they kindle great fires on all the hillsides, and jump backwards and forwards through the blaze. What is this but a hideous continuance of the worship of Moloch?

On the day following Christmas the young men gather together and make a long pole, on the top of which they bind a cage of twigs containing a live wren. Then they go from house to house, and ask money for the burial of the wren. If it be true, as I hear, that among the ancient Druids the wren was held king of the birds, and that the first Christian teachers permitted some such celebration of the victory of the Cross over the emblem of Paganism, they are surely in the bonds of dark superstition, darker than even the common gloom cast by the shadow of Rome.

Woe is me that I am constrained to dwell with Meshech! My habitation is a lovely one, but it grieves me that I have it among the tents of Kedar. I can but hope to be surrounded presently by godly neighbours, each of whom will exercise a blessed Christian influence over this unhappy land, to the healing of her long sorrows. But sometimes I doubt whether any settlement will have its due effect that is not carried out more entirely than this.

Joshua made peace with the men of Gibeon, and made them hewers of wood and drawers of water; but alas! they and others who were spared became thorns in the sides of the Lord's people, and helped to win their hearts to the worship of Chemosh and Ashtaroth.

I would fain, since they are to be allowed to dwell among us, bring the Irishry to a better mind, not only in things spiritual, but in those which concern their worldly interests.

So I have given them much good counsel, and they have ever received it with a smiling willingness, to amend which has greatly rejoiced my heart, since I expected to be at first refused, and to be compelled to work my way slowly and in the face of opposition. But I have been sorely disappointed to find that this ready acquiescence of theirs is only the willingness of him who said "I go, sir," and went not.

Moreover, in all seriousness, they return the strangest reasons when I would have them give up foolish or hurtful practices.

For example, I spent half an hour yesterday in exhorting one Donovan to weed his field of pease, full of the hateful yellow rag-weed. "For," I said, "the weeds are choking your crop; they take room, and use the nourishment of the earth."

All which the man confessed to be true.

"But then," said he, in the tone of one who advances an argument that cannot be refuted, "they are such excellent sticks for the pea plants, and save endless trouble."

Again, it grieves me sorely to see horses fastened to plough or harrow by their tails, and compelled to draw —a most cruel and also a foolish custom.

"But we have done it from time immemorial," say the people; "and if we take a weary horse from the shafts and set him to draw by the tail, straightway he is fresh again."

How can one meet such arguments?

Moreover, their moral code is so hopelessly low. "To steal a little thing is no sin," their Church declares, and to white lies no blame attaches. So that I am often compelled to consider whether a statement is likely to be true or not. If they have seen a fine salmon, it was the size of a shark; if they have heard a strange story, it is repeated with so many new details embroidered, so to speak, upon it, that the original groundwork is scarcely to be recognised.

Nor will they do any work thoroughly. So long as it will serve, the less labour the better; and the stitch in time of the housewife's proverb is seldom taken.

Thus a man will plant his field of grain, and will fence it after a fashion, and dig a kind of ditch round, but seldom so effectually but that his own cattle or his neighbour's will have a merry night there before his crop is harvested. He will spend more labour on patching than a first thorough making would have cost. Has he a gate? he ties it up carefully and walks through his hedge. When the opening thus made becomes inconvenient, he stuffs it with briars, and then makes a fresh one by degrees.

Nothing has an appointed place, or an appointed time. Nothing is used for its proper purpose, but serves an immediate need, no matter what, and for its own purpose has to be replaced by something else. Thus, if the spade be taken to mend the fire, the potatoes for the next meal may have to be dug with a hurly-bat, or perhaps with the fire-shovel.

All this and more I could say of the faults and follies of the Irish—of their fighting for pleasure, of their love of vain plays, and of dancing, that procession of the devil, as a worthy divine has so aptly called it. So great is their love of this folly, that they have professed dancing-masters, who go from house to house and give instruction to assemblies of both sexes for the sum of fivepence quarterly. Professed card-players there are also, who wander from place to place, haunting especially the houses of the richer sort of people, and joining themselves to the endless train of retainers and hangers-on of the gentry, whose wasteful luxury in consnming sheep and beeves, and casks of French wine and Wicklow ale without number, to feed their swarms of guests and menials, has cried to Heaven, a shame to the country.

It is well that this should have an end.

"Bogs, purgatory, wolves, and ease by fame,
Are counted Ireland's earth, mistake, curse, shame,"

wrote one who understood well the nature of the country and of the people.

All this and more also I could tell of the Irish; but when all this is told, I must even with shame confess to the experiencing of that spell which Master Giraldus the Welshman declared to be cast over the English who came in his day to dwell among these strange people, so that they became degenerated from the very nature of an Englishman, and were indeed like those who had drunk of Circe's cup, and not only were turned into beasts, but had no desire to take the shape of men again.

For I must own that a kindly feeling towards them springs up ever afresh in any natural heart, in spite of the knowledge that they are not truly to be called the children of Sion, with whom alone we should delight to dwell.

I go into one of their houses, with its walls of mud and thatched roof, on which darnel and wild oats spring. The best seat is brought for me, the best food is offered. The children come shyly about me; and I cannot but own that they are fairer and better fed than those of our labourers in England. Never, never have I heard an angry word spoken to a child. Love and kindness reign in the cabins, and the inmates have enough of food and clothing, and are content.

Every woman can spin and knit, many men can weave, and most have some knowledge of carpentry and tinkering. None have the careworn look and stooping gait of an English peasant.

Whether to regard me as friend or foe, they seem to doubt. I am in their eyes the persecutor of the O'Connors, their dearly loved lords, and therefore they must needs hate me. On the other hand, I am as a guest amongst them, and I have dealt justly by them, and so they indine to love me.

Therefore it is, I suppose, that while they welcome me with all possible cordiality, on the other hand they do me much harm. I can call nought my own except it be under lock and key.

Of late I caused a car to be built for me. The two wooden wheels which I had made with spokes—not mere discs, as they mostly are—these, being painted, were set aside to dry one evening, and in the morning their place knew them no more, nor could I ever hear tidings of them.

My trees they break for fuel. In truth, I think a tree in every stage of growth is to their mind chiefly a thing to steal. The little sapling they will take for a cudgel, or even a walking-staff; a little older, and it is needed for an oar; again for a pike-handle; again, when greater, for a Maypole, or for the rafters of a cabin.

Iron is almost as uncertain a possession, whatever be made of it. One of my neighbours is apt to find that he requires the thing, and it ceases to be mine straightway.

Such is this nation—a people hard to deal with, hard to guide, harder still to improve. Many times I have felt ready to lose heart, feeling that it would be so easy and so pleasant to leave my fruitless work among them, and, as their old lords have done, to let them live as they list.

But when I think of the infinite patience of our Maker with even the best of His servants, I chide myself that I have so little patience with my brotherman. And, indeed, the task will not always be so hard; for, since all priests are banished from the country, under pain of confinement in certain islands on the wild west coast, and the saying of the idolatrous mass is become a crime against the law of the land, there is a door open for the entrance of the true faith, and with it of liberty, the true liberty from the slavery of superstition, the freedom with obedience of the Lord's bondservant.

So I have a good hope for them. But that godly man, Isaiah Heston, blames me for so saying, and declares that there can be none.

Oliver grimly offers them, as is commonly said, "Hell or Conn aught."

"Oliver was to blame," said blunt Isaiah to me one day, "in that he gave them the choice."

"But have you ever been in Connaught, my friend?" I asked him; "for I think if you have, you will own that the choice was not great after all."

"Say you so, indeed?" said Isaiah. "Indeed, I wondered that our wise Oliver should seem so to fall away from the steadfastness of his obedience to the

Lord's will."

Thus I have lived, therefore, striving to be faithful in all things, as a good steward of that which is committed to my care, praying always for myself and my brethren, that, having now been made to possess houses which we have not built, and vineyards which we have not planted, we may not forget the Lord and His goodness to us in the time of our distress. And that it is to be feared some among us have done, so that the Papists have had some ground for their bitter saying, that they have hunted with ns, diced with us, drunk with us, and fought for us, but have not been called to pray with us.

May-day, which the Irish count the first day of summer, is again a day of merry-making. Every family sets a thorn-bush at its door, the thorns being stuck with yellow field-flowers; and in the morning the young men and maidens go forth in their gayest dresses, with music and singing, to plant a slender tree for the family of O'Connor.

Madam O'Connor sent a message, begging that I would dine with the family, and taste the May-day stirabout, which I gladly promised to do.

This old custom of eating on May-day a dish of flour and milk boiled thick, which some do call stirabout and some hasty pudding, seems intended as a proof of good housewifery, whereby the old corn of the land is shown to have been made to last till almost the coming of the new. But rich and poor alike have it, so that the custom only remains, the cause being almost forgotten.

After the social meal, it was proposed that we should go down into the woods and walk, and then having taken boat, should row down the lake to a fair island at a lovely part of its labyrinth of woods and water, and there drink a dish of coffee.

Madam O'Connor would not go. Her heart was heavy, I think, though she would at all costs seem cheerful She and her daughter had been graciously dispensed from transplanting till the harvest should be gathered in. The son was awaiting news from his father, to say in what part of Connaught an assignment had been made to the family, that he might join him there.

Mistress Ethne was present, having returned from her pilgrimage. I looked upon her face and wondered what had passed in her heart. The seed of the Word has had fair soil to spring in. Has it sprung up? and what fruit will it bring forth?

That painted butterfly, the empty-pated gallant Maurice Burke, was also there, and hovering like a butterfly continually about the maiden. If he were worth the hating, I would hate him for his empty flatteries and foolish converse. It grieves me with a grief that is more than reasonable when I see Mistress Ethne smile upon him, for though she laughs at his idle compliments, yet I fear she likes the taste of them.

I would she were an Englishwoman. She has a brave heart, and, I think, an earnest soul, and truly she is marvellously fair of face. Such tender love does she show her parents, such cheerfulness when their lot seems dark, such patient forbearance to her passionate brother, that I think the man would be happy who

L should call her wife, and bring her as a daughter to his parents.

If her heart should have turned to the Lord, might she not even be as Ruth the Moabitess, whom Boaz did well to marry, and who became not only one of the chosen people thereby, but also was highly honoured in being permitted to be an ancestress of the Saviour?

But the maiden is merry-hearted, and loves gaiety and brightness. I grievously fear that the suit of yon gay spark may at last find favour in her eyes, for women are light-minded, and easy to be won by flattery, and will choose a gay and painted toy for its mere beauty. Happy is the man who is not led astray by them, who makes a covenant with his eyes, and will not look upon a maid.

T was May-day when I came home again. My father was still in Connaught. All else was much the same at home, except that Father Ambrose had been ordered to repair to the nearest port, and thence along with many other priests, some of whom had languished long in jail, was to be shipped for Spain.

He had left a letter for me, which my mother gave me with the seal unbroken.

"My daughter," it ran, "your soul has been as the clove which ventured forth from the safe ark of the Church, and found no rest for the sole of her foot till she returned again. As I told you of late, I am no longer near to put forth a hand and take you in; but the way is clear, the door is not closed against you—not yet. "

So he wrote, as though I had nothing to do but to fly back to the old abiding-place of my spirit, and there be at rest—all the more at rest, perhaps, for having once wandered. But it was not so easy. No; I can never be as I have once been—never again.

What I actually am is hard to say; I know not very well myself. I know that Father Ambrose's banishment, which is a bitter grief to my mother, is truly a relief to me. But for the first time in my life I must dissemble with her, and assume a grief I would not feel. At least that is the convenient and easy thing to do, though not the most truthful, and I have learnt that all deceit is of the Father of Lies.

What then? Shall I add to the heavy burden of grief and anxiety that bows my mother's dear silver head? or shall I wait a little and see what the next few days will bring forth?

These thoughts were in my mind this morning while I helped to deck a Maypole for the children and crown the prettiest of them queen. A hard matter it was to find the prettiest among all those curling heads and clear eyes—windows of innocent souls—and smiling rosy lips whose corners have not yet been drawn into bitter lines.

I turned slowly back, and found that Captain Standfast had come to be our guest and taste the May-day dish.

May-day used ever to be one of our merriest days. Great dishes of roasted meat smoked on our table then, followed by our daintiest jellies and pastries and cakes, all in the largest quantities, for our invited guests; and the uninvited, who knew themselves sure of a welcome, were sure to be very many. The dishes were emptied, rivers of claret flowed, and, when all was done, the remnants of the feast used to be carried out for me to the gate of the castle, where the needy thronged in eager troops, among whom with much gratitude and much merriment the substantial remains were divided.

But this year our only guest was our supplanter.

I am sure Pierce was thinking thus, for his brow was overcast, and he was, with more warmth than could be necessary or wise, defending the national mantle against Captain Standfast, who appeared to have began the argument by expressing his agreement with Master Spencer's opinion that the mantle ought to bo abolished.

"Consider the uses of it," argued Pierce. "If it rains, the man is dry; if it is cold, he wraps it about him and is warm; if he is weary, he rolls himself in it and sleeps soft and warm, though he have but the bare ground for his bed."

"Just what I said," interrupted the other. "The dress is calculated to make outlaws of men, or vagabonds at the least."

The hot flush crept to Pierce's brow. It did not matter to him what opinion this Englishman had of the Irish mantle. But he cried—

"Ay, in sooth, when you take from us our houses of stone, we may as well have the tub of Diogenes, that was to him all things in one!" And the speech seemed cruelly ungracious, since it was only by the officer's forbearance that we had yet a roof to shelter our heads. "Since we are like to be left altogether without clothing, soon we shall be glad of the mantle as a covering for our many rags."

"It is at least an apt garment for a thief," said Captain Standfast quietly. "What thing cannot be hidden under its ample folds? And in battle there is our target already provided for us; wound round the arm, the folds make an admirable protection against cut or thrust."

"The cut or thrust of an important foe," said Pierce; "but there be some weapons of some foes which cannot be resisted thus, because their weapons are but paper— sharp ones, however."

"I will grant," said the officer, with perfect composure, "that against the stings of the gnats which swarm out of your woods the mantle may be a useful defence. But civilised man does not live in the woods, and I say it is a savage garment, and ought to be renounced."

"And I say," shouted Pierce, "that it is graceful, rational, and useful, warm, weather-proof, and defenceful. I would have our people keep to their quilted jackets, of gilded leather, their cord wain shoes, and, above all, their mantles, and follow no English fashions. I pray you what good has the coming of anything English done to us?"

Then my mother hastily interfered, for anger was gathering in the Puritan's eyes.

"We that have loved our old customs find reason for them, Captain Standfast. My son does indeed defend them over vehemently. But you in England, who have striven to make the nation wiser and better, must have found many a hindrance in the reluctance of even the best people to leave that which they learned at their mother's knee."

"It is true indeed!" responded the soldier readily. "Even I myself"— and he paused.

But I thought that it was true, as I have heard it said that good people of convictions the most opposite have almost always a ground of agreement, if only they will seek for it.

Pierce made no apology, but he showed his penitence by taking pains to make the meal pass pleasantly for all, and especially for our English guest. And, when it was over, we four—for Maurice had joined us—went down to the lake and took boat, and drifted in the golden light of the afternoon about the still waters, to whose very edge the trees come down as if to look at their own untroubled reflection in the tide.

Now and then a sound of singing came to us upon the wind, or the skreed of a distant bagpipe, to which the young folks were dancing, came pleasantly mellowed to our ears.

On the banks here and there sat children, fishing with a packthread and a crooked pin, and taking home good baskets' full of little silvery things. For our lakes are full of fish, and we have never had the custom, of which Captain Standfast tells, as in England, where the Lord of the Manor keeps fish and fowl for his own use, and the poor man is grievously punished, or even hanged, for taking the wild things which God Almighty sent to be food for man without reservation.

Certainly it were to be wished that our people would refrain from eating salmon when unwholesome, since this is said to be the cause of the hideous leprosy that is to be found here and there in our island. But since we must all die, I suppose we must all ail, and it may be that hunger would bring other evils as great as this.

Very happily we drifted about the lake, and landed, and lit a fire, and had a gipsy meal. Here Pierce caught a lizard, of that strange sort which we call Arglogher or rush-pig, in shape like a miniature crocodile. At which we were greatly delighted, for whosoever takes this creature and draws the scales of it three times against his tongue, is thenceforward able to cure any burn or scald by licking the part affected.

Over this worm Pierce and the Captain almost quarrelled again, for Pierce would have had him try the plan, and ho refused, saying that such things were idle and vain superstitions. Nevertheless, when I ventured to say that medicine certainly showed that the Creator had given us in plants and animals many remedies for the cure of disease, he was willing to agree that it might be so, and that at least the notion was a harmless one.

It was altogether a trifling matter, but that which happened before many hours were past made me remember it, as I think I shall do as long as I live.

Among the woods we wandered, and gathered handfuls of flowers—pale primroses that grew so thickly, you could scarce see the ground between them. And Captain Standfast pulled a great bunch of the lovely star-like wild leek, and brought it to me, but threw it away again in some disgust because Maurice held his nose and called loudly to imaginary servants for *eau-de-luce*. We were very merry altogether; but late in the afternoon it happened that Pierce and Maurice had both roamed away, and that Captain Standfast and I were left alone—I sitting in the slanting sunshine on a fallen tree, binding flowers into a wreath, and he holding a great handful of them till I should be ready.

Then suddenly all my merry mood died away, and a constrained silence fell between us. A heavy bee crept from his winter sleep, buzzing a drowsy grumble, shook his wings, looked about, and flew away with a contented hum, out of the darkness into the light. That thought brought me to speak what was in my mind, and I lifted my face and said—

"Captain Standfast, the reading of the Bible brings pleasure to you. Is it not so?"

"More than the finding of rubies and much hid treasure, Mistress Ethne."

"And to me it has brought only pain. You said you knew it would. And—and you did not seem greatly to care."

"Does the wise surgeon shrink from giving some pain with his healing knife?" I laughed, but not merrily.

"In truth," I said, "your work is surgery. For if my mind goes whither it is drifting, what lies before me but severance from all I have held most dear? My father"

He stood looking down upon me with an earnest, searching gaze.

"Yes," he said. "But when the Lord called the sons of Zebedee, they left their father with the hired servants. They heard a higher call, that was more imperative even than that duty. And it is not written in vain—' Come out from among them, and be ye separate, and I will be a Father unto you, and ye shall be my sons and daughters.'"

A more imperative call? I hid my face in my hands and thought, feeling as though I stood on the brink of a great precipice.

"They were *men* whom the Lord called to forsake home ties," I said, looking up again.

"But women followed Him, even to the Cross. They were there, though men had forsaken Him and fled."

"Yes," I said; and there was silence again, when a squirrel ran up the tree beside me and peered down at us, as if to ask what there could be in the world to be so serious over. Perhaps he concluded that we had no store of nuts, as he went away, the poor mortal creature that knew neither the hope nor the terror of a beyond.

Captain Standfast's eyes were on the dead leaves at his feet—the dead leaves through which fresh green things were springing. He lifted them and looked down into the troubled face which I had turned to him, and spoke in a low tone that trembled a little.

"Put your hand in mine, Mistress Ethne," he said, "and come away from the idolatries and the follies of your people. I think it is to this that the work of the Spirit in your heart is to lead you and me." He spoke slowly, and as if weighing every word.

"I am not speaking hastily," he said. "When first this was borne in upon me, I fought against it day and night, with strong crying and tears, believing it to be a snare of the Evil One. But I fear that I fought against the Lord's will. Do not you do so."

For I had sprung to my feet and stood facing him, my cheeks burning, my flowers scattered all round.

"Now, by Our Lady above, Captain Standfast!" I cried, "surely this is the strangest wooing ever maiden had!"

And my indignation broke into a sob.

"I should never have spoken to you as I have done! Oh! how dared you?" I cried, scarcely knowing what to say.

But he stood looking at me with a troubled gaze.

"My tongue is not as the pen of a ready writer, I fear," he said; "nor have I ever cared that it should be, till to-day."

"It is fluent enough to say what you mean," I said. "Do not think I fail to understand."

"You *do* fail to understand, my lady," he answered, with gentle patience. "You fail to understand that I would have you leave that which your heart has already forsaken, and live by my side, a godly Christian matron among the Lord's people."

So he spoke, and stood tall and straight and grave before me, waiting my answer. It was not a very dignified one, for it came with a little sob—

"Other maidens are wooed with words of love," I said.

"I have said my tongue is not used to honeyed phrases," he said, almost sternly. "If you desire these, have you not every day a surfeit of them?"

"Indeed Maurice is very foolish," I said quickly, for I would not have him think that Maurice's ceaseless flatteries were what I desired.

"And you would have me the same to win your favour? You would rather be treated as a pretty plaything than as a woman of discerning mind?"

"No, indeed, Captain Standfast," I answered, feeling ashamed that the sudden surprise of so strange a wooing had made me so confused and so foolish.

"I like you far better as you are. Honestly, I will answer that I think none could fail to respect and esteem you. But you will understand, sir, that it is no light matter for a maiden to give her whole self away. And, moreover, your people are not my people."

"You have spoken wisely and well, my lady," he said; and as before he said *my lady* in a tone that seemed as if he would have said "my love," and that went much more to my heart than if Maurice Burke had said "my love" a hundred times over.

"You will think—and you will pray, as I shall, that you may have a right judgment. And, Mistress Ethne, you said that my people were a strange nation, and that the thought of severance was hard. But whatsoever my help can do for your father and mother, and for your brother"

"Indeed, you are very good," I said; and I looked into his grave earnest eyes and found courage to smile. That his promise included Pierce I thought the kindest part of all.

"So it shall be then," he said. "To-morrow, if it please you, I will come for my answer. Or, if not to-morrow"

"It shall be to-morrow," I said; and I sat down upon my tree again and picked up my flowers by handfuls, while Captain Standfast knelt before me and did the same. It chanced that our hands touched, and suddenly he caught mine in both his, and laid it upon the palm of his strong right hand, that had done much hard service, and was very brown and very firm to feel.

"It looks like a flower dropped on a piece of rough wood," said Captain Standfast; and then our eyes met, and he smiled, and I drew my hand away very quickly, for I saw Maurice Burke coming through the trees with a load of May-blossoms.

I knew not whether he saw that the Puritan soldier was kneeling at my feet with my hand in his, but he began to carol some foolish rhyme about the spring-time and a merry ring-time, and such matters as poets make songs upon, with something of love to flavour their verses.

"Let us be going," I said to Pierce. "The evening grows cold."

"Warm hearts should be never a 'cold,'" declared Maurice. But I had no answer ready for him, and he was strangely quiet as we rowed home again.

SURPRISE was in store for us when we reached home. My father had returned, and was sitting in his arm-chair by the fire when wo entered.

He looked weary enough, I thought; and when Captain Standfast asked how he had fared, he answered, in a hoarse and tired voice—

"You had better ask that of your brethren the Commissioners at Athlone, sir," he said, "who kept me waiting their pleasure for many days before they would so much as attend to my case."

"Doubtless they had much business on hand," said the Englishman.

"Doubtless they had," returned my father grimly. "So much so that the wheels of their machinery have grown clogged, and must needs have golden oil before they will move."

Against this Captain Standfast, as in duty bound, protested that he was sure his friends at Loughrea were godly folk, and would do their best. But they were only men, and their work was hard, and doubtless there was much opposition.

"There was opposition certainly," my father said. "The soldiers were occupying places, and laying out the three-mile belt, and the reserved lands round the larger towns. Certain proprietors who had to be dispossessed, and were to receive lands in Ireland instead of those they gave up, were opposing the entrance of the unhappy transplanters, whose prospects seemed to grow more and more hopeless. Those who had some store of ready money were obtaining good lands by bribing the officers appointed to set them out."

"And as for me" But there he stopped, and seemed unable to proceed.

"As for you, sir?" said Pierce.

"My lot fell in the barony of Burren, in the county of Clare, where, as they say, there is not wood enough to hang a man, water enough to drown him, or earth enough to bury him with. I had no golden bait wherewith to catch better fish. With this news I have come back. *If* a faithful servant or two will go with me I will take them, but I shall advise them rather to become tenants under Captain Standfast. For to hold even thirty acres here is better than to own two hundred in that desolate place, where the low grounds are marshes, and moss replaces our rich green grass; where the rock crops up at every step one takes, and the fields are covered with the hateful yellow ragweed—the sure sign of a miserable soil."

There was silence when he had finished—a silence of dismay. Captain Standfast broke it.

"Sir Gerald, I am truly grieved for you."

Pierce, standing with folded arms, glared at him from under his dark brows, as if he would say—" How dare you pity us?"

But my father lifted the grey head that he used to carry so proudly.

"I thank you, sir," he said. "Old and broken as I am, I can at least be grateful. Nay, I could—I can—even stoop to ask a favour. I learn that many proprietors are living as tenants under the adventurers and soldiers. And since the lands of Connaught cannot possibly suffice for all that will be left, even when the flower of the nation have sought military service abroad, I think they will be allowed to remain. I have never stooped to ask a favour in my life—but I ask one now."

"Father!" broke out Pierce. But my father lifted his hand.

"My son, for you Spain and France remain. There you can be welcome as a soldier, welcome as a citizen. For us who must remain, it is deliberately intended by the English nation that we should by degrees sink to the level of peasants. I may cut my own turf, but I shall still be O'Connor."

"Come over seas!" cried Pierce; "you and my mother and Ethne. I will win what support I can for you."

But my father shook his head.

"I am too old; for me it cannot be. By your sword you can earn your bread, or in the cloister there is a welcome. You were not bred to be a physician or a lawyer; you cannot be a merchant. Only the sword or the pen remain, and your hand fits best to a sword-Mlt."

Pierce stood still with downcast face, and my father looked to the English officer for his answer. And I looked also, but I would not look entreatingly, so I turned my eyes to the floor, though I felt that he was questioning my face. At last he spoke.

"It is true, as you say, that many have done so, though it is altogether against the Act, and I fear that it will not long be tolerated. Nor do I think that the adventurers and soldiers have acted quite uprightly in permitting it. Nevertheless, I am willing, and I make you welcome to take a holding, as you proposed."

"I thank you," said my father, in a low choking voice.

I knew what it must cost him to say that. But Pierce strode from where he stood, and came between my father and the officer, looking from one to the other with naming eyes.

"I cannot believe it!" he said. "Father! speak and tell me that it is all a horrible dream! You cannot accept such an ungracious permission as this, nor lower yourself to be a tenant of his—of yours, you canting, hard-faced regicide! What name can I call you that is apt enough—you"

"Pierce O'Connor," said Captain Standfast, in a low, harsh tone, "your evil passion does not harm me, but it harms your own soul. I counsel you to do as your father says, and convey yourself straightway into Spain, where your energy may be better spent, or at least less misspent."

Pierce's dogs had risen from where they lay by the window, and came forward growling, and only waiting his signal to fly upon his antagonist. Pierce quieted them by a look.

"I thank you, sir," he said. "I thank you greatly. I will indeed rid you of my odious presence as soon as I can, sir. And as the rest of my family seem to be handin-glove with you, I look to be little missed. Oh, father! mother!" he said, turning to them, and speaking in a voice that trembled, "I would I had died before this day."

"My boy! my boy! control yourself!" said my mother, pale as death.

"Control myself! I *have* controlled myself. I have striven to forget all, and to treat this man as our guest, and even to persuade myself that better times might be at hand. I will control myself still, and go in silence so soon as may be. But I tell you, sir," and he turned again to Captain Standfast, "I would our house had been burned to the ground before ever you entered it"

He turned and tramped from the room. His fosterbrother, Teague O'Rnark, standing at the door with a hand on the collars of the two dogs, had been drinking in every word. He gave a malevolent glance at the officer now, and followed his young master from the room.

"Take me with you, my Drinan Dhun," I heard him say. "I will follow you to the end of the world."

I know not how the evening passed. I know that I was thankful when at last I found myself alone in my own room, and could throw my little window wide and look up at the sweet May moon, and let the soft May air blow upon my brow and soothe the tumult of my thoughts.

Roger Standfast—we have almost forgotten the addition to his name,—except in the mouth of Isaiah Heston we never hear it, and him we seldom see. Of Roger Standfast I have to think.

"He may be a heretic, but he is a good man and a true," said my mother tonight. And the knight, my father, answered—

"If he be so in thine eyes, sweetheart, I think he must be so indeed."

And she smiled back at his tender words and answered softly—

"Nay, what a man is in the eye of his Maker, that is he, neither more nor less."

I threw myself upon my knees and prayed, long and earnestly, as *he* had bidden me, that I might know the right in this matter, and do it. And as I sat down by the window again, I saw that though it was midnight a light burned still in the tower chamber, which I knew Captain Standfast used as a sleeping-room in Lara Castle, as Pierce had been wont to do.

He too was praying. He would read in his Bible

H too. There was a word of guidance there for those who thought of marriage.

Let them be married to whom they will, *only in the Lord,* commands the apostle.

But in that little sentence lies the root of all the matter. The wedding at which the Lord may be a guest must be one He would approve.

I could not put down on paper all the thoughts that passed through my mind. For this was indeed a strange wooing, and many a question had to be faced—not merely the usual simple one a maiden asks her heart, "Is he a good man, and dost thou love him?"

For my parents the protection of Roger Standfast's influence; for my own soul his faith. Those were clearly to be set down as gains, but that was not enough for my heart.

I could not put my hand in his and promise to be his wife, unless with all my heart I could love him, and be content to give all myself and all my life to him.

From my window I could see the great beech at the terrace corner, a dark mass against the sky, its outermost twigs silvered by the moon. I could not see now, but I knew that in a cleft of its great roots a little rose-tree had, from some chance seed, sprung up, and was dwelling and blossoming there.

I had often thought the little rose-tree happy. I thought now that I too could be happy in the shelter of that strong arm—in the love of that true heart.

And yet I was afraid, for Roger Standfast was very stern. If so stern even as a lover, what would he be as a husband?

Then I thought of Maurice, and I laughed aloud, and felt that, while any maiden might have Maurice for a lover, so her face were sufficiently fair, Roger Standfast's heart was assuredly not lightly given. And I felt honoured by his love, and proud of it, and I thought surely I could love him in return.

Yet in the depths of my heart there lay a great fear. The teachings of my youth rose up before my mind, and made me tremble. How could I break away from them utterly and for ever?

So I sat pondering; and sometimes the step seemed too hard to take, and too doubtful of success, and sometimes it seemed hopeful and happy. And between the two it seemed too hard for me to solve.

So I just sat still, and tried to think of God, and to let my soul, as it were, lie still before Him, without even a prayer. For how can the soul hear His voice, except it will be silent to listen?

It was very still as I sat. The silence seemed to tingle through the room, so that I could almost hear it, or feel it, as some mysterious presence. All nature was resting in the calm moonlight There was nothing to be done now. By-and-by the sun would come back and bring the need for care and toil—by-and-by, when strength had been renewed. And from the exceeding calm came a sense of divine peace to my agitated heart.

"O rest in the Lord; wait patiently for him!"

The dawn would come; all living

things would have light to find their work by. And I too. To me also strength would come, strength to tell the truth at all costs as to my newly found faith. And when Roger Standfast came for his answer, I would put my hand in his and promise to be his wife. Would he smile and kiss me as a lover should, and call me by endearing names? I knew not—his wooing was altogether so strange.

A little rustle broke the utter stillness. Probably it was a bat among the ivy boughs on the wall of the castle that caused it. But surely that was a step on the gravel?

I leaned out a little and looked. Yes; there wag certainly a figure stealing along the castle wall in the shadow. Captain Standfast's light had gone out some while ago; no one was stirring inside the house. Now the figure came to a corner; it must certainly be seen as it rounded a turret where the moonlight lay.

I watched anxiously, and then I called softly—

"Teague! Teague!"

The figure stopped and seemed to hesitate, then went on again more stealthily and quickly than before. It was an odd thing certainly. I could have sworn that it was none other than Teague O'Ruark stealing along in the darkness.

But I saw nothing more, for the figure lost itself in the dark shadow of some shrubs at the further corner of the house. I wondered what Teague—for I felt sure it was Teague—could be doing in that place at that hour. I had enough else to think of, however, and my thoughts were busy with my own affairs, when I suddenly saw Teague return to the corner, stand looking up for a moment at the window of the officer's chamber, and then again he disappeared and returned no more while I was still watching.

It was certainly Teague. I saw him this time quite distinctly, although he was closely wrapped in a mantle— that curse of Ireland, as Roger Standfast had declared it to be. It seemed to me that he might very probably have been pilfering from some of the Captain's tool sheds, but he did not appear to be carrying anything very bulky. What could he have been doing? Mischief, I feared.

Now Roger Standfast had often complained of the disappearance of his iron nails. Wherever he might happen to have them they were sure to vanish, and he gave our people a bad character for honesty in consequence.

We never locked up anything. The practice was inconvenient; and, after all, if a poor man did want a nail or two, it was a great matter for him to buy them, whereas we should not miss them out of our store. We were never much plundered, but we allowed a margin for this kind of consumption, which seemed a most undesirable arrangement to the Englishman.

"You might have had the grace to ask my leave," he said one day when he caught a malefactor in the very act.

The man was immensely surprised. He never dreamt, so he candidly answered, that any *gentleman* would care to be troubled about such trifles.

Teague was something of a carpenter, so I made up my mind that nails must be the object of this strange nocturnal prowl; and having thus settled the matter to my own satisfaction, I lay down in my bed and soon fell asleep.

I am not used to dream till morning, when the world comes slowly back in those chaotic shapes which are sometimes so pleasant that we are sorry to come back to the prose of real life. But to-night I had not been long asleep before I had a very strange dream.

I dreamed that my life was over, and that I felt tired, for it had been a toilsome one. And that as I entered a glorious and restful place, and stood a little dazzled at the entrance, Roger Standfast came to meet me. Roger Standfast indeed, but changed, so changed that I could not help telling him so. At that he smiled and took me by the hand.

"Ay, dear love," he said, " I am changed, for I have become what God would have me be, and so have you. All the sorrows of earth have been to us cleansing fires. We can look back now and bless the purging pain."

"But see," I said, "it is here!" For as I looked down I saw that my feet were upon the sea of glass mingled with fire, which pulsed and shot towards me with an angry glow.

"Nay," he said, and his smile told of deep and peaceful happiness. "We stand *above* it for ever and ever. Those fires burn still, but not for us."

So he spoke and smiled, but suddenly, with the strange metamorphosis of a dream, I thought that I was in the abode of the lost. Dreadful faces looked at me, and a wild cry came up, and the flames rose and shot wildly up, and roared and crackled close to me.

I was awake and standing by the window, and before my eyes Lara Castle, the only home I had ever known, was on fire. And there I stood voiceless with dismay and gazed on the most fearful sight it had ever been my lot to behold.

We knew afterwards that the house had been kindled in many places. Nothing else would account certainly for the terribly rapid way in which they had spread.

The night was very dark; the moon had set, and clouds had come up and covered the stars. I looked at the heavens, which seemed inky black with that blaze below. If only it would rain, there might even yet be hope.

A faint hope indeed. The fire had possession of the building, and was greedily devouring it, and roaring like a wild beast over its prey. Dense masses of smoke belched forth, heavy and choking; it seemed almost as if they ought to smother the flame. But no; it crawled about the windows and sent forked tongues to lick up the woodwork of the frames, and run up the hangings within. Greediness, eager haste to devour, seemed to possess it, as though its time might be short. But what could our people do? To run to and fro with buckets to the lake would be utterly vain. There was no hope except in the heavens. And as I thought that, a whispering rain *did* begin to fall, and a cry went up from the people who had assembled hastily in the yard, a great gathering already.

But scarcely had that shout of hope died away before there arose another shout, this time of terror or dismay.

"The Captain! Where is Captain Standfast?"

There was a hurried calling, a running to and fro, a pause of terror. And still the rain fell lightly—so lightly! Sometimes in the midst of hay harvest the heavens will open and the rain descend in bucketfuls, drenching every field, soaking the hay so that a fresh making must be gone through, laying the corn flat on the ground. We cannot understand the ways of God. How hard it seemed now to watch this soft gentle shower!

But all eyes were turned to the upper window, that window where I had seen the light burning for so long. All was dark there, and the flames had not reached so high as yet. But what of the staircase?

"Oh, save him, save him!" I cried through my window, but no one heard. Then suddenly I saw a man force his way through the people straight to the tower door, whence a staircase went up to that room. Over his shoulder the man carried a coil of rope, and I was astonished as I looked, for I saw that this man was none other than my brother Pierce.

Pierce, who hated Roger Standfast, was *he* going to the rescue? My heart thrilled with gladness for a moment, and then almost stood still with renewed terror; for Pierce had scarcely disappeared through the doorway before a little puff of smoke came through a window above the door—a window that lights that staircase.

There was silence now—a silence broken only by the rushing sound of the fire, and now and then a crackling, bursting noise from within the house, when, doubtless, the flames had got some fresh hold, accomplished some new mischief. That, and the rustle of the rain—no other sound, for the crowd below me were holding their breath.

I saw my father come down and join them. My mother came presently and joined me as I watched. And just as she came, a new shout broke from the mob, and as they shouted, I saw a bright light gleam through the window that looked on the staircase. The stairs were on fire!

It was at the same moment, I think, so far as I can recollect in that time of terror, that a figure at last appeared at the bedroom window. One figure only—that of Roger Standfast.

Bis brown face was very pale as he looked out— perhaps the glare of the fire made it the paler. He looked down at the people below him, and then up to the sky, and I am sure that he was praying.

"Pierce!" shouted my father. "Where is Pierce?" and we all waited breathlessly for his answer.

"Pierce!" he called back. "Your son? Is he here?"

"My son, my only son! He went to save you. The tower stair!" cried my father in a tone of anguish.

Captain Standfast was gone from the window in a moment. It seemed a long time indeed till he reappeared, and when at last he did so his face was blackened with smoke, and in his arms he carried my brother, whose ghastly white face fell back helplessly over the strong arm that carried him. To all appearance he was dead, and my mother at my side smote her hands together and went away into her own room, where I am sure she fell upon her knees and prayed.

I could not leave the window. I could see that smoke began to fill the room in which those two were—not fire as yet, but a thick ominous cloud of smoke. Then I saw Captain Standfast, with, as I thought, a strange slowness of movement, uncoil the rope from poor Pierce's shoulder and fasten it to something inside the room. He was partly out of sight as he did this, and my horror and desperate impatience grew with every moment, for we could see that every now and then he was compelled to lean out and draw long breaths, so thick and choking the smoke had become.

At last—at the long last—he leaned out with Pierce's still helpless figure in his arms, and we could see that the rope was most carefully knotted round the poor boy's arms. Slowly and carefully the soldier lowered him, and there was a cry of joy and thankfulness when Pierce, still unconscious, but mercifully still breathing, was in my father's arms.

Straight into my parents' room he was carried, and there both hung over him. He was only suffering from the smoke, in which he had fainted before reaching Captain Standfast's door, and their attentions soon brought him to himself. He was their son, their only son—it was natural enough—but to me at that moment it seemed horrible that they should appear almost to forget that other life that was still in danger.

For my part I remained at the window in an agony of suspense that seemed scarcely abated by Pierce's safety. I had doubted before, but in that moment I learned what Roger Standfast was to me. If none but he could have heard, I would have called across to him—

"Roger, Roger, I love you! Do you hear? I love you!

But there I could but stand and watch, as women so often must. Indeed neither man nor woman could help now. The staircase was evidently a mass of flames, and now suddenly in the dense smoke behind my lover a brilliant flame burst forth.

He had tied the rope to some piece of furniture within, and now climbed upon the window sill and took it in his hands.

A moment and he would have slipped safely down— all would be well.

Alas! before he had grasped it, suddenly the whole rope fell down among the crowd. The upmost end was on fire. Evidently it had been burnt off from its fastening.

That cruel rain fell still, lightly, uselessly. It hissed as it dropped on the hot stones and spurting flames. It beat the smoke down in great clouds.

"Master, Master," cried the faithful fishers as they tossed in imminent peril, "carest Thou not that we perish?"

I could have cried thus to Him now. Was it nought to Him that His faithful servant should die when the world had need of him; for there are not many such. And I had such sore need!

The flames filled the room now. Roger Standfast stood outside on the window sill. He could breathe there though the hot fire and the choking smoke were trying to pursue him. There was nothing to climb down by, nothing to climb up to. The distance to the ground would be certain death to jump, but now some of the people brought mattresses and laid them on the ground, calling upon him to jump.

His eyes were upon the dark heaven for a moment, then for the first time, as I thought, he looked over to me and waved his hand with a smile. I think he was bidding me a last farewell, and tears filled my eyes, so that for a moment I could not see, and I drooped my head upon my hands. As I lifted it again, for I could not choose but look, my eyes met another pair of eyes that were gazing from the crowd with an unearthly expression, and a horrible suspicion came to my mind as I recognised Teague O'Ruark, who was looking at me with every emotion of the wildest dismay and surprise painted on his ashen face.

A moment more, and he had elbowed his way to the front, and was calling up to Captain Standfast—" Do you see that pin? Can you reach it?"

The tower wall had been thought a little unsafe. It had been pinned together with iron bolts, each one of which had a large head to it. One of these was not far from the window; but it could not well be reached, being near the upmost corner, but some way to the right.

It was a giddy sight to see Captain Standfast on tiptoe at the very verge of the narrow ledge reach slowly up till his hand held the iron knob.

I heard expressions of wonder from the people below. "He must be as cool," they said, "as if he stood on the solid ground, or he could not do it. He cannot get back. He will fall and be dashed to atoms. He will—he *has* done it! Holy Mary! Did ever any one see the like!"

And mingled with these came other words that implied that the speakers would not have sorrowed overmuch if the Puritan—the Cromwellite—had been dashed to pieces.

A hand came upon my arm. I started and turned round. Teague O'Ruark stood beside me. It was no time for apologies. In his hand he held the bow and arrows which Maurice Burke brought me home from England years ago. I have practised the use of them much. My mother loves to see me take the exercise, which she holds to be healthy and graceful for a woman, and I like it myself, though my father has grumbled at the Sassenach sport.

"Lady Ethne," cried Teague, or rather he whispered hoarsely, "I would never have done it if I knew you loved him. My Drinan Dhun wished it; he could not bear to see the stranger in the home of his fathers. If he is your Gille Machree, will you draw a bow for him?" He held up an arrow to which a piece of fine twine was tied, and the rope was fastened to that.

"0 Teague!" I cried, "God's blessing be about you for ever. Let me shoot at once."

I turned to go. Never till now had I remembered that my feet were bare and my hair unbound. My shoes were quickly put on, and my mantle cast about me, and Teague and I were in the yard before many seconds had passed.

A chorus of voices greeted me. My intention was buzzed from mouth to mouth, and shouted to the soldier who stood leaning his back against the wall, his feet on the window ledge. Burning rafters from the roof were beginning to fall; it would soon be scarcely possible to stay in the yard. The crowd had pressed back already. I set my arrow upon the string, took careful aim, and shot. Alas! my hand was trembling; the arrow went wide of the mark, and a murmur of disappointment arose.

Teague pulled back the arrow by the string, and I said to myself with shame—

"*He* was perfectly collected, though his life was in peril. You cannot save him unless you are quite calm, Ethne."

With that thought, and a prayer for strength, I set the arrow in its place again, and, as slowly as if shooting for a prize at a very small mark, I drew my bow and watched the arrow's flight.

Thank God! Right through the window, so that Roger Standfast caught the string, amid the vociferous joy of the eager watchers.

Ah well! I have lingered long over it all.

I know that there was yet some suspense till at last Roger's steady hands had tied the rope firmly. I know that he slid down it, and stood on the ground in safety; but before he could come to me to thank me I was in my own room again, and my overwrought feelings found relief in a passion of tears.

Through the night the house still burned. The roof fell in, and the inside became one mass of glowing heat. Happily, what little wind there was, blew smoke and sparks away from our abode. The flames became less wild, the smoke less heavy; the glowing mass remained, causing the stones to start and crack, so that great rents came here and there in the walls.

Then at last, when all the mischief was done, just as the skies were beginning to brighten for the dawn, down rushed the rain in torrents. It was too late then; it was too late, grievously late, and it would have been so welcome earlier!

For I think it was only when I saw our dear old home next day—that is, the charred ruins of it—that I realised fully how sorry I was, for though they were no longer ours, nor ever would be again, to see the dreary smoking heap within the skeleton walls was to me as it is to look upon the corpse of an old familiar friend!

CHAPTER XIX. cfrom t&e BUcorti of Eocer StanUfact. HE Lord gave, and the Lord hath taken away; blessed be the Name of the Lord!

Thus I must feel when I think of the house which He gave me, and took away again after His good pleasure.

It may be that I took too much pleasure in it, and pleased myself so well with the thought of an earthly home, that I began to think less of the heavenly one, and so I sinned.

But here I touch upon the skirts of a great mystery. God cannot be tempted with evil, and yet He uses the evil passions and evil deeds of men as instruments to carry out His will. By the hand of man He has now been pleased to chasten me.

For /, walking sadly in the ruins this morning, heard voices close to me, and my own name spoken by them. I paused to listen, and this was what I heard.

"You desired it; you said so, my foster-brother, my Drinan Dhun! It was not only your lips that said it; in your heart I knew you wished it done," said the voice of Teague O'Ruark.

Pierce O'Connor groaned aloud in answer. "And now you are angry with me for doing it. Why? Because the Buddagh Sassenach 1 had the dove's heart 1 The Saxon churl.

under the kite's feathers. You might have seen that sooner if you would." Again Pierce groaned.

"Well, then," said Teague O'Ruark, "I did wrong. But it was all out of love to you!" And indeed there was love in the poor fellow's voice as he spoke. "I thought all was fair to an enemy. Anyhow, I had better not be at home to visitors awhile, I suppose," he said, between laughter and tears.

The cinders crackled under his feet as if he had turned to go.

"I suppose you will not take me with you into Spain, or where you'll go?" he said, in a hesitating tone.

"No, no, Teague. You stay at home and marry your Nora in a bit, when bygones are bygones," said Pierce O'Connor, in low broken tones.

Teague's feet crackled away, and I, ashamed in part of having heard that which was not meant for my ear, came straight to where young O'Connor stood, lost in moody thought.

"It is you, is it?" said he. "Are you come to reproach me with burning your house down?"

"Not so," I said. "The sin is against Heaven. He who committed it will bear the burden of it."

"I shall, then," said he. "My hands never kindled it. But I wished the house to be burnt, and that wish started the blaze. You saved my life, and so I confess it freely."

"And I forgive you," I answered, " as the Lord would have us forgive our brother."

"What!" he said; "you will not have the incendiary brought to justice?"

"No; I will not," I said. "I cannot see how he who drags his brother before an earthly judge can be a Christian in truth. Our Master said—' If any man take thy coat, give thy cloak also;' but if we at once go to law with him who does so, are we Christians?"

"It seems not," said Pierce slowly. "Yet the doings of your country in taking away our lands"

"Are the will of God, even as the spoiling of the Egyptians by the chosen people."

"A very sound parallel, sir, and a very satisfactory one—to the favoured nation. But we, being in the place of the Egyptians, are a little inclined to doubt, ay, and to cavil, may be."

"*Bare* not to question His dispensations," I broke in. "Therefore it is that He so often needs to smite once and again, even because men will not confess His chastening hand."

"H'm!" said young O'Connor. "But doubtless the really faithful will not fail in that particular;" and he looked round meaningly.

"To see error is the first step towards renouncing it," I said quietly. "And for you, Master O'Connor, if I may counsel, I would have you repair as promptly as may be to Spain or to France, where you will no longer have the temptations that beset you here, but an honourable career will be open to you."

"Ah ha!" he cried passionately, "that is how you manage to forgive me, is it? You make that a condition—that I should get out of your sight?"

"God forbid," I answered hastily. "*That* is not forgiveness, else what would become of us? No; He makes no conditions when He forgives. How should I dare do so."

"I thank you then," he said, with sudden gentleness; and he turned away and left me among the ruins, from whence I went down to the wooded way by the lake where Mistress Ethne had promised to meet me and to give me her answer.

She came presently, moving in a white dress over which flowed a long scarlet mantle, under the chequered light and shadow made by the trees. As she came I could not but think how fair she was—tall and graceful, not too slender, but with a certain dignity of carriage that is in my eyes a great charm in a woman. At least I have learned to think so of late. Her dark hair waves upon her forehead; her eyes are thoughtful and serious; her mouth smiles often, but has a certain seriousness too.

So I watched her as she came, and I remembered that it was said in the Holy Book—

"He that findeth a wife findeth a good thing."

I have been cool and calm in battle; it is also but two days since that I looked Death in the face and feared not; but now my heart beat fast and my hand trembled, so strange is the power of a maiden over the stout heart of a man.

She came up to me proudly yet modestly. She laid her two hands in mine and said with steady voice, though her colour deepened a little—

"Captain Standfast, I have come to say that I will be your wife."

It seemed to me that I had never known how fair the earth is until that moment, when a glory seemed to be shed upon the trees and the shining water that peeped between them, and the sky that looked down, and the commonest things that crept or grew, as I looked into my lady's face and pressed her hand to my lips.

But a fear took me that she scarcely understood what manner of life must be hers as my wife. No vain dance, no idle singing, but a grave assembling together of them that fear the Lord; and for sweet melody the songs of Zion, which are framed rather to support the soul than to tickle the ear. So I told her all this. Her face grew grave and perplexed while I spoke, and at last she looked in my face.

N

"Captain Standfast, do you repent you of your offer, or fear you were too hasty?"

"The Lord forbid, maiden! But do *you* repent of too hasty accceptance thereof?" I said earnestly.

Then she smiled and answered me in the sweet words of Kuth—

"Where thou goest, I will go....

Where thou diest, I will die.... The Lord do so to me, and more also, if aught but death part thee and me!"

That she answered me from Holy Writ was a joy; that she gave her whole self to me so frankly and lovingly was yet greater joy. I clasped my lady in my arms and sealed our betrothal with a kiss.

She might not tarry long, so for a few glad moments we walked beside the lake. Then my lady left me, when I had promised to seek her father that afternoon and tell him of our love.

I would have gone with her at once, but she desired first to speak to them herself. She would not seem to need one to support her in declaring her new convictions, she said, lifting her head proudly. So she went, and I watched as long as I could see her. Then I took boat and rowed down the lake, desiring to be alone with my own thoughts.

I suppose an hour had passed, or it might have been two hours, when I returned. As I neared the landingplace I saw that gilded dragon-fly, Maurice Burke, roaming to and fro as though waiting for me.

I had no mind to talk with him, but I must needs tie up the boat, and while I was making her fast he joined me.

"I learn that I ought to wish you joy, Captain Standfast," he said, and I answered briefly that I thanked him.

"Ay," he continued, "I would have wished the fair Ethne joy too; but when she brushed past me and went forth into the woods alone, I had not the heart."

"Let me advise you, Master Maurice," I said, "to meddle chiefly with those matters which concern you in this life."

"I am grateful for the advice," said he, bowing; "and in truth it is what I am doing, for the matter does greatly concern me, since even I myself"—he heaved a deep sigh—" well, it has been the dream of my youth, and I trusted my hope was very near fulfilment. But women are ever so, and shall I—
'Wastynge in despayre,
Die because a woman's fayre?1
Not so. My motto is—
'If she bee not fayre for me,
What care I how fayre she bee 1'"

"An exceedingly wise conclusion, and one that shows a prudence beyond what I should have expected from you," I said.

"Ay, indeed, but you do flatter me. And I fear that I cannot be quite callous to the sufferings of the only woman I have ever loved, indifferent though I would be."

"Sufferings, sir?"

"Ay, sufferings, good Sir Dragon. But perhaps your studies have not been wide enough to embrace the story of Perseus and Andromeda, so that you know not how once, when a certain land was devoured by a certain dragon, and many had fallen victims, at last the king's daughter, the fairest maiden in the land, was given over to the creature. They say she went most willingly, hoping to profit her parents and others. A praiseworthy maiden, sir, though she was not devoured after all."

"In consequence of the interposition of Sir Perseus. The fable is well known to me, Master Burke, and a mighty pretty tale it is. A pity it were not true," I said.

"There is much truth in fables, sir."

"And a good lump of falsehood," I said; and having fixed the boat to her moorings, I was about to walk away.

"Nay, kind Sir Dragon, but hear me a moment," said Maurice; "for I think the tears of so fair an Andromeda might well move the scaliest heart. I wish you had been with me, sir, as I stood with my ear glued to the door— I own it, for all is fair in love—and heard the wrath of our good father loudly rolling.

"'A creature like that'—he would not so much mind the heresy—' but his family! Pray you, whose scullion was his mother? Had he ever a grandfather?' asked the Knight of Lara."

"Pray you," I said, striving to be calm, "keep the confidence which you so honourably gained, *as* honourably."

"For her sake I will share it with you," he said, and a scornful smile curled his finely-cut lips. "Said then her mother, ' Be not so hard on the child, Gerald. Do you not see that she is sacrificing herself for us? As for her faith, let that be. Young hearts are sometimes led away, only to return with eagerness to the safe fold of Holy Church. But for us, the man has promised us shelter, protection, room to abide here.'

"' Ethne,' said Sir Gerald, 'I am to believe that it is for our sake you have done this?'

"I glued mine ear the closer, but I heard only sobs.

"' He will not hold you to such a promise,' condoled the mother. 'The sacrifice is too hard, my child; we cannot ask it of you.'

"I was sure by Ethne's tone that she raised her head proudly.

"' Not too hard for an O'Connor,' she said. 'What we have promised, we perform. Father! mother! my mind is made up. You will not refuse your consent?'

"I only heard a murmur from the old people in answer.

"' No, you will not/ said Ethne. 'Think of it. My part is harder than yours, but I can fulfil it with a smile. If you wish to make your Ethne happy—as happy as she can ever be—you will consent willingly!'

"I heard that they kissed her and blessed her, and I had but time to move as if I were just coming upstairs, when she swept past me and out of the dwelling. Her eyes were red, as I said; but I have wearied youi patience, sir," and he lifted his plumed hat and bowed low, then walked away without another word.

"Stay, sir," I called after him, and he came back a step or two. "You are a gentleman—a man of honour, I suppose?"

He bowed, laying his hand upon his heart.

The young jackanapes! I could have crushed him like a painted moth, without effort.

"*Gentlemen* always are men of honour, sir," said he.

"Oh, indeed," I said, keeping down wrath, lest I should sin in being angry overmuch.

"Then, sir, perhaps you will give me your word of honour that this is true, word for word, to the best of your recollection."

Master Butterfly laid his white be-ringed fingers on his sword hilt.

"Am I to understand that you call me a liar? If so, draw and defend yourself!" and his blade leaped from the scabbard.

"I fight in no such foolish quarrels," I answered, and I unbuckled my sword and threw it on the ground. "If your story is true, your honour will not be tarnished by being appealed to, precious thing as it is."

"It is precious, sir," he answered, leisurely putting up his sword; "a precious pearl it may truly be called, and there are certain animals before whom it is not wise to cast pearls. A good parable truly, sir, and one which I am sure you have not failed to consider."

The same scornful smile curled his lips as he went, and my carnal pride rose up so that I could have followed him sword in hand and thrust his insults down his throat. But I forbore, and walked swiftly away into the wooded paths to think on the story I had heard. And there, leaning my back against a tree, and looking upon the soft mosses at my feet, I strove to perceive and know what I ought to do.

There was a little pool among the mosses; it was clear enough to reflect my figure as I stood. I looked at myself, and at my worn clothing that had no beauty about it even when new. Then I thought of Maurice Burke.

"Ay, there is not much in me for a woman to desire; it is like enough that young Maurice spoke the truth."

As I thought thus, I heard a strange sound not far from me—the sound of a woman weeping. And, going towards the sound, I found Mistress Ethne sitting upon a fallen tree, her face hidden in her hands.

"Ethne!" I said; and she lifted her head, and at sight of me rose to her feet and stood trembling with downcast head like a child that looks to be chidden.

I had no mind to chide. I pitied her in my heart, and I felt disappointed, for I had thought the maiden possessed of a braver spirit.

"Mistress Ethne," I said, "I have come to release you from your promise. I ought not to have asked for it, that is true, but neither ought you to have given it."

She lifted her head and looked at me, but did not speak.

"It is well," I said, "that persons should at least learn their own minds before they are irrevocably bound together, and find they have made a promise which they are not able to fulfil."

She threw back her head proudly.

"I at least make no promise that / will not undertake to fulfil, Captain Standfast."

"I think you would try," I answered. "But I have no courage to ask such an effort, after what I have heard."

"What you have heard—what is that?"

"The *truth,* maiden," I said, sternly enough. "The truth of what passed between you and your parents, related to me on undoubted authority."

She looked me straight in the face as I spoke, but when I had finished she dropped her eyes to the ground at her feet, and watched with great apparent interest the ways of a snail that was slowly making its way along the mossy path. So she sat in silence for many minutes. Then she held out her hand.

"Good-bye, Captain Standfast. I trust yon may yet find a wife after your own heart, who will be to you all that you desire."

She spoke with steady voice, and went away with a firm step. But as I watched her go my heart rose up and cried that this could not be, that there must be some mistake. I followed her therefore, and she, hearing my hasty steps, turned and looked at me in the same quiet way, so that I stood before her embarrassed, and not knowing well what it was that I would say.

"I pray you," I stammered at last, "grant me one request. Tell me yourself why it was that you wept but now?"

"Methinks it matters but little to you why I wept," she answered, speaking gently, but with sparkling eyes.

"But it does matter, my Ethne;" and now I stood before her wholly abashed and humble. "I pray you tell me, sweet Ethne, for without you the earth would have no beauty in my eyes."

At that my lady laughed, with that pleasant low laugh of hers.

"Do you know, Captain Standfast," she said, "that that is the first lover-like speech you have ever made me? It is strange that you should utter it now, just when you have ceased to be my lover."

"I have no right to ask, I know; but yet have pity on me, dear Ethne. Tell me why I found you in tears?"

"Yes; I will tell you. Why not? It was because Pierce, my brother, has come to tell us that he goes to Spain with the troop that is being gathered in these parts. And it is hard to part from Pierce, my father's only son, and my only brother."

"0 Ethne, Ethne!" I cried, "was that why you wept? Not because, after you had promised yourself to me, you found the sacrifice too hard, and you looked back as did the wife of Lot?"

She drew herself up proudly, and spoke more coldly than I had ever heard her do.

"Captain Standfast had, after all, but a low opinion of the woman he professed to love."

"0 Ethne, Ethne, forgive me!" I besought her. "I was told; but it was a lie. Forgive me, and let all be as it was when we two talked together this morning."

But she drew her hand from mine.

"Nay, Roger Standfast," she said; "I fear me you would make no woman happy. If you can thus readily think evil and entertain suspicion as a lover, what would you be as a husband?

'And Bo without more circumstance at all,
I hold it fit that we shake hands and part,'
as I have heard my father read in a book he loves well."

She spoke thus, and then turned away and left me standing there. I would not follow her again nor call her back, for I felt very wroth. If only she had given me time, I think I would have humbled myself before her, saying—

"Nay, my Ethne, we will not so part. 'Confess your faults one to another,' says James the Apostle, and I confess that I have wronged you by the suspiciousness of which you justly complain. But if you could find it in your heart to forgive me, my Ethne, I would strive against the temptation to hardness of heart, and daily I would thank God for the good gift of your love."

But she was gone; and though I thought I heard once and again her returning step, it was only some rustle among the trees, and at last I turned and went away, feeling grieved in spirit, and yet thinking that doubtless all things were working together for my good. For he that is unmarried careth for the things of the Lord, but the married man must often care much for the things of the world, how he may please his wife. And Paul himself, having considered the question of marriage, and given utterance thereon, turns away as though the subject, which fools think so all important, were indeed but petty and vexatious.

"But this I say, brethren, the time is short." CHAPTER XX.
JFrom the Rrcotn of Roact Standfast.
UNE is upon us.
Sir Gerald O'Connor has for his own possession this year's crops of his own planting on the part of the lands of Lara which he himself farmed hitherto. He has, therefore, for the present continued to dwell in the offices of the Castle, while I, at the invitation of Isaiah Heston, have been dwelling with him at Glendour Halls. Alas! it falls to me now to mourn as David over the sorrow which mine own familiar friend hath wrought for me.

How often we have taken sweet counsel together, and have walked in the house of God as friends! How often as boys we played together on the low meadows by the silver Severn, delighting in trials of strength, and in all the madcap sports beloved of boys and young men.

It is hard to part from a friend who goes over seas for many a year. It is sad to part when Death leads our friend within the veil, whither not even a message can follow him, leaving us altogether lonely and wistful. But harder still are these partings of the spirit. Hand may clasp hand again, but the souls are separated for ever by a great gulf which we cannot bridge, and would not if we could. Thus it is now between myself and my old friend Isaiah Heston, and thus the severance came about.

The measuring of the land with chains and rods hath been going steadily forward, the land allotted to each troop or company being now divided into each man's portion. Of late many soldiers have come to see their settlement. There has been some murmuring, since the thing to be divided was not a pudding of which each man should receive a slice, certain to be of the same quality as that of his neighbour. Here are patches of wood, valleys that are a mere basin to hold bog, bare hills, and rich pasture or corn lands mixed up together. It must of necessity happen that one man's portion will be better than that of his neighbour. Herein is no cause for complaint, since the disposal of lots is from the Lord. Nevertheless, some have been exceeding wroth, and others greatly elated and triumphant.

I myself bought of several soldiers their debentures, which they were glad thus at a fair price to sell. Isaiah Heston would gladly have done the same, but he lacked the ready money needed for the bargain. Many of the soldiers, moreover, were not then willing to sell, so that Isaiah had failed to arrange for himself that which he desired, namely, by adding house to house and field to field to make himself a great estate.

One bright June afternoon, therefore, while I abode with him, a soldier, named Robert Dixon, rode into the yard and called in a lordly tone to an Irish lad to take his rein and tell him where the master of the house might be. Isaiah came forth and led the man into a room which chanced to be just below that wherein I was, and offered him food and wine.

The windows were open. I could hear their talk, and listened idly to it, without thought of being an eavesdropper.

The soldier, having eaten and drunk, produced a paper, as I could hear, and smoothed it out.

"To me have fallen," he said, "a hill called Monery, and the valley of Lack. Barbarous names enough. Will it please you tell me where they be, Lieutenant?"

"In truth, my friend," I heard Isaiah answer, "I am, from my heart, sorry for you. Lack said you, and Monery? Then those two together make up Lack Money, unless yon have a mind to put your shoulder under the stones that lie upon the hill as thick as the quails sent to murmuring Israel, and roll them down to fill up the wet valley. Plenty of stone to build yourself a house, my friend; plenty of fuel to warm yourself withal, and to cook your food, if food were yours to cook. But there is the crux, for nature will need pursuading—nay, even constraining, before she will produce for you the scantiest subsistence."

"Say you so indeed?" asked Robert Dixon; and then there was a pause, and in a low tone he muttered a profane word, and struck a heavy fist upon the table.

"It is hard upon us poor devils," he said, "that this is all the recompense we are to get for risking our lives, for marches, wounds, hard fights! I could wish there were a king again in England to pay us in good red gold, and not in pieces of paper which admit us to a bit of bog and a precipice."

"Good friend," said Isaiah, "you are profane and also disloyal. Remember that in the sweat of your brow you may yet—say after twenty years' good steady work —make this wilderness rejoice and blossom like the rose."

I heard the soldier give a growl of disgust.

"Twenty years, Master Lieutenant. You talk as if a man had the life of Methuselah, so that some twenty years were just a slice easily to be taken out of it. And I pray you how will Damaris Bryce, my betrothed, look by the time I am able to make a home for her? I would sooner leave the army to follow again mine ancient trade of wheelwright. I was a skilled workman, and could yet make a good living at that."

"Why not, indeed!" echoed Isaiah. "For how will you buy plough and harrow, good Dixon, and other things needful for farming?"

"There again!" cried the soldier, with another thump on the table. "I swear that now at this very moment if one were to offer me—say a barrel of beer, for which liquor I have a great longing—this paper should be his."

I heard how joyful Isaiah's tone grew, though he spoke slowly, and as one reflecting.

"There be even now *two* barrels in my cellar—the one of beer, the other of prime Gloucestershire cider."

There was a rustle. I think the soldier threw the paper across the table to him.

"Done with you, good Lieutenant!" said he. "The paper is yours, and the cider is mine, and the beer, if you will add thereto something in money—enough to convey me happily back to mine own home at Moreton-in-theMarsh in happy England."

Now I had all this time been exercising my memory about these two places—the hill of Monery and the valley of Lack; and with the soldier's last words the recollection of them came suddenly to me, and I remembered that Monery was one of the fairest and most fertile slopes for miles round, and that, as for the valley of Lack, though there was yet a small piece of bog in it, which was indeed no hurt, but only a benefit, as supplying fuel, the rest of the valley was exceeding fertile, and held at this moment a fair field of oats, thick and green, and a most hopeful promise of potatoes, with some flax, the last being an exhausting crop, and one which requires that the ground which has grown it should be handsomely refreshed. This would be an expense to the incomer; but one receiving so fair a little farm as this great valley and the fine pastures on the low rolling hill might well be content to spend the small sum that might be required for the next year's profits.

I could scarce believe that mine ears had heard aright— that it could be mine own familiar friend Isaiah Heston who had thus attempted to overreach the poor soldier. And I strode downstairs with anger in my heart, and joined the two men.

The soldier was in the act of signing his name to a paper which Isaiah must have hastily written—a deed of gift.

"Hold!" I cried; and both started to their feet, and, truth to tell, one looked as guilty as the other.

"Robert Dixon," I said, "beware how you barter the inheritance given you by the Lord for strong drink. And you, Lieutenant Heston, think you that the noble hill of Monery and the fertile valley below are thus to be exchanged? Is this their value—a few quarts of poisoned water for those good lands?"

"*Good lands,* Captain?" said the soldier; and he looked from Isaiah to me, and threw down the pen on the table before him.

Isaiah laughed aloud.

"Nay, then," said he, "we know that Captain Standfast is much enamoured of this land, so that he judges— how shall I say, Captain?—leniently, overfavourably, of its worth. But if you will come forth with me, Dixon, I will e'en show you the farm; and we will take this paper along with us, and if the place likes you well, why, then keep it; and if not, I will buy it at whatsoever price we may agree upon."

"I am content," said the soldier; and they went forth, and I continued at some carpenter work that I had in hand, for I hold it sin to be idle when aught can be done.

I suppose an hour had passed when I heard steps, and Isaiah Heston came towards the house alone. I left my work and went to meet him, for I was grieved at heart, and felt that I must withstand him to the face, because he was certainly to blame.

"Where is Robert Dixon?" I asked, as he came near.

"Oh, he has gone away," said Isaiah, and he laughed again. "The poor fellow had no mind to dwell in this country, and who can blame him? Not I, for one."

"And the price, Isaiah?" said I.

"For the price, so long as he was content with it, I pray you what matter is it of yours, Captain Standfast?"

"It is my matter," I said steadily. "It is very much my matter to see that a man be not defrauded and overreached. And now I bethink me, friend Isaiah, how is it that you come from this side the house? This is neither the way to nor from the hill of Monery."

"Oh, it was a pleasant walk," said Isaiah; but I felt certain that he was not speaking the perfect truth, and a fresh suspicion flashed into my mind.

"The barren hill of Cawhoo and the boggy valley below it lie on this side, Isaiah Heston, and I greatly fear you have deceived the poor man into the notion that they were his portion," I said.

"You are very stern, Captain Standfast," said Isaiah. "Pray you be not so ready to think evil, for that a Christian should not do."

I bethought me of Ethne's words when I had been deceived about her. Indeed such suspiciousness seemed to be in me a besetting sin.

I held my peace, therefore; and it was Isaiah's own doing that I learned how right I had been in my judgment, for he said, in a coaxing kind of tone—

"' Live and let live' is a good motto, friend Roger. If my hands are not quite clean, you will lend me your gloves. None of us could bear to have quite all our little matters closely looked into, could we?" "What do you mean?" I said, very angry. "I have done nought at which I have cause to be ashamed."

"Oh, pardon me! but I thought there was a—well, no matter; but he was a strong man and a servant of the Lord who was enticed in the valley of Sorek."

"I will not pretend to misunderstand you," I said; "but the maiden whom I would have taken to wife was no Delilah, but rather a Ruth whose heart the Lord had turned to Himself, and who I trusted would have become a godly matron among the Lord's people."

"Ay," said Isaiah, "we can make the following of our own desires seem wondrous godly by a fair use of language; but I cannot think that direct disobedience to the laws is so very blameless. It is true that Israel kept some of the idolaters among them, but they were as thorns in their sides."

"You mean that I am to blame for sheltering the O'Connor family and admitting them to be my tenants?"

"In plain terms, friend Roger, I do mean it. If I am to blame for smoothly arranging matters with a soldier, to the perfect satisfaction of us both, you are more to blame for tampering with Popery and sheltering the rebels and traitors to our country."

"Nay," I said, "I think not. A false weight is an abomination to the Lord; that justice should be tempered with mercy is well pleasing unto Him. The man O'Connor is old. His wife is also old. Their days cannot endure for ever. For the present they will" sink to the level of the peasantry, and when they die they will be blotted out, for their son is gone forth as an exile already, and will not return."

"Plausible, assuredly," said Isaiah; but he smiled as he unrolled a paper which he carried. "This, friend Roger, I received from Robert Dixon. It was published but yesterday. Fleetwood, the Lord-Deputy, being at Limerick, hath discovered that this same joining hands with the Gibeonites and taking them to hew wood and draw water hath been done in many places, and he proclaims that all officers are at once to search out all transplantable persons, and to cause them to remove as promptly as may be into Connaught, on or before the day three weeks of the proclamation, which is dated June ist."

I looked at the paper, and found that it was even as he had said. While I stood pondering he came close to me, and said in mine ear—

"Ha, friend Roger! what say you now? Shall it be 'Live and let live'? Tush, man! we all eat and wipe our mouths now and then, you and I and our betters also; no need to pull so long a face over it."

It was hard for me to find words wherewith to answer, so wroth was I.

"Master Isaiah Heston," I said at last, "a man may be led away by strong temptation and may fall into sin, a sin not unto death. But to make a mock of that which destroyeth the soul, this is to turn one's back upon Zion. Take heed lest ye be as Demas, who departed altogether from the fellowship of the saints, because he loved this present world.

At that Isaiah changed his tone altogether, and would have had me believe that he spoke but in jest. How is he fallen, mine own familiar friend! His presence o became unbearable to me, though I wrestled long in prayer for him that night and the next, but the third day I bade him a sorrowful farewell, for they who travel by the narrow way had need keep closely to the path, lest their feet slide suddenly.

CHAPTER XXI. from t&e Diarg of ffitfcne sD'Connor. HE flax is to my mind the prettiest crop that ever grows on hill or dale. It waves so gracefully in the wind, and the green is so soft and pale, there can be nothing prettier than the plant in blossom, with the dainty blue bells nodding on their stems no thicker than a thread. They look frail enough, those stems, but if we pull them to pieces, we find how tough is the fibre that composes them. I think we women had need be like the flax, nowadays at least, with a steadfast spirit within our fragile bodies. I was standing this morning with a flax blossom in my hand and these thoughts in my heart. I had been weeding in the fields, as I often now do. I choose this work, and give for a reason that we are but tenantfarmers now, and I ought to do as a farmer's daughter does; but in truth the work is hard and wearies me, and I am glad, for from sheer weariness I can fall asleep now, and have no need to lie with my own sad thoughts for company. Yet I like also to sit spinning or embroidering, for while the hands are busy the thoughts are free, and by day I can think more cheerfully. I know not why I should be so sad. I am not sorry that I sent Roger Standfast away; I could not do otherwise. But I am sad. I have no heart to sing; I try to be cheerful for my parents' sake, but the effort oftentimes seems almost too great.

For our faith, it comes little into question now. Father Ambrose, being discovered in Dublin, was seized and taken to the storm-beaten isles on the western coast, where he, together with many more priests, is kept in confinement, as we believe.

I have often found that the things to which I have looked forward with dread have not been so terrible after all when they came. I had been sore troubled at the thought that I must confess to my parents that their faith was mine no longer. But when, with a voice that I strove vainly to steady, I had owned my conversion, my father said only—

"Why, what stuff are these girls now made of that the ways of their forefathers are not good enough for them?"

And then he groaned, and said—

"All is changing, all is changed. All except me, and I am too old to change. I trust that in heaven their will be no more changes; there can be none, I think, for they are ever for the worse, and always give pain."

And when I told him of Roger Standfast's love, he said—

"Ay, my child; then what must be must. Marry him an thou wilt; his home will be better for thee than Connaught."

I think he was almost grieved when I told him that Roger Standfast would not come now to ask my hand. He answered me then almost with anger.

"Why, what is it? I thought the girl had a spirit and knew her own will. And now, look you, she is as weak and changeable as—as other women."

My mother followed me from the room.

"Ethne," she said, "if it be in some mere pique that you have sent away your lover, I counsel you to think well. He is not the husband I would have chosen for you, my child—far from it, alas! But the love of a good man is not a mere trinket for a woman to deck herself withal, or to fling away at her pleasure."

"Nay, mother dear," I said, "it is not mere pique. I think I could not be happy with him, and you would not have your Ethne wed a man except in perfect certainty that she could love him."

"Love deepens with the years, as I have found," said my dear mother, smiling out of her own happiness of love.

"Surely you have found it so. But I think you sowed much love to reap this fair harvest," I said. She smiled again.

"The human heart is a wonderfully fertile soil for that crop, my Ethne!

Whoso sows love shall find it spring up and blossom and sow itself again a hundredfold. The heart is never exhausted by love, it only gains strength to love better."

"But it loves in many ways," I said, thinking that the love of a woman for her husband must be very different from all other kinds of love.

"Ay, my child," she answered; "and I *have* seen one love fill the heart so that there was no room left for any other. But I think that can never be true love to narrow the heart thus; it must be a mere selfish delight in a being who gives us pleasure. In the heart of God there is room for love of a whole creation, doubtless even of other whole creations."

"In the heart of men there is room for much hatred," I said sadly. "Ob, mother, if I had been God I think I *must* have made all men to be good, and to love one another and be at peace. How can He bear to look down and see the hatreds and strifes—not so much of the wicked, from them He might turn His eyes away— bnt of *good* people?"

I suppose I spoke passionately, for my mother laid her hand on my brow with that gentle touch which has ever had power to soothe me, and, answering my thoughts rather than my words, she said—

"My Ethne mistook esteem for affection, perhaps. She honoured a man for his goodness, and was grateful to him for his kindness, and she thought these two together made up love. Was it so, my darling?"

"Indeed, I know not, mother," I said; "but I think love must have respect in it—*true* love."

"Most surely it must; love were little worth having, else—it were merely the fancy of the child for its toy, of the butterfly for the rose."

It was of this talk with the sweetest and wisest of mothers that I was thinking as I stood among the pale-green stems and blue blossoms of the flax. And as I stood a musical voice called my name, and I saw that Maurice Burke was coming up the hill. Maurice, in satin as blue as the flax blossoms, slashed and plumed with pearly white, a short cloak of russet velvet over his shoulder, a very prince out of a fairy tale.

"Well, my Lady Ethne," he cried, coming up to me. "I wonder the sun troubles himself to shine to-day. What waste of light when your eyes are open, my Samela.

'As fair Aurora in her morning grey,
Decked with the ruddy glister of her love,
Is fair Samela!,

sang Maurice. But I cried impatiently—

"Have some sense, I pray you, Master Maurice, and remember that I am no Samela, but now only a shepherd maiden, or rather scarcely anything so poetical as a shepherdess, but just a farmer's wench. One who pulls weeds, sir, and soils her hands withal; who binds sheaves till she turns brown or scarlet, as the sun and her complexion may arrange it, whose feet grow wide with much walking"

"Spare me," entreated Maurice, his hands on his ears. "Nay, my Samela, talk not of such horrors—wide feet, brown hands, red face—away with the very thought! If hard fate has willed it so, we may at least have the poetry of rustic life—

'And we will sit upon the rocks,
Seeing the shepherds feed their flocks,
By shallow rivers, to whose falls
Melodious birds sing madrigals.

And I will make thee beds of roses,
And a thousand fragrant posies;
A cap of flowers and a kirtle,
Embroidered all with leaves of myrtle.

A gown made of the finest wool,
Which from our pretty lambs we pull,
Fair-lined slippers for the cold,
With buckles of the purest gold.'"

"Nay, for once I am even with you and your rhymes; for once and for ever, Sir Maurice," said I, and I laughed, as I well might. "One who was not to be won by such pretty fooleries as yours made once an answer to that same rhyme, as I read in one of your books, and remembered it well, as you see.

'If all the world and love were young,
And truth in every shepherd's tongue,
These pretty pleasures might me move
To live with thee and be thy love!'

Ah, Maurice! if you could assure me constancy on your part and the weather's, what might we not do! But—

'The flowers do fade, and wanton fields
To wayward winter reckoning yields;
A honey tongue, a heart of gall
To fancy's'"

But Maurice looked so sad that I had no heart to end the severe saying.

"Nay," I said, "I think I must leave out the ' heart of gall.' I am sure no such bitterness lurks in yours, my old playfellow."

"If it does, sweetheart, it is but the bitterness of a wounded spirit in which your arrows are rankling," said Maurice; and then of a sudden he caught my hand and fell upon one knee to kiss it as though I were a queen.

"Maurice," I said, with all the gravity I could muster, "I think you cannot guess how much I should prefer to be treated as a woman and not as a goddess. I am human, I assure you—very human indeed you will find me if you plague me too much."

Maurice laughed his gay laugh, but there seemed a little constraint about it, and again he took my hand as he stood beside me.

"Ethne! my love, my life!" he cried, "you tell me continually that I say too much in your praise; but I tell you that is impossible! I could not, cannot tell you —not if I used all the words in our language, what you are in my eyes, maiden most beautiful, most perfect, most peerless. I love you, my Ethne! I will sing of you till the birds of the field hide their heads for shame that they cannot equal the melody and variety of my music. I will make songs to you, so that the fame of Laura shall grow dim. I will love you as never lover loved his lady before, so only you will be mine, Ethne! Nay, do not stand looking at me with those grave, troubled eyes! How long have I been drawing the toils of my love round you—laying siege, little by little, to the too well watched citadel of your heart, where Captain Coyness and General Pride have kept spy upon my every movement? Do not tell me you did not know I loved you, Ethne, for you would not tell the truth in so saying. Of that I am very sure."

"Yes, I should be telling the truth, Maurice," I made answer slowly. "I did not know you loved me. I think you loved to be in love, and I did as well as another to sing to and make verses on. I think I have been a doll dressed to your fancy with gifts and graces, and labelled ' Samela.' That your Samela should *possess* the graces was quite unimportant. Tou could call them hers; that was surely enough. The true lady of your worship is the lady of your fancy."

Maurice laughed.

"What! would yon have a poet search his lady's face for a wart, or measure every feature to see if it accord with the canon of beauty? No, my Ethne, the poet and the lover have the only open eyes; they are the world's seers, and all the joy and beauty of the world is open to them."

"Then they must see the sorrow too more plainly than others, and the sordid ugliness."

"Not so, my beloved. Look into the world as into a duck-pond; you can see the stars shining there and rejoice in their light. But some there be who look in and see but the weeds and the mud of the bottom. Poor souls!"

"Or their own faces mirrored," I said; and I laughed, and Maurice's face grew grave again, and his eyes put on a beseeching look.

"Ethne, it is useless. As King Midas made all he touched into gold, so you make all into mirth. What shall I do? bow shall I persuade you of my love? how entreat you to have pity upon me? What shall I do to win you? I would drink up Esil—eat a crocodile: but I doubt if you would love me better."

"Nay, Maurice," I began; but Maurice went on— "Or shall I become anything but what I am?

'Bid me to live and I will live
Thy Protestant to be.'

Ay, one modelled on the exact pattern of Captain Lookwhere-you-go yonder, if you will."

"Maurice," I said, and in my folly I spoke hotly, "there is no need for you to bring in Captain Standfast to this talk."

"No, that is true," said Maurice lightly. "It would be as fit to bring a carthorse fully harnessed into a lady's pleasaunce."

At his careless, insulting tone, a passionate anger sprang suddenly up in my heart, and without thinking of the unwisdom of my words, I cried—

"You can call Captain Standfast as many ill names as you will, Maurice Burke, but they will not harm him, nor will they make him aught but what he is— a good man and true, a better man than many whose outside"

"Truly I have seen many a choice fruit in a plain russet coat," said Maurice. "But Ethne, why so hot?" Then suddenly a new thought seemed to strike him, and he cried, with troubled face and voice—

"Ethne, it cannot, it *cannot* be! I know he seeks your company, I can well believe he loves you, for who could help it? but you will not tell me that your heart is given to that—that man of iron with a tongue of lead."

"And a heart of gold?" I asked softly.

But Maurice grew deadly pale at that word.

"Anything, anything but that! You are not going to marry him, Ethne?"

"O Maurice! I never thought you loved me so," was all I could say.

"It has been my fault that you have not, I suppose; but at least you know it now. Ethne, my beloved, I do love you with all my heart and soul. If you will be mine, I know I shall grow into a nobler man for your sake, if not—why, the devil may make me into what he pleases, for my wretched self would not be worth my own care."

"Maurice! Maurice!"

"It is true, as true as that we two stand here together. Ethne, you are not going to wed that man?"

"I *was* going to wed him," I said slowly.

"But you are not now? You found that there was no warmth in him, no love that blesses the heart of maiden as sunshine upon a flower? You wearied of his cold homage; who could endure it long? who but a woman made in his own mould? The love I offer is— it is *love,* and that is all, the first word and the last, the fount of all joy, all beauty, all poesy.

'What thing is love, which nought can countervail?

Nought save itself, even such a thing is love.

All worldly wealth in worth as far doth fail,

As lowest earth doth yield to heaven above!

Divine is love, and scorneth worldly pelf,

And can be bought with nothing save with self.'

Say then, my lady, can the whole sum of my love not buy a kind look, a little word, a single sigh from you? If not, why, away love; thou art but dross after all, and no gold as the poets have feigned."

"Maurice," I said slowly and with hesitation, "I never heard words that gave me so much pain as these of yours. Truthfully I tell you, I never dreamed that you loved me, save in a kind and brotherly fashion, as Pierce might. But now you stand here and speak as if this love of yours gave you some claim on me"

"I take no such lofty tone," he broke in. "I do but supplicate most humbly that the earnestness of my affection may find grace in my lady's eyes."

"I am grateful to you for your offer of love," I said more steadily. "I would I could love you in return, but I cannot, save, as I said, in sisterly fashion."

"But what is there in *me* that you cannot love," said Maurice; and now his voice was hoarse and unsteady. "Because if I knew that, Ethne, I would go from your presence with a good courage, and spend day and night in shaping myself to that which you would have me to be. I would truly, with 'The tried intent

Of such a truth as I have meant,

My great travail so gladly spent,'

to make me, ay, even a Puritan, if that please you, or aught else."

"And what truth would there be in this new being of yours, merely put on for my pleasure? Maurice, I think you yourself have told the reason that you cannot win my love"

"Because I am not a man of iron like yon English fellow? So you will none of him because he is overhard, and none of me because I am over-soft, perhaps. So there is nought for me to do but to take my dismissal and go."

He lifted his plumed hat and bowed low with his courtliest air, and parted from me. But he had gone only a few steps when he returned, pale and with piteous eyes.

"Ethne, Ethne! *can* you not love me? I love you so dearly, Ethne; you are all the world to me. Do pity me, sweet Ethne. I am unworthy I know, but I love you, I love you, I love you!"

I was pale too, I am sure of that, and I answered with trembling lips.

"I *like* you well enough, Maurice. Do not ask me to *love* you; it is not in me."

"You that like and I that love," said Maurice. "Well, so be it, since so it must be;" and Maurice went away and left me standing alone in the flax-field, with tears raining down my cheeks.

Maurice and Roger Standfast—I had sent them both away, and it seemed that I could not do otherwise.

Yet Roger Standfast's strong arm would have shielded us all, and with Maurice I might have made a better home for my parents beyond seas. Perhaps after all I was but selfish and proud, as maidens are sometimes said to be.

At the thought I wept, and then I grew angry with myself for my weakness and folly. I had done what I felt to be right. Of what use was it to grieve over a might-have-been? There are so many might-havebeens in life that our whole time might be spent in vain sorrow. I left the field and walked swiftly homeward, determined to sit down and spin diligently, and put all selfish thoughts behind me.

The black ruins of our home are cool now. When man leaves any spot, it seems as if nature at once and gladly took back the usurped possession, and tenderly wrapped the seared thing in a mantle of her own making, blotting out as fast as she can all trace of the work of men's hands.

So it is with our ruined home now. Already green things are springing and sprouting everywhere among the 222 broken masonry and charred remains of woodwork. I suppose bub a year or two will pass before the whole becomes a thing of picturesque beauty, dear to painter and poet, unless indeed the new owner should elect to raise for himself a home on the ruins of ours. In truth the new prosperity of these invaders is all founded on the ruined happiness of others.

As I entered the courtyard on one side, Captain Standfast entered it on another, and with him came my father, who held in his hands a paper, which I knew at a glance to be one of those simple white sheets with the thick black printing, of which we have so much reason to dread the veiy sight, the proclamations of Cromwell, or of his Lord-Deputy, Fleetwood.

My father was talking eagerly, remonstrating as it seemed, while the Englishman looked grave and troubled, and seemed to be listening silently.

I came near, and my father gave me the paper.

"Read that, Ethne, and join me in telling Captain Standfast that we would rather endure anything and everything than suffer him to fall under the anger of those to whom he owes obedience."

I read the edict hastily. It was couched in sufficiently wrathful terms. The sheltering of poor transplantable proprietors was severely denounced as a great dishonour to the army and a gross breach of discipline. If they were to be received as tenants, the country would not be properly planted with English and Protestants. Finally, any officer persisting in such sheltering of the transplantable would be punished by the articles of war, as negligent of his duty, and the punishment would be proportioned to the heinousness of his offence.

This broadsheet had been found by my father thrust under the door of our dwelling—the cottage which was now our not unbearable substitute for home. By whom it was put there he could not guess, but / knew in a moment that this must be Isaiah Heston's doing.

"You see, Ethne," said my father, as I gave back the paper, " drowning men have no right to pull down others with them. So—good our friend and good our enemy, both at once—we thank you for your kindness, and we will e'en take leave and go to that spot of God's earth which He meant for seagulls and rabbits; but to which men dressed in a little vain authority consign us, to burrow and nibble like the rabbits. Well for me that I have no pride left—none!"

"If only "—began Roger Standfast, and his eyes were fixed on my face; but the talk was broken asunder, for there was a great clatter of horse-hoofs, and an officer of Cromwell's army, followed by Isaiah Heston and a soldier or two, rode suddenly into the yard at a round pace, and pulled his horse sharply up in front of us as we stood.

"Here, churl, take my rein," cried the officer, dismounting.

"Well, good Captain, it gives me joy to see you; but how? what is this? You have not made of your house a burnt-offering and sacrifice by fire?"

Isaiah Heston laughed aloud at the grim jest. My father had not caught the rein thrown to him, and the horse started at the sound, and, finding his head free, suddenly made off by the way he had come.

Two of the dragoons were out of their saddles and after the beast in an instant, while the officer turned angrily to my father.

"What is this, fellow? Art not able to hold a rein? Nay, by thy sullen look, I think thou wert not willing. No answer? Take that then, sullen dog that thou art"

And, as if he had indeed been a dog, the officer struck him over the shoulders with his whip.

"Nay, Colonel," broke in Captain Standfast, "the man meant no barm, I am sure."

In my father a wild fury blazed up. He clenched his fists and set his teeth, while his eyes flamed. He made a step or two towards the Colonel who had so grievously insulted him, then suddenly his hands dropped to his side, and he bowed his head on his breast.

"No pride left," he muttered, "none—for their sakes," and he stood aside with humble air, like a servant who has been justly corrected. Only the great vein that swelled on his forehead showed what that effort must have cost him.

The Colonel looked at him and then at me.

"Captain Standfast-on-the-Rock/' he said grimly, "we have ever reckoned you one of the strongest of the faithful. Tour very name betokens that the Lord hath saved you from the miry pit and hath ordered your goings. But now it seems that you have gone down into the valley of Sorek and your feet have slipped. What! could you not dwell among the Philistines unscathed by their abominations? Is it not written, 'Thou shalt smite them and utterly destroy them, thou shalt make no covenant with them, nor show mercy unto them'?"

"That was the command to Israel," said Captain Standfast; "but if of the people of this land there be some who will turn from idols to worship the true God"

The Colonel had little eyes that twinkled. He looked now upon Captain Standfast and then upon me.

"Of a truth, and indeed," he said, "very pretty work it is for a man's leisure to reclaim these pretty lambs of the devil's flock. As for you, old bellwether "—he looked at my father—" the task in your case must have been harder, and more meritorious, therefore"

"Ethne, come," said my father; "we have stayed too long."

"Why, what insolence is this?" cried the Colonel. "But I see how it is. Ay, Goodman Proud, you *have* stayed too long. Before the setting of another sun you will do well to get you on your road to Connaught. I see who you are; the coat cannot make the peasant."

"Nor the jerkin the gentleman," said my father, as he turned away. I suppose the Colonel was not of gentle birth, for, as we went, we heard him storming against "pride in birth and breeding, fit, forsooth, for cattle, whose price is according to parentage."

As for us, we went away to our cabin. It was a poor hut, but harp and spinning-wheel and a few household treasures had made it pleasant. My mother was sitting there; she looked up with a smile, but tears were in her eyes.

"We have news of Pierce," she said, and held out a letter.

It was no news to cheer us; such sorrow and bitterness breathed in every line of the narrative, from the moment when the troops with whom Pierce went marched from their rallying point with bursting hearts.

"Ha til, ha til, ha til mi tulidh,"1 played the wild pipes, and wild thoughts filled the hearts of the exiles, and anger and grief became so vehement that the officer commanding the levy called to the pipers and bade them Btrike up *Gairy Owen,* and to that merriest of strains the march went on. Bran, the faithful wolf-hound, had followed Pierce. At least one friend would share his toils and cheer his lonely hours. But as Pierce passed on shipboard the tide-waiters came to him.

"We must keep your dog," they said.

"Keep my dog! Nay, then you had better keep me too, for we will not part!" cried Pierce. But they told him this was the order of the Lord-Deputy. In the 1 We return, we return no more.

P desolation their own hands have spread, the English are sorely troubled by the increase of wolves, so that they are hunted even in the suburbs of Dublin. Henceforth no wolf-dogs are to be allowed to follow their masters into exile. Was ever a bitterer comment on the acts of a government?

F any man will do His will, he shall know of the doctrine," said the Lord while He walked on earth. I think I did His will in refusing Maurice Burke, although he declared himself willing for my sake to set his face whither I would. I think I have striven to do that will of late, on our long and weary journey towards our prison-house, where the wide rolling sea lies westward, and eastward the land is to be filled only with our foes.

The Lord who knew not where to lay His head has felt for us, I think, in our weary pilgrimage, and has cared for us; for oftentimes when the rain fell in torrents, and our weary beasts could travel no further, or night came on and we could see no shelter—even then help has come; a friendly hand perhaps has been reached to us, even from among our enemies, and shelter, if only in a dry barn, has been afforded us. Or the rain has ceased, and a warm sun has shone out, suffering us to dry our clothes and warm our stiff limbs in its pleasant rays.

I am grateful to Roger Standfast for that parting gift of his. It seems to me that whatever need of speech the Christian soul may have, *somewhere* in that blessed Book are words for it—in the Book which he sent me the night before we left, with a brief message that he had another and needed not this. "When thou passest through the waters I am with thee," I say to myself again and again when the sorrow seems heaviest, and often I have had occasion to remember with joy that "The Lord is my Shepherd, I shall not want."

It seems now that His parable of the lilies is the best lesson of all for ua. They are clothed; the birds are fed. Just now it is a hard trial of faith to rely upon the care of that same Fatherly Hand for us.

For we have left one or two faithful servants behind to care for our' crops, and have come with three waggons piled with household gear and clothing, and with such cattle as we have kept, driven painfully all the weary way by ourselves and two kind helpers. Those tenants who still desired to remove with us, barren and miserable as the place of our banishment is, came after us with their own chattels and live stock. A strange sight indeed the roads have been, crowded with delicate women and children, with the sick and the infirm, with thirsty and lowing cattle; everywhere we overtook caravans like our own, although this exodus has been slowly progressing for months past. Those who have been allowed to remain for a few months are beginning to go now; others are yet waiting for the harvest; and we learn that in a few weeks the officers will march their men to the lands appointed for them, while from England come some of the adventurers and persons who desire to farm under them. So all the land is a scene of journeying, and oittimes of inconceivable confusion and misery, when waggons break down, when children cry for weariness and hunger, when sickness takes man or beast, or hapless women fall in labour.

And here the misery is as great, or greater. O God! behind Thy blue sky, how canst Thou see it patiently!

We found no house. The two noble-hearted servants who came with us, helped by my father and by such labour as the poor old blind harper and I could give, have raised a kind of shed, of which the back wall, and indeed part of the sides, are made of the very earth hollowed out, a steep bank having been chosen, for wood is scarcely to be had here. Long since—some time in the reign of her whom in England they call Good Queen Bess—other adventurers, or soldiers, or temporary possessors, had cut down every stick of the pleasant woods that clothed these now dreary hills. They sold the timber, doubtless, very profitably. They did well to make the most of their time.

If it be any consolation to have partners in misery, then certainly that consolation is ours; for round us on all sides are people gently born like ourselves, who must build their own house, tend their own cattle, dig their own ground, strive with Nature, who is in some spots so generous, but here so niggardly, to wrest from her their daily bread.

In this struggle we have spent the long summer days, rising early and resting early, because lights are costly, and even of such expense we must be very frugal.

It seems a sad lot; but even here we have found some pleasure, my parents and I, because all that had to be faced has been faced *together,* and all that we do for each other seems brightened by love.

But in the last week a new sorrow has fallen upon us. My dear mother has long been suffering grievously in unselfish silence. We who saw her grow paler every day and more worn thought her thus oppressed by sorrow, and knew not that disease was slowly eating away her very life.

Now, because she cannot any longer rise from her chair, the sad truth must be told; but with a calm face that often smiles but never frowns, she sits in the miserable place which to me is glorified by that beautiful presence as though an angel sat there.

Through the long hours, while my father and I are out doing what we can, she has read in the little Bible. She was not afraid to read it now, she said, and I, with a very anxious heart, have waited to know whether she could read that Book and yet hold our ancient faith.

This question I asked of her with much anxiety at last, one evening when I came in and found her with the little Book open before her.

"My Ethne," she said slowly, " I have just been reading the story of the Saviour and the Samaritan woman. A most lovely story it truly is, and with tears I have read how He sat by the well as one aweary. He knew what it was to be tired, weary almost to death, as I am now. Nothing of all that we feel seems to have been left out of His load."

"Sometimes weariness is so great that it is as hard to bear as pain," I said, for she could scarcely speak, as it seemed, for exhaustion.

"I have heard Father Ambrose say," she said, "that in the Litany of the Eastern Church is a very touching prayer —' By Thine unknown sufferings, good Lord deliver us!' Besides those which are recorded for us, there must have been so many sufferings, so many. That Church is heretical, I believe, or at least in schism, but it has herein at least one lovely thought."

"Heresy!" I said, desiring to lead back her thoughts. "It is heresy to be— to be a Protestant; and reading the Bible makes people"

"Protestants? Well, my Ethne, I was reading, as I said, the story of the Samaritan woman. She was ignorant, she had had no teaching, and she could not understand the meaning of the mystical living water. She seems to have been strangely dull; but when those who had companied long with the Saviour returned, even they could not understand what He meant by His mystical meat, which was to do the Father's will."

"But oh, mother!" I cried, "the truth in this matter seems plain to me."

"Then follow it, my dear one. For me, I am too old to be rooted up from the foundations of my faith, and set to grow afresh in other soil. I have walked by the light the Lord" gave me, and have never dared to doubt or dispute it."

"Then it seems wrong to you that I should question aught that I have learned at your knee?"

"Not so, for we live in days of change. The Christian confession of faith that we have held must remain firm, for it is faith in One who cannot change. But there are other matters. Ethne, my child, may God steer your tempest-tossed spirit into a sure haven! For me, I am going beyond it all; I am going to see for myself!" Her face shone with happiness as she spoke, then sadly she said—

"I would I could come back from the dead to make you wise, as I shall have then grown, my darling," she said; and my father came in, and for that time we talked no more.

I know not how it was, but before last Sunday morning there went a kind of whisper from house to house that all would gather in the rath upon our hill soon after sunrise. No one named the purpose of this gathering—it was not even spoken of as a gathering; but it began to be known that so-and-so would be there with wife and child, and others also. We too went, my father and I.

It was a splendid summer morning, the air most sweet and fresh, the heavens deeply blue. Dew lay yet upon the grass, the birds sang lustily, chiefly tho larks, for the tree-dwellers Lave grown scarce with the trees. There are trees in the old fort, and the ditch is deep, with a high and steep bank inside it. The summit therefore is a flat, round, and well-shaped expanse of green sward. Here in the stillness of the morning words of prayer were heard; here a little altar was set up, and the worship of the old faith offered by a priest who braved all dangers that he might minister still to those who longed for the familiar rites. My father knelt and worshipped, with tears falling down upon his furrowed cheeks, and I knelt and prayed that in His own good time the Lord would cause all His servants to agree about the truth of their Holy Faith.

The priest ventured to our dwelling to visit my mother. She thanked him for coming, but she made at that time no confession. She did not refuse to do so at a future time.

"But of late," she said, "I have had no sacrament or other help. And it seems as if God in His wonderful goodness has made up for the want of them by speaking Himself to my inmost heart. I sit here through long hours alone, and He is near, and I tell Him all. How can men doubt if there be a God? They would not if they could *feel* His presence as I have felt it."

"Captain Standfast says there is no Purgatory," she said to me at another time. "That, too, I shall learn; I am content to wait. Only bid your father, when I am gone, to spend no money on masses for my soul. I will trust to the mercy of God; He will not let me suffer in vain."

It was thus that my dear mother spoke of herself now and again, but more often her thoughts were for others.

"It is sad enough here," she said; "we ought to do what we can to cheer our neighbours. Ethne, do you gather the young people together.this evening; and you,

Malachy, do you take your harp and play for them that they may dance."

So in that strange and dreary place when evening came we gathered together and sang the old songs and danced to the old melodies, as we were used to do in the merry careless days that are gone for ever!

CHAPTER XXTTI. JFrom tfe EUcorD of Eooer StanbTaat. IKE other officers in command of companies and troops I was ordered in the late summer of that year, 1654, to return to Killegar for the last time, and thence to march my men to their place of settlement, all things being now in order, and the proprietors transplanted. I rode forth, therefore, as was commanded me, from Lara Castle, as ever and anon I had ridden back and forwards when my presence in the garrison was needed, a few officers at a time taking in turn the duty of remaining in charge of the men till their final disbandment.

It was a two days' ride, and the sun set on the evening of the first day before I could reach any house of shelter. Truth to tell, many a home lay now in ruins, where formerly the heartiest welcome was ready for the traveller, whoever and whatever he might be. The twilight was deepening as I entered a little wood, a dark and lonely spot in a country mostly open enough, and varied only by the countless lakes that are fringed about their swampy shores with tall reed-mace and wild water-plants, haunted by snipe and teal, whose cries came mournfully through the stillness, and sent back my thoughts to those younger days of my life, when such cries would have stirred every pulse in mo with desire to pursue and kill the creatures over whom the Lord has been pleased to give man dominion.

Even now—as I thought of long days spent in fowling or in riding after hounds through the crisp wintry air over my own Gloucestershire hills and down to the broad plain of the Severn, with its wide water-rhines, noble leaps for a horse—even now my blood began to tingle, and I spurred my good horse and rode deeper into the shadows.

I have said that the cries of the wild birds were mournful in the stillness. But a cry arose in the wood beside me so wild and so lamentable that my very heart stood still, and I drew rein and peered into the darkness to see if aught that lived could shriek in so unearthly fashion.

Truly they might have been spectres who came flitting towards me, too hurried to walk, too feeble to run. A band of women and of children; but utterly unwomanly, nnchildish.

"Dismount!" they cried. "Give us your horse that we may eat him! Pull him from his saddle, the accursed Sassenach! Food, food; hasten, children, here is a feast!" they shrieked.

Thus crying in their native Irish, and brandishing long skeans that glittered in the dusk, this strange ghoulish band gathered round my horse and strove with their skeleton fingere to pull me from my saddle.

I, seeing no help for it, drew my sword and cried to them to desist, for I should be compelled to defend myself and the life of my good steed. At the sight of my naked blade they withdrew a little and cried to me to kill them if I would, one by one, for that the pangs of the death-in-life which they were now enduring were worse than the sharpness of death by the sword.

I could well believe it, for truly their voices were faint and hollow, as though ghosts from the grave cried upon the living; and for their faces—truly when the Almighty made man in His image, His heart must have been grieved at the foreknowledge that man's sin could reduce him ever to such a shape as this!

I had money with me and a little food. I gave the food among them. But alas! it seemed almost a mockery, so insufficient was it. Nay, more, the horrors it caused were as great as the misery I would fain have relieved, for the wretched creatures fought desperately for it, snatching it from the blue lips of the children. I cannot paint the scene. I have seen war and its cold afterbattle fields, death in all its forms, and have not shrunk. But I think this scene will never altogether fade from my memory, but haunt me at times like an evil dream.

What money I had I gave, and the wild troop spared the life of my horse, and flitted away as fast as their shrunken limbs could bear them, huddling together and gibbering like a host of spectres. I looked after them till they were lost in the shadows; then I shook the reins that lay on the neck of my noble Hampden, as I proudly called my charger. But as he sprang forward a heavy hand fell upon his bridle, strong hands grasped me also before I could draw my sword, and a voice that spoke in English bade me not stir or struggle if I valued my life.

Bound, gagged, blindfolded, I was presently being conducted whither I knew not. A man had mounted behind me, and, after one desperate effort to set myself free, I found it well to be still and keep my strength for a time when I might need it.

My captors exchanged only hurried words in Irish now and again. He who rode behind me spoke not, but only now and again drew my bonds a little more tightly and felt the knots with care. So I was hurried on for a long distance—a mile or even two miles. At last my horse stood still; I was lifted from the saddle, and the movement having deranged the bandage over my eyes a little, I could dimly see that we were at the foot of a high rock surrounded by trees, while below I could hear the rushing of water. Then there was some altering of the cords that bound me, and presently I felt myself lifted from the ground and drawn upwards along the face of the rock till other hands grasped me, and I was hauled or dragged into what seemed to be a cave in the face of the precipice.

So I found it when my bonds were removed. It was now almost dark; moreover bushes grew about the entrance, so that the cave was chiefly lighted by smouldering logs, which threw a faint red glow upon the faces of the inmates. There must have been some outlet, however narrow, else the smoke had been more dense. As it was, the man before whom I was led, and whom my gaolers addressed as captain, slouched his beaver hat more deeply over his face before he turned it to me. No doubt I had fallen into the hands of some of the Tories, or mountain robbers, who infest the land.

"Who are you?" he asked. "*What* you are your dress plainly shows; tell us therefore your name."

"Roger Standfast-on-the-Rock," I said, "the friend of the Lord, the enemy of his foes."

The Tory captain laughed aloud.

"Truly a fine name and a fitting," said he. "That is, Roger Standfast-m-the-Rock would exactly meet the present case. Canst stand fast beneath the tree whereon thou shalt hang, good Roger?"

"As fast as anywhere else beneath the dome of heaven," I said. "I am in God's hand there or here, or in my English home."

"Methinks you are in our hand now," said the Tory chief, and his brow darkened. "Thou hast taken thy last meal on earth, Roger Standfast. Art ready to start for the next world before dinner?"

There was a laugh at the grim jest; it came from the shadows, and sounded so harsh and weird that I thought the robber chief himself shuddered as he glanced round for a moment.

"Art ready?" he had asked, and I thank God that with a willing heart I could answer—

"I am ready. 'Blessed is he that shall eat bread in the kingdom of God' is true now, as it was long ago."

"Then our sentence is spoken," said the Tory chief, "and as you shut your eyes on the land you have laid desolate, remember that we whom you have driven to despair and crime are only taking just vengeance upon you for crimes which your single death cannot atone."

"Just vengeance!" I felt constrained to lift up my voice and bear witness that the word was false.

"Woe to them who work their own vengeance and are not instruments of the wrath of heaven!" I said. "'Vengeance is *mine,* I will repay, saith the Lord.'"

"Friend Standfast-in-your-own-wisdom," said the Tory sternly, "you are a bold man to speak so with the cord already round your neck. A truce to this vain parleying. Ho, Morrish, Flanahan! lead the prisoner to his doom!"

Two of my captors came towards me, but a man stepped from those dark shadows whence the laughter had come, and standing before the Captain, asked a boon, speaking in his own tongue.

"Willingly granted, so it be but reasonable," said the Captain, and the man hurriedly, and in a low tone, so that I, being indifferently acquainted with the language, lost most of his speech, explained his petition.

"It is well," said the Captain, turning to the rest. "Our faithful henchman here has a special grudge against the prisoner, and prays to be his executioner. Morrish and Flanahan, are you willing to resign your work to him?" "In truth I have no desire to be hangman, though ready enough with my skean," said one, and the other laughed and said that the only necklace he cared to fasten was that of a pretty maid.

"Go then," said the Captain, waving his hand to the petitioner, and one from behind replaced the bandage on mine eyes. I was lowered once more down the rock, lifted on my horse, and hurried on again, my gaoler riding behind, along a wooded path, as I could feel when Hampden's feet stumbled now and again at the roots of the trees.

I know not if we went far, for so many thoughts coursed through my mind—sins to repent of, and in my heart to confess, and old memories that came flooding my mind in strange disorder. Mine own people would perhaps never know the manner of my end; I thought of them, and then I thought of those strange old wives' tales of visions seen or voices heard of the dying at the moment of their death. My mother, in our home, with the woodbine yet in flower on the porch, would she see me stand pale and speechless before her, or hear my step and call to me, or know my hand on the latch? Now before I was summoned away to the war, I had it in my mind to set a new latch on that door; the old one was long since worn thin and crooked. I pray God to forgive the folly and lightness of my spirit, for truly I believe that in that hour of death the matter that came most vividly to my mind was the broken latch on the door of my peaceful home, at Oldbury beside the shining Severn!

Before we left the foot of the cave my bonds had been yet further strengthened. "He is in a desperate case, he may make a desperate struggle," said the Tories, and they made me so fast that my captor pulled me all helpless from the horse, and I stood a moment to gather all my strength for one last effort, truly with little hope, since the man before me was armed to the very teeth, as I saw when he pulled off my bandage once more.

I had not seen his face—the slouched hat and a piece of his mantle thrown across hid it from me; but now he threw off the hat and threw back the mantle, and I was face to face with Teague O'Ruark.

He looked at me so long in silence that I think I almost smiled as I said—

"Well, Teague, doth the task of hangman not please you after all?"

"Captain Standfast," said Teague, in a low hoarse voice, and in my own tongue, "*I* set fire to the Castle for Pierce O'Connor my master's sake. I was glad to think you would burn in it, like a wasp in the honey you never made. It is a strange world—that story had a strange end. And now, I would string you up to that tree, but for the sake of one whom I worship like one of the blessed saints. I played false once to kill you, now I have played false to save you, not for your own sake, no, for your cold hard heart does not deserve it, but for *her* sake. Because her warm Irish heart is given to you, and you go rooting like the pig you are, and don't heed the jewel on the ground before you."

"Teague," I said, "I fear your wild and sinful life has made you mad. If you mean to kill me, make an end. unless" And with that I strove with might and main to free myself, but Teague caught me by the arm with an iron grip and held his bright skean to my throat.

"Because she might cry after you, and the whole world's not worth bringing salt water into the Lady Ethne's eyes for," said Teague. "So I'll risk my own life now to save your wretched skin, and it's all I ask that you'll either love her as you ought, or go your ways back to your own land, so that may be she'll forget you."

"I think you err grievously, friend Teague," I said; and Teague shrugged his shoulders as he answered—

"Ay, so said the mole when one told him it was daylight;" and his eyes twinkled as he looked at me. But with the sudden change of mood common to the people of this land, he clasped his hands together and said entreatingly—

"I pray you, Captain Standfast, by the love of Our Blessed Lady—or since you despise her, by whatever love can touch your heart—tell the Lady Bthne that I have atoned for the mischief I did. I tried to kill you to please my master; now I have saved you to please my mistress, my soul is white again."

At that I lifted up the protest I felt I must make.

"We cannot reckon debtor and creditor fashion with sin, poor erring soul," I said. "Not against me nor your mistress is the wrong—against Thee only have I sinned, and done this evil in Thy sight!' is the confession of a Christian."

"There is no confession now—you have left us no priests," said Teague bitterly; and I would there and then have sought to show him all the way of the Lord, but he stopped me and would not hear.

"If you are grateful for the present I have made you of your life, tell her what I said," he cried; and having cut my bonds with his skean, he bounded back into the wood, and though I cried loudly after him to return, for that I would be to him a friend and protector, no answer came back, and I was fain to turn away sorrowful, and after giving thanks to Him whose hand had kept me in so great danger, I mounted my horse again and rode in safety to the town of Killegar.

Here I found that a great and strange thing had been wrought by the Lord.

Many Popish artisans had remained in their dwellings,

Q partly encouraged to do so by our own men, who, like Israel, when all the smithies were in the hands of Philistines, found sore need of their enemies' work. A fire has at last broken out in the town; it has swept away almost every dwelling of a Papist, leaving only those standing which are inhabited by Protestants or by our soldiers quartered therein. Howbeit it seems that these houses are the better sort, and are slated, whereas the others were but of clay, and roofed with rafters and straw.

It was not without some delay that my men, whose discipline has naturally become somewhat relaxed, were gathered together, and under my command, with the help of Isaiah Heston, were marched to the neighbourhood of Lara, around which their settlements lie, and there disbanded and left to settle themselves, which some did with pleasure and thankfulness, but others with much murmuring and grieving of the Spirit, supposing their neighbours' portion to be better than their own, or hating the unaccustomed labour and cares of a farmer.

All being done, I had now leisure to bethink me what I should do, and more especially in the matter of the strange communication made to me by Teague O'Ruark.

Many and grievous have been of late my searchings of heart concerning the maiden Ethne. At times I doubt whether she may have been sent to prove me, even as it is written that wine was set before the sons of Rechab to prove whether they were faithful in the very depths of the heart. Then do I in spirit turn away from her, even as the true knight of Master Spencer's allegory of The Faerie Queene turned away from the loathsome image of sinful beauty showed to him by the wicked enchanter. Many a time have I thus hardened my heart, and cast forth thence all thought of the maiden. But then her tender care for her aged parents returns to my mind, so that I think within myself—

"What if the maiden be as Rahab, the daughter of Canaan, who, in the destruction of her people, was saved alive, and saved all her family and household? What if the Lord have shown signs of grace in the heart of this maiden, that she may be saved from among the idolaters, and with her kinsfolk also? Yea, and what if it please Him, who maketh the hearts of men for vessels of His will, to use me, His unworthy servant, to pluck her as a brand from the burning? Shall I then fight against God?"

Again, when Master Allfrey speaketh again in the fulness of his unction against the dark and subtle wiles of the Delilahs of this land, who have stolen the hearts of many of the Lord's people, then my spirit is afraid, and a voice speaks within—

"Come out from among them; be ye

separate."

If God will to save the maiden, if she be one of His elect, is it for me to meddle in His doings? Nay then, how but by the hands of men doth He work? and have not I myself been turned from darkness to light by His Word, spoken through the mouth of Master Jabez Allfrey, whose voice cried in my unregenerate ears as the voice of John Baptist, saying, Repent!

Thus through three long days and nights have I pondered the matter, kneeling on my knees and wrestling sore with the God of Bethel, saying as Jacob, I will not let Thee go. And now, after one more and a longer struggle, the thought has come to me, I will kneel and open His Word, and wheresoever my finger shall light, there it has been revealed to me that I shall find guidance.

Shall I rejoice, or shall I fear and tremble? Yea, I will do both, and will give thanks to the God in whose light we see light. For this is the word of His message to me—this is the word on which my hand, opening the Book blindly, has fallen—" Whom shall we send, and who will go for us?" Go with me then, 0 Lord, as Thou wentest with Elimelech, servant of Abraham. Grant me to find the maiden, as he found Rebekah, willing to be led home, or if she will to abide in Connaught, may it be unto her as a Goshen, and she as a candlestick to bear Thy light in that most dark and desolate place, or at least to move, as an Israelite maiden in Egypt of old, with the light of day shining around her, if others must perforce walk stumbling in the darkness that can be felt. I will rejoice, therefore, though it be with trembling, since it may well be that he who is bidden to pluck a brand from the burning may kindle his own garments at that fire.

Six days have passed since I wrote thus—days passed in riding from the centre of this island even to the remote west, where with much difficulty I sought out the apportionment of Sir Gerald O'Connor. Travelling first to Athlone,1 I found a strange settlement there—the widow and the orphan have been cared for fitly and wisely, those left behind by such of our soldier-brethren as have departed this evil world being assigned lands and dwellings in and around this town, together with the widows and orphans of Irish proprietors.

True, there were amongst them women who bemoaned their situation and pined after a home in England, and did not scruple to lift up their voices even against Oliver himself. But it may well be, methinks, that in this matter also all hath been ordered for the best, since these women being without husbands, who might restrain their tongues by due reproof, and being no longer kept in subjection, are well bestowed in this remote place, 1 Hence, no doubt, the charms of the proverbial Widow Malone, "Who lived in the town of Athlone, alone."—*Editor't Note.* where, at the worst, they can but clamour each against her neighbour, and trouble no man's peace.

Though I think thus, I must add in all truthfulness that here I was most kindly and graciously entreated and entertained by Mistress Damaris Strong-i'-th'-arm, widow of one among mine own comrades, a woman of goodly presence, and one that ordereth her household well, who yet hath learned a greater sharpness and even lightness of speech than beseems a godly matron. Thus I found, when I had supped with a thankful heart, but I trust with due restraint of carnal appetite, seeing that I would fain have eaten again of her hot oaten bannocks, but forbore. For then Mistress Damaris, having swept her hearth and set a seat for me beside the embers, said, smiling—

"I pray you, Master Roger, own the truth. Are not a pair of grey eyes, or it may be blue eyes or brown, mighty magnets to draw men westward over the broad Shannon?"

"I know not," I answered, as coldly as the courtesy due to mine hostess would allow; and remembering that it is written, "Answer a fool according to his folly," I said, "That over which the magnet has power is drawn by it—nought else."

"And are not all sons of Eve of the same metal, I pray you?" asked Mistress Damaris again, with a smile of much meaning, at which I was very wroth.

"All men may be fools from their birth, but a fool may forsake his folly," I said. But Mistress Damaris laughed outright, saying—

"Ay, Master Roger, and a wise man may leave his wisdom."

"It were indeed a loss of wisdom to bandy foolish jests," I said; and Mistress Damaris perceived my displeasure, for she said with humility—

"Nay, Master Roger, be not wroth. 'He that findeth a wife findeth a good thing;' and that hath mine own husband said many a time, so that I am glad now in the thought that he could say so."

At this mention of her husband the good woman's eyes filled with tears, so that I repented me of having roughly handled a bruised reed.

"Yea, my sister," I said; "so it is when husband and wife are brought together by the hand of God, as Isaac and Rebekah. And truly Paul himself teaches ns of the New Covenant that we are at liberty to be married to whom we will—only in the Lord. Should so grave a matter be made food for unseemly jesting?"

The widow hung her head and toyed with her apron string; then she looked up again with a face that threatened laughter.

"In truth you are a stern man, Roger Standfast," she said. "Have not the ways of young men and maidens about whom they hover been evermore a subject for harmless mirth? Are we to have no mirth now to brighten our lives? Surely they are sad enough at times."

And again her mouth trembled and her eyes filled, as is the weak way of women if only the shadow of sorrow touch them.

"Mirth?" I said. "Nay, my sister. Mirth is a crackling of thorns fit only for children and fools. We know that the Man of Sorrows wept; we learn not that He laughed."

To that she gave no answer, but sat in mournful silence for a long time. Yet her lightness of spirit prevailed over this better frame of mind, for rising at last she said—

"Well, Master Standfast, if all tales be true, there is Borne hope that you may find your Rebekah sitting by some well or other water, of which in good sooth there is somewhat overmuch in this country. I pray you, therefore, when you have found and taken her home, let her laugh, if it be but now and again, and when you are out of hearing."

"I pray you, Mistress Damaris," I said, with exceeding sternness, "keep your counsel till such time as it is needed."

"And welcome," she answered; "but lest I may not be able to give it then, I say but this, that if you drive a young colt with too heavy a hand it may kick over the traces."

And she departed, leaving me in much anger and perplexity, chiefly for this, that idle tales had seemingly been spread abroad, and such tales are indeed as words set on wheels, that run hither and thither through the earth, ever doing such harm as lies in their power.

As I rode on my way next day my thoughts were busy with this matter; and in truth I think men would do well to fear the tongues of women, and so far as may be to defend themselves therefrom, since there seldom was mischief done in this world but the tongues of women had to do with it, whether by way of provocation or of tale-bearing.

When, having crossed the broad, beautiful Shannon, the rampart behind which we have driven these evil people, I found myself in Connaught, there was much else to behold and wonder at.

In my own heart I question whether we have not been as Saul, who spared of the Amalekites that which his erring heart saw fit, and destroyed the rest. For here are many turbulent and wrathful spirits cooped in this small province; such of them as have not fled to fight in foreign countries left here to chafe against this dispensation, and to be a thorn in the sides of the peaceable colonists.

Also I noticed the exceeding poorness of much of this land. Rocky ground, where only moss can grow; great bogs, needing years and years of cutting and then of reclaiming before they can sustain life; low and wet marshes full of reeds and moss, costly to drain and cultivate; barren hills, countless lakes. How is such a land to maintain so many?

Doubtless the pride of the race will be broken; and it may be that in the days of want and starvation which must come upon them they will bethink themselves and turn to God, knowing this to be the punishment of their sins. If they be of His elect, this they will surely do; but if not, both we and our rulers may have brought wrath upon ourselves in failing to destroy utterly the enemies of God, whose iniquity is full. And if this be so, both we and those who come after us will surely bear the punishment, and be plagued as was Israel by the remnant of the Philistines and other idolaters.

It was again evening when I reached my destination, the wild and lonely barony of Burren, and, after asking many times for guidance, found myself in a boggy valley which had neither the pleasantness of fertile land nor the wild beauty which often is given to barren places, but was utterly and entirely dreary and unpleasing. And in this sad place I heard of a sudden the sound of a harp playing a melody which I had oft times heard from the fingers of old Malachy at my first coming to Lara Castle.

It was Malachy who was playing. He sat upon a little rock, his sightless eyes gazing heavenward, and before him on the green a number of young men and maidens were dancing.

"How hopelessly vain and foolish is this race!" I Baid in my heart. "Even as the soulless African they will dance in any circumstances, as they in the bonds of slavery."

The old harper, with the quick hearing of the blind, was aware of my coming. The music ceased, and the young people stood still and looked at me. And there in the midst of them, to my surprise and grief, I saw Ethne O'Connor—Ethne, of whom I would have said that I felt sure she was employed in no such vanity, that by the waters of Babylon she might sit down and weep, although I think her spirit too brave for mere useless grieving. I had never thought Ethne could sing and dance—here!

Her colour deepened, but she came towards me with her light and graceful step.

"Captain Standfast, we can give you but a poor welcome here; nevertheless, to what we can give you are welcome." ISTRESS ETHNE desired Malachy to continue the dance, and led me to her home. Her home! A shed such as we in England might deem good for pigs or asses, but not fit for so noble an animal as the horse. It was half house, half burrow, yet the deft fingers of a gentlewoman had decked it in such a way that the wretched place had something of the air of a *home* about it.

And there sat Madam O'Connor, worn and wasted, as I could see even in that dim light, by disease, and my heart was glad, for on her knee lay the little worn Bible I had given to Mistress Ethne.

There was not much wherewith to make a guest welcome, Mistress Ethne had said; nevertheless as fair a welcome as man could wish was held out to me, and the painful scene of our last parting seemed by them forgotten, though to me there was at first a painful constraint.

"My mother is dying," said Ethne to me the next day. "You see it, Captain Standfast?"

Her eyes searched my face as if for a contradiction of her words, but I could not give it.

"I see it," I said; and she said farther—

"I think she is like a well-rooted tree that cannot be transplanted, but needs must die. I hope my father will die too; it would be best for him to go with her."

"And leave you utterly alone?" I asked, wondering that she spoke so calmly.

"Oh, I must not think of myself," she answered, almost as if she would reprove me for suggesting so selfish a thought, and as she spoke I felt my love for her deepen and widen and glow within me.

"You thought me wickedly frivolous last night that I could dance," said my lady, and her clear eyes were upon my face, and again I could not contradict her. "But it was for *her* sake that we danced, at her request. And yet I know not why I should justify myself to you;" and she lifted her head with a sudden touch of haughtiness, for which I fear I liked her none the less.

If she could be haughty in this fashion, assuredly my lady was not overproud. For with her own hands she toiled like a farm wench, milking kine, seething porridge, and doing cheerfully all that she could do, and more than I thought she could have done. But all these tasks she did as a princess might have done who could not lose her ladyhood thereby, and I, with a stammering tongue, besought her that I might be allowed to help, fearing that she would laugh at my offer, which in truth she did.

""What!" she said, "an Egyptian bend his back to an Israelite burden? A Spartan take on him the duties of a Helot? Nay, my lord, we are already but too much honoured that you have thought fit to visit us, so only you have not come to spy out the nakedness of the land?"

"Do not, *do not* think I came with such a base motive," I began, and she, looking over her shoulder at me as she laid fodder for the goats, laughed again.

"Nay, my lord, I will seek a better cause for your coming. Shall we say that your health needed the fresh sea-breezes that blow on our coast? The traveller in search of health is ofttimes willing to be poorly entertained so he find that which he came to seek."

Then, seeing perhaps that I looked ill-pleased, she said more gravely—

"Nay, then, I will hold my peace, for the tongue is an unruly evil, and men seem to think ever that a *woman's* tongue is specially to be condemned."

"Mistress Ethne," I said, "I pray yon strive against lightness of spirit. Truly a light *heart* is said to be a good thing, if one can compass it, but there can be no good in the light *mind* that makes a mock of all things."

"I think you fail to understand, Captain Standfast," she said, answering meekly when I thought she would have been angry. "My heart is heavy enough. But" —and she was silent and bent over the rude manger, and I thought a tear fell upon the grass in her hands. But it may have been only a dewdrop, for she was quite composed as she turned and told me that if indeed I had a mind to help, though a guest should hardly be suffered to do so, I might draw water and sprinkle the young cabbage-plants brought from her home and set in hopes of a late crop. The water-buckets were heavy, she said, with a smile, and when I lifted them I was grieved to think that her back should ache with the heavy and weary weights.

As a few days have passed, and I have seen the life of the settlers here, I have wondered more and more over the strange plan of our inspired leader in thus planting out a nation of emigrants. Some have put their hands to the plough and their backs to the burden; others, who find it hard in a moment to change from gentry to peasants, have portioned their appointments out among servants and tenants, and will live, even though in a hovel, yet in their former manner, keeping up the shadow of their state when the reality is gone, and taking even greater pride than of old in their family and ancestry.

A few days passed, I have said. For the flickering life of Madam O'Connor made all wooing appear unseemly, and I have dwelt with the family, and each day have done an increased share of their work, keeping myself apart from their neighbours, many of whom look upon me with no friendly eye, though outwardly courteous.

At length last night it grew plain that the darkness of death was gathering round Madam O'Connor, and she prayed to see me for a few moments and alone.

The little Bible was in her hands when I entered.

"Captain Standfast," she said, speaking with difficulty, but with a smile on her wasted face, "they say that death sometimes gives a new clearness of sight and certainty of knowledge. It is death that tells me I am right in what I am about to say. She paused for breath, and went on, laying her hand on the Book.

"I have read your Book with an open mind, much of it I have read many times. I find in it much that is beautiful, much that is true. Yet I die in the faith of my fathers, though I may not have the last rites of my Church, and that grieves me. But it was not of myself that I would speak, but of my Ethne. The whole world is changing, changing. It may be that the outward form of faith must change too, though never the heart of it. My Ethne finds peace in the new faith—let it be hers; I can die content. That is half of what I would say. For the rest—whatever has risen between you, I know that you love Ethne, I know that she loves you. Have I spoken truth?"

"Yea, I love her well and truly," I answered, and a smile of great happiness came over the mother's face.

"How good is God to me," she said, "that I may leave my child to one who will care for her. But one word more—while—I—have strength."

I bent down to hear her earnest words, low and broken. "You are a good man, but stern. Be kind to my child—she has never known aught but kindness— promise—me."

"I promise," I said, and a lump rose in my throat. I am a man of strife, for unto that the Lord hath called me, but how could any man be aught but kind and gentle to my Ethne!

I went out and found her, and spoke loving words to her, and besought her to be my wife. And when she had promised, with maiden modesty, but without doubt, I led her back to the room of her dying mother, where some of the neighbours and the little household were gathered already, and my soul was grieved to see that they held lights, according to the superstition of heathenism and of Rome, to light the departing spirit on its way. Madam O'Connor could not speak, but smiled upon us, and Sir Gerald sitting by her, lifted his head, which was bowed upon his hands, and looked upon us, and spoke dreamily, and, as it were, to himself.

"A good man and true," he said. "But

of no family. Well, neither was Adam."

And his grey head dropped upon his hands again. But in that short moment I saw that a strange change had come over the old knight—that change which is as though the Angel of Death had marked beforehand the tree that he will shortly lay low—a nameless change, that one cannot put into words, but which is seen upon the face as plainly as a signature. And I said in my heart that it were well if those two might enter into rest together, as did Tristram and Iseulte in the old profane tale, or rather as the fabled Philemon and Baucis, who after long wedded life could not bear that either should be left lonely upon earth.

So we stood, my Ethne leaning upon me, who prayed earnestly in my heart, and the old knight motionless, and the retainers with their burning candles and smothered weeping, till with one gentle sigh the silver cord was loosed, the golden bowl was broken, the spirit had returned to God who gave it

Then the stillness was broken by the caoine1 that rose from the watchers—an awful cry, and unbefitting those who in their sorrow have hope. Far and wide it thrilled upon the air of that desolate place, that all might know of the passing away of the beloved lady.

Then my Ethne went to the old knight.

"Father," she said, "I am left;" and she looked at me and said, "we are left to you still. Come with me."

But as she lifted his hand it fell heavily upon the bed again. And I saw that that which I had hoped was fulfilled—the two who had been so long together in life, in their death were not divided.

1 Caoine, pron. keen—the death-lament. AM alone in the world! Thus I began to write. "Alone but for Roger," I would have said, but even so much as that I cannot find it in my heart to say. For a husband who truly loves his wife is to her a wonderful replacing of other earthly relationships. So he be but a good man, she can honour him as a father, and trust him in some measure to care for her as a mother, while lie gives her the daily friendly companionship also of brother and sister. Something, at least, of all these I think every true husband must be.

The days of my mourning being ended, Roger sought to arrange our marriage, and to that end rode many miles to consult with one Master Allfrey, a chaplain, about the time and place of the ceremony. It was with a somewhat grave face that he returned, and with hesitation he spoke to me.

"My Ethne," he said, "I have learned what I ought to have known sooner, namely, that according to an ordinance of the Lord-Deputy, no marriages between the army and the maidens of this country may be solemnised till the bride has before a board of godly men and ministers given proof that her conversion is no mere cloak, but a true working of the Spirit in her heart. It is a hard matter to ask of thee, sweetheart; nevertheless "—and there he came to an end.

"Nevertheless I will do it," I said; and I smiled in his troubled face, which brightened to an answering smile. "I am no theologian, but I trust I can give a reason for the hope that is in me—the hope I have learned from you, or at least by your means, Roger."

But I was somewhat tremulous as I stood before the stern-faced men who sat at a table, and lifted their eyes to look searchingly at my face, as if they would read my heart through it.

"For Roger's sake," I told myself; and I sat down, as they *bade* rather than invited me to do, and waited to be questioned.

"You are one of those, maiden, who have come to ask your way, as was said of old, with your face set to go to Jerusalem," began Master Allfrey the chaplain. "We would therefore first know from you why you elected to leave the City of Destruction, even Rome, the Mother of all Abominations, set on seven hills."

I found courage to answer quite calmly—

"I desire to leave the Church of my fathers," I said, "because through reading of the Gospel I find the Christ to be the only and the eternal Way of Salvation, whereas in Rome I find ever some rite or some priest set between the soul and God."

"Good, so far, and yet not altogether good," said the minister, "since you can yet speak, maiden, of her who is filled with the blood of saints, of her who deceiveth men to the destruction of souls, as the 'Church of your fathers.' How comes this?"

"Because I have seen holy lives and true lived in her, and the love of God filling the souls of those who dwelt in her," I said.

"Take heed," broke in the minister sternly; "take

R heed, woman, lest you be as Lot's wife, who looked back and hankered after the evil city whence she had just been delivered. I will put to you a closer question. We know that the Lord hath predestined some to be vessels of salvation, to dwell with Him in everlasting glory, and hath chosen others as vessels of wrath, to be finally cast out and chained in darkness with the evil angels for ever. Now, do you feel and know in your heart that you are indeed foreknown and called to everlasting salvation, that you have been converted, and are once and for ever in a state of salvation?"

The four pairs of eyes fixed themselves upon me waiting for my answer, and in the back of the room I knew that Eoger Standfast listened also with eager expectation. On the old wooden mantel a clock ticked slowly and heavily, measuring out the silence. That silence seemed long and terrible before I found words at last wherewith to answer, in a low and trembling voice.

"Good sirs," I said, "I am no theologian. I cannot feel such a knowledge of the Divine purposes as you seem to require of me. All I can say is that I have heard the voice of Jesus Christ saying ' Come unto me, and I will give you rest. ' And I *have* come to Him, good gentlemen, and in Him is all my hope;" and my voice grew steady, for I felt that in this I spoke but the simple truth.

"An unsound answer," cried Master Allfrey, knitting his brows. "What, maiden! know you not that Christ must dwell in you, or you must be reprobate, one or the other. You must have assurance of that salvation, else"

"Nay, Master Allfrey," said the Colonel, who sat at the head of the table, "I think the maiden has answered wisely and modestly, as a maiden should. Pray you, gentlemen, do you think with me?" and he looked at the other two.

And to my exceeding relief the others answered that they thought even as he did, though Master Allfrey muttered angrily that it was easy to feign this kind of conversion. The stern faces looked more kindly upon me, and I found courage to answer a few less hard questions put to me by these my judges; and then in their presence, and with hearty if grave words of goodwill from them, Roger Standfast and I were, by the mouth of Master Allfrey, made man and wife.

I said that Roger, my kind and loving husband, seemed to me father and mother, and kinsfolk too in a measure. Yet when to-day, having reached Bristol after a long and weary sea-journey, full of many discomforts—although it was summer and the sea fairly smooth—I heard around me only the English tongue, and saw but English countenances, I longed sorely for the sight of any old familiar face. We sailed slowly up the winding Avon, between great rocks rising high above the vessel and taking the wind from our sails, so that men pulling by a rope carried over to the shore were our only hope of progress. Fair woods there were, clothing the gorge almost to the water's edge; and among them Roger told me the nightingale was to be heard—that bird of whose song we in Ireland have no knowledge, but which Roger says is wondrous sweet and pleasant to hear. So up this sluggish and mud-coloured stream we came to Bristol, a fair town and busy, with fine houses of the wealthy merchants behind its quays, and a great stir and bustle, as of much merchandise. Above the city rose pleasant and wooded hills, and as it was yet early when we landed, we took horse at once to ride that very day to Roger's home at Oldbury, by that wide and shining Severn on which already we had sailed to the mouth of the little Avon.

So we rode forth, and after some miles we came to the brow of a fair hill at Almondsbury, and there Roger drew rein, and I saw that he looked down with great joy and gladness npon the plain and the wide and noble river with the blue Welsh hills behind it—a fair landscape and peaceful, rich also as it seemed.

"There, Ethne," he said—" there lies my home and yours. My God, I thank Thee that I see it again in peace," he said, in a low and fervent tone.

I looked over the fertile plain, the rich and well-wooded happy English country, not wasted by fire and sword like so much of my own dear land. There beside the river, on a little hillock, rose a church, white-walled and with a comely tower, which, as Roger had told me, was a welcome beacon to the salmon-fishers out on the broad river or estuary. Smoke rose from houses half seen among the trees, hills stood round about as a pleasant shelter, and nearer to us lay the greater town of Thornbury, under the hill of Almondsbury, or Amesbury, as men used to call it. Truly it was a fair scene, and one that spoke of home and a friendly welcome, and therefore I blame myself that the tears flowed down my face, and in answer to my husband's question I could but stammer forth—

"Yes, I am very glad it is beautiful—but oh, Roger, I would it were Lara!"

"My wife must not be so foolish, so childish," said Roger, somewhat sternly. "Bethink you, Ethne, it is no *home* that you have left behind you."

"I know, I know," I said, and dried my tears. "I am sorry to have grieved you, Roger."

"You must be wiser in future," said Roger, and my foolish eyes filled again. He did not know, he could not tell, how sad I felt, and how at that moment I longed for a kind word. Else I know that I should not have looked for one in vain. He only glanced at me as I dried my eyes, and we rode on in a constrained silence, which Roger at last broke by saying—

"I trust my mother will be prepared for our coming, having received the tidings I sent her of our marriage; but in these troubled times such matters are uncertain. The letter may not have reached."

"0 Roger," I said, "I shall be so glad to have a mother once more! I feel as though already I loved her dearly. I hope she will love me."

"I hope so too," said Roger; but I fancied there was a touch of doubt in his tone, and I wondered.

"I will try to be to her all that a daughter should," I said; "indeed I will, Roger. And what I do not know of English ways I will soon learn; you do not know how quickly I will learn."

"Ethne," said Roger, with a little hesitation, "you knew when you married me that I was not, as the world reckons, your equal in station. You will find none of the dignity of Lara Castle here, therefore I would warn you not to look for it"

"Foolish Roger; *ymi* are foolish now," I said, and laughed and clapped my hands at his ignorance. "What! have I served an apprenticeship in Connaught to no purpose? Is it not to tne grandeur and dignity to have a floor of boards and a casement that can open! I think howsoever many of the deadly sins I may commit, I shall at least not fall by that of pride."

"Take care in my mother's presence to keep that tongue of yours in due subjection, my Ethne," said Roger; but this time he smiled as he spoke, and we rode on with pleasant talk through that cheerful country, till at last we reached the pleasant village with its scattered houses. Soon we turned in at a little gate, and dismounted at the door of a pretty farmhouse, with woodbine and roses about the porch, and latticed windows in the snow-white walls, looking upon a little garden wellkept and full of sweet flowers, mingled with homelier but more useful herbs of many sorts.

There was a cry of "Roger!" and "Welcome!" and a pleasant little bustle, a barking and jumping of dogs, a running to and fro of servants. So that for a few moments all was confusion; then suddenly there fell a dead silence, and

I was standing in a parlour, primly set out, and a tall gaunt woman somewhat past middle life, with another who I knew must be her daughter, but who looked scarce younger, were standing gazing upon me, while the household in the background looked also, and I longed that the earth would open and swallow me up.

"Your *wife,* Roger?" said Mistress Standfast at last, in the tone of one who scarce believes the evidence of her own senses, much less what she is told.

"An Irish wife?" said Hester; and her voice was the harsher of the two, and I thought her grey gown hung in stiffer folds, and her white Puritan cap and the linen at her neck had severer lines than those of her mother.

The moment was too trying. I remember only that I held out my hands beseechingly.

"Oh, I pray you," I cried, "do not blame me that I am Irish; I will be all you wish!"

"Mother," said Roger, going to her as she sat down in her straight-backed chair, as in a judgment-seat, "I entreat you bid my wife welcome. I am grieved that you heard not of our marriage. But I think when you know my Ethne you will find her to be all that you would desire your son's wife to be."

"I trust so," said Mistress Standfast. "Of herself I cannot judge yet, but as my son's wife I make you welcome, *JSthne,* if that be your name. A Pagan name it sounds to me," she said, scanning me from head to foot.

Anger gave me back my voice.

"It is not a Pagan name," I said. "It was borne by the mother of the blessed Saint Columba, and I am proud to be called by it."

Mistress Standfast rose to her feet and held up her hands.

"Roger!" she cried—" *Roger!* Do not tell me that you have brought to my house a wife who is Papist as well as Irish? From that at least may the Lord have delivered you!"

"Nay, mother," said Roger, " Ethne finds it hard to free herself wholly from the speech of that bondage from which she has mercifully been delivered.

Columba was a servant of God before Rome held sway in Ireland, and I have heard that he preached the Word of Life without some at least of the corruptions that she brought in."

"It is well," said Mistress Standfast grimly. And she took three steps towards me and kissed my forehead, and after that Hester did the same, but more coldly still, and then a servant-maid was bidden to show me the Pink Chamber, a sleeping-room exquisitely clean and scented with lavender laid among sheets and in drawers. There I was thankful to be alone, and to lay my weary head upon the pillow, where I lay listening to the voices of Roger and his family below, till presently kind sleep came to me, and I awoke only when Hester came to call me to the evening meal.

"Is Rachel well?" asked Roger, as we sat at table; and the talk was chiefly of what had passed since Roger last saw the village.

"You have not quite forgotten her, then," said Hester; and she looked at me, and then at Roger, and then looked at her mother with a smile on her thin lips —a smile without mirth or even kindliness.

"Surely I have not forgotten her," said Roger gravely. "Rachel and I have been friends from childhood, and I trust we ever shall be."

"Oh!" said Hester; and Roger asked again as one who would have an answer—

"Is she well?"

"She is well," said Mistress Standfast. "She lives with her grandmother still, who is indeed an elect vessel and rich in grace, but somewhat deafer and more feeble than of old."

"I must go to see her," said Rogef, "and Ethne must come with me. She and Rachel will surely be friends."

"Hardly, if old proverbs are true," muttered Hester under breath, yet not so low but that I heard; and Mistress Standfast said in her decided tone—

"Your wife could not do better than to make a friend of Rachel Eversley, Roger. I trust you will see to it." And she looked reprovingly at Hester.

"As though friendship could be made

by decree," I said in my heart; but I held my peace, for I would fain be meek, and give no cause for displeasure to these stern women, my husband's kinsfolk, who look askance at me.

I used to take a pride in my Irish blood. Here it seems at least a drawback, if not a disgrace. Yet I cannot blame them entirely, for doubtless in this quiet village they have heard strange and horrible things of my nation —the enemies, as they think, of God and of England, worse even than savages, in that they have had better chance of amending.

CHAPTER XXVI. JFtom GEtljite'o Diarg,

ilT is wonderful how soon one can settle down to any new mode of life, so that it seems to have been going on for a long time, and as day follows day it seems as if the yesterdays spread far behind.

So at least it has been with me. The household goes on like some great wheel of which Mistress Standfast is the pivot. There is no time for song or laughter or any kind of pleasant idling; every hour is filled with its appointed task, steadily and willingly, though not joyfully, performed. For prayer and reading of the Word much time is found, the household being gathered together, the maids from their churns, the menservants from the harvest—all are brought together morning and night, and an hour or two hours spent in reading, in exhortation, and in prayer, wherein one after another may have utterance if moved thereto. On Sunday we all go forth to the little white church by the waterside. Of late the pillars of hewn stone have been hidden under whitewash, and various windows, broken in tho godly zeal of some fiery reformers, have been filled in with white glass in place of the soft warm colours that were there before. From religion, as from dress and from the inside of their houses, all ornament is rigorously put away. The melodies of olden time are to be heard no longer; only the songs of Zion, slow and long drawn out psalmtunes, are to be heard, and as for a poem, a play, or even, as I think, a nursery tale, they are never spoken of. Life is made to be a steady disciplining of the spirit to gravity and sobriety in all things.

I am as one who has entered a world that is altogether new. At every moment I have to watch my tongue lest it should utter any forbidden thing, my feet that they may move sedately, my eyes that they may not sparkle with mirth. Foolish talking and jesting, which are not convenient, are ever severely reproved by Mistress Standfast, but it is not often that she has occasion to administer any such reproofs, for such young people as come to the house are awed into quietness by the mere influence of her presence. Yet she strives to be just to me, as I think.

"That is your Irish temper, Ethne," said Hester yesterday, when at last, by a continual east wind of bitter words, she had stirred me up to anger, and I gave a hotter answer than I ought.

"Nay, Hester, it is you who are to blame," said Mistress Standfast, who had heard all, and I was thankful to her. For indeed it is hard to be simple and natural if one is ever as it were before the judgmentseat, and life becomes sadly constrained.

I dare not be merry, lest I should be condemned for yielding to the frivolity of youth; nor dare I be quite silent, lest I should be blamed for being sullen; while aught I say or do that is not quite what Roger's mother or sister would say or do is set down with a kind of pitying scorn as "one of Ethne's Irish ways."

For Roger's sake I am willing to please his mother. I am willing to bear many things from her—those reproving glances, for instance, which she shoots at me if in presence of strangers I utter my thoughts too freely.

"Child," she says, "you are too young to have any opinions."

And when, I pray you, shall I be old enough? Truly if I am to wait till my locks whiten, I may never see that day. And for that I have no wish to wait, if that other saying of hers be true which she repeats so often—

"At my years you will know that everything in this world is vanity and a snare."

To which she is apt to add, with a sigh—

"Poor Ethne, I trust before then you will have learned that all earthly joys are but as that Dead Sea fruit which they say turns to dust and ashes in the mouth, though it be fair to look upon."

So she said only this morning. And I turned away and went about my morning tasks.

The poultry had to be fed, and the calves; I went out into the fresh morning air. Below the house the great Severn seemed to dance in the sunshine. Our colt Brownie was loose in the field; she could not eat in quiet, but must needs spring and dance on soft grass. Under the thatch the swallow had hatched her little ones; she was teaching them to fly, and far overhead a lark was singing as though earth had sent him up with a message of gladness to heaven. The children laughed as they went to school; some reapers' sickles sounded pleasantly; grasshoppers chirped near me.

I leaned against the late roses that clung about the porch.

"How good, how good it is to be alive!" I said aloud. A woman went by—a gipsy woman that carried a child on her shoulder and sang to it. And the child drew a red shawl across its mouth when it saw me, and showed me only its eyes that laughed. With that came its father, and caught it to his own arms and kissed it, and all three laughed and went their way. At that sight a great joy and a great longing came over me. If I too might carry a little child in my arms, to laugh in my face and touch my cheek with its pink fingers— my child and Roger's! If I might!

Why then, the world, already so bright and beautiful, would simply brim over with gladness.

How good it is simply to be alive! and why should I pull a long face and speak of Dead Sea fruit? I laughed aloud at the thought, and my laugh brought Hester to the door with a cold reproof for my levity and idleness.

I shivered as though an east wind had suddenly arisen and chilled the very sunshine. But I answered her defiantly as Roger was not near.

"Am I never to smile and be glad?" I said. "I think if He who made this fair world were to look down and see us going about like so many scowling thunderclouds, it would not gladden but grieve Him."

"A contrite heart is His delight," said Hester, and the corners of her thin lips went down.

"When a child sins and is sorry, its father forgives and kisses it," I said. "He would not like to see it look the more miserable for his kiss. Is He less gracious who saw the world He had made, and called it very good? Did He not smile upon it, as His sunshine is smiling now?"

"It was a woman's foolish tongue that persuaded man to his hurt, and brought sin in to corrupt the world," said Hester grimly; and I drew a long face and went off to the calves. But I must needs bite my lips to keep from laughter till I was out of her hearing, for I knew that she made of poor Mother Eve a stalking-horse from which to shoot one of her spite-poisoned arrows at me.

Oli, these hard-faced women! I look at Mistress Standfast and ponder on her face, wondering how it looked when it smiled in its cradle. Or did it ever so smile? Did she not come into the world ready wrinkled, made in some strange mould, and born like that Pallas of whom I have heard my father tell, ready girt for warfare?

To Roger his mother is, I suppose, the very pattern of all that is noble and good in woman. My thoughts had reached this point by the time I had reached the farmyard, where I caught sight of my own face reflected in a bucket of clear water. I am afraid that Hester would have found some cause for her continual reproaches of frivolity had she seen me set down the calves' food and fall to work to try if I could pull my rounder, rosier face into the set shape of her own, or the stern outlines of Mistress Standfast's countenance. At least I am sure Mother Eve, looking guiltily round before tasting that fatal apple, never would have felt more abashed or have crimsoned more hotly than I when Roger's voice spoke behind me suddenly.

"Ethne! What is this? What do you?"

I stood so abashed and ashamed that I could not utter a word.

"Child, child!" said Roger, "have you no mirror at home that you must study your looks here and thus?"

"It is not vanity, Roger. I was not thinking of my looks," I said hurriedly, vexed to be thought capable of such vanity by him—I who, God knows, care for nought so long as I may please his eyes and keep his love.

"Then—then what are you doing?" asked Roger, the least touch of sternness in his voice—that touch which always makes me think of his sister Hester. If he had not spoken so I should have answered meekly; as it was I answered with only too faithful an imitation of his sister's coldest tones—

"Trying to make myself look as beseems one who is in the gall of bitterness."

"Ethne!" said Roger, and his voice was now exactly like Hester's, and I felt vexed.

"It is always Ethne, Ethne! So long as I am daily taken to task like a child, you cannot wonder, Roger, if I long for wrinkles to spoil my face and increase my dignity," I said, with a pettishness worthy of a child. But in truth it is hard to be for ever chidden, either by Mistress Standfast, or by Hester, or by Roger himself. Not that I should mind his chiding sometimes—at least I think not—if he would but refrain from reproving me in presence of his women folk, shaming me before them, and bringing a look of grim satisfaction to Hester's steely eyes.

"I did not look to hear such folly from my wife," said Roger; and now there was a touch of vexation or disappointment in his tone. I stole a glance at his face, but that was still stern.

"Well," I said, "I know that you would have me shape myself on your mother's pattern."

"I would have my wife shape herself on the pattern of all godly matrons," answered Roger coldly, or at the least so I thought. His eyes were on my face; I did not look up, but tore a flower with impatient fingers. I would show him for once that I had the spirit of my race, and that he might lead me by gentleness if he would, but that he should not for ever chide and repress me with impunity.

"Then I will shape myself on the pattern of my own mother," I said. "Her sweet calm face showed much more like that of the blessed saint she now is than if the mouth were hard and set and the brow and cheeks drawn into"

"Ethne!" said Roger, in his deep grave voice, "it is written that the tongue is an unruly evil, and set on fire of hell. See that you learn to bridle yours betimes."

And Roger turned and went away, and a great lump rose in my throat. I offend him with my tongue!—I to whom a woman's bitter tongue hath been ever a source of dread. In my own country we fight not with words that sting and rankle; our hearts are tender, and we fear to wound the heart of another. Indeed I have sometimes thought that we should do well if it were but now and then to speak our wrath more openly, for an Irishman will answer softly and with a smile, though a wrathful thought lies like a burning coal in his heart, and may smoulder there for long unnoticed, to burn afresh if but a straw fall on it.

His mother's tongue and Hester's seem therefore all the more cruel to me because I am not used to hear bitter speeches. Nor could I ever see the joy of uttering them. If one have cause for anger against another, let the truth be told and the complaint spoken out; there need be no quarrel, for either knows the other's mind.

Thus at least I have ever thought, and now to be blamed by Roger for the very fault that is most odious in my own eyes! And Roger was sorely vexed; I could see that by the set of his shoulders as he walked away. All the sunshine had gone out of my day—it always does if Roger has been displeased; and then I feel myself such a waif in a strange land that nothing has any gladness for me.

But at all events it was too bad of Roger to be so displeased. If I had indeed done amiss, why, I could endure to be found fault with; but all my crime had been a childish fancy. He forgets how young I am—not old like his mother, not middle-aged like Hester. I stood sadly by my bucket, my eyes on the ground. One moment I glanced at the water, and thought the process of ageing would go on fast if Roger continued to treat me so, my face looked already so grave and downcast.

Steps came slowly across the yard—steps that I could not mistake. Roger was sorry; he was coming back to tell me so. That was well, all was well; I would kiss him, and he would kiss me. He would come and help me to feed the calves; how happy the day would be!

I looked up at him as he came close, with a smile all ready for him, and a kiss ready too. But his face wore no smile to answer mine.

"Ethne," he said, "still idle here? Methinks you forget that time is a precious gift, and will need to be accounted for."

"Then you should not waste your own time in coming to tell me so, Master Standfast," said I; and I laughed because I had a mind to cry.

Roger's tone was cold as ice as he asked—

"Why do you laugh, Ethne? If there be good cause for mirth, tell me, that I may share it."

"I laugh at *you,*" I said stoutly, though I was somewhat afraid of his stern look and tone.

"If I thought you needed mirth as a rest from long toil, I would gladly afford food for your merriment, Ethne."

"But as it is, my lord desires that his slave shall carry buckets. Well, my lord taskmaster, I suppose I shall do well to obey, shall I not? Then perhaps for once I may pass the day unchidden."

"The work is of your own choosing, answered Roger. "Having chosen it, you will do well to fulfil it, remembering that the night cometh wherein no man can work."

"Oh me!" said I, "are you so weary of me as to wish my days shortened, Roger?"

"Ethne, you cannot know how you grieve me by your heedless talk."

Fool that I was. I spoke the words that rose to my lips—the words of the loving wife that God knows I am at heart—
" Dear husband, I would die sooner than

grieve you."

I had better have uttered the angry answer that rose with them—" Not so much as you grieve me by continual fault-finding." I wished I had spoken so.

For Roger answered—

"Do not think to please me with such a thought as that, Ethne. The natural man is ruled by the fear of man or by earthly love, but she who is regenerate must remember that whatsoever is not of faith is sin, and that they who are elect 6hall be blessed—where they neither marry nor are given in marriage."

"Even for loving you, you blame me. O Roger, Roger!" I cried, "what shall I do then? If in heaven I may not love you, then I solemnly declare to you that there is no joy in such a heaven as that for me."

And I broke into bitter weeping, and fled from him, rushing back into the house, passing Hester like a whirlwind, unheeding her cry of " Ethne! what now?"

Upstairs I closed the door of my own room, threw myself on the bed, and wept my fill.

"I would, I would I were at home with mine own loving, large-hearted people," I wept; and there I lay, hiding the sunshine from my eyes, and feeling truly that I had cause for weeping.

I wept till I was tired; then I rose and looked at my face—so much of it as I could see at one time—in the tiny mirror that hangs upon my wall.

Red eyes enough, red and swollen. If mine own people saw this, they would know that Roger had not sought to make me happy. They would—ah, no! I know well that if they came they *should* not see me thus. I would smile and look my best, howsoever sad.

S

They should know that I am happy with Roger, my husband, whom I love.

Though he will not let me love him! At that thought my tears flowed afresh.

"I *will* love him in spite of himself," I said. "Ay, and he *shall* love me. I will not believe he is not to love me in heaven, for I think if we might walk hand in hand down the golden streets there would be a double glory filling all the happy place; but at least he *shall* love me here."

Foolish Ethne! If he did not love me, why did he lead me from Connaught? My beloved is mine, and I am his.

I rose and bathed my red eyes, and smoothed my rebellious hair. Roger loves to see it smooth and tame. Woe is me for the little curls that will creep out on my temples, so that I dread to stir forth in any wind.

I brushed and pinned and stroked my locks; I took out the soberest grey garments that my little store contains. My saffron gown lay there—the dress in which Roger saw me first. Ah, in which he learned to love me! I should like to put it on. What influence would it have on Roger now? I wondered where Roger was; I looked from the window and saw him. He had done all my morning tasks for me, it seemed, for I could see the fowls feeding, and the calves; and from the garden he had gathered fruit, and was bringing it with the eggs of my fowls into the house.

O Roger, kind of heart, if sometimes stern of voice, how ill I have behaved towards you!

Hastily as might be I finished dressing, and went my way down stairs to seek my husband, going out quietly and by the back door that I might not be heard by Hester.

That was Roger talking in the orchard. I followed the sound of his voice to the gate, and there, looking in, I saw that he was speaking with a maiden, tall and very fair of face—none the less fair for her stiff Puritan dress, which rather seemed to mould itself to her graceful figure and take the beauty of the wearer.

That was Rachel Eversley. I had seen her in church and in the village, and had thought that in her I might indeed find a friend. But now I was not altogether well pleased to find her talking with my husband; and coming near, I heard something of their talk. "As we did in the pleasant old times," Rachel was saying, and Roger seemed happy as they talked. A twig snapped under my foot as I moved, and Rachel looked round and saw me as she finished speaking. I drew back a little, feeling almost as an intruder, but she smiled as one whose eyes light suddenly upon a dear friend, and came to me holding out both her hands.

"And as we will do again in the pleasant new times, if you are willing, dear Ethne—if so I may call you. We were speaking of gathering blackberries, your husband and I."

Under the spell of her eyes and voice the bitterness at my heart melted in a moment.

I threw my arms about her neck and kissed her. "O Rachel, be my friend!" I cried; "I am so lonely here!"

"What! lonely, and a bride?" said Rachel, when she had returned my kiss; and she turned smiling to Roger, who said gravely—

"Judge for thyself, Rachel; is it a solitary place to which I have brought my wife?"

"Nay," said Rachel; and she slid her arm about my waist, standing by me as tall as myself, but of more slight and fragile build. "Not a solitary place in itself, but among strangers the heart is lonely. Is it not so, dear Ethne?"

The thought seemed new to Roger. He turned and looked at me with the tender smile which so wonderfully beautifies his face. Surprise and some regret were there.

"Ay, is it so?" he said. "Then, Ethne, I must be more to you than I have yet been." And to Rachel he said—" Some day I must tell you, if my wife will not, how, when first she found me, I was not only solitary, but in sore peril, in which her woman's wit and woman's kindness saved me."

"Tush!" I said, and coloured at his praise of me, and all our past bitterness was forgotten, and we three went in together, and even Mistress Standfast seemed to speak more gently and Hester to be less sharp than usual while Rachel Eversley was there.

I am sure when the Lord dwelt on earth every bitter or false or ill-natured word must have died away where He came. People *could not* utter them in His presence, I think, except their hearts were hard as millstones. Certainly those who are most like Him on earth restrain much evil by their mere presence, and thus does Rachel Eversley.

I was not slow to avail myself of Rachel's entreaty that I would come to see her. I went one day when all I ought to do was done, that Roger's mother might not have cause to call me idle.

Flowers only bloom perfectly in the garden of one who loves them—so I have heard it said; and if the pretty proverb be true, Rachel Eversley must love her flowers very dearly, so luxuriantly they grew in the garden before the house, and about the walls, and in the rooms too, for I saw them peeping through the windows as I went up the garden path. Yet I know she plucks them continually for the sick and others, and that in great handfuls. Perhaps the flowers know her kindness and reward her!

Rachel sat at her sewing, and as she sewed she sang.

"If any be merry, let him sing psalms!" said the apostle. Hester often sings psalms, but not because she is merry; every song of hers is a De Profundis. Rachel's was a Magnificat. She sang as though indeed her spirit rejoiced in God her Saviour.

"Rachel, Rachel!" interrupted a querulous voice; and Rachel ceased to sing, laid down her work, and went over to an arm-chair by the fireside. "My pillows!" complained the voice, doubtless that of the old grandmother.

"Are they not easy?" asked Rachel, leaning over and gently arranging them.

"Easy! No, not they. They are never easy; but because I do not complain you think I must be at ease. Thoughtless, inconsiderate, girls ever are."

"Dear grandmother, you know ten minutes since you would not let me set them right, and told me I was troublesome," said Rachel gently.

"So you were," complained the old woman. "A maiden with her wits about her knows when to be still and when to be useful. Now I suppose you think me hard to please—girls always fret if they are blamed ever so little."

"I think I would go barefoot round the world to please you, dear grandmother;" and Rachel kissed the old face, and set a posy of her flowers a little nearer to the grandmother.

"There, are they not sweet?" she said. "There is lavender among them, and rosemary."

"I detest rosemary!" said the old woman. "Have you lived with me all these years and not learned that? But there, girls never remember."

As she spoke, she impatiently pushed away the cup so vehemently that it fell from the corner of the table and was shattered on the floor.

"Never mind, grandmother dear," said Rachel, who had just sat down again. "There is not much harm done; the cup was mine, and not so over-precious."

"Harm done! with the wet about my feet ready to bring on pain! And no harm that I should be affrighted 278 and my heart made to beat so hard; but you have no knowledge of illness—of old age and weakness, Rachel."

"There, it is all done," said Rachel, who had dried the floor and gathered up the fragments; and as she rose again she saw me standing in the porch, and greeted me with the kindest welcome.

"Grandmother," she said, "this is Roger Standfast's wife—Mistress Standfast-on-the-Rock, if you would have her called at full length."

"I would that godly name so lately taken were not forgotten again so soon," said the grandmother; and she sat up in her chair and scanned me with bright but sunken eyes. The faces of the old are a written book, and tell truly enough what the guiding motive of the life has been. If love, why then the face is as fair as a summer sunset, but if self-will and discontent, then it is deeply lined with a record which only death can efface. My mother's face bore furrows which pain had ploughed, but when she lay in her last sleep these were all but gone, and a smile was in their place, as though the first glimpse of the Beyond had availed not only to wipe out all sorrow, but even the memory of it. But her face was furrowed by pain and sorrow, not by ill-temper, and was no less sweet for the lines in it.

"So this is Roger's wife," said the old woman; and she raised herself in her chair and peered into my face. "Fair to look upon—ay, beauty that is skin-deep. And after all, no handsomer than Rachel. Well, I looked that Rachel should have been his wife, but she chose rather to be a burden to me in my old age, when I ought to have had done with the care of children—ah, a heavy care, a heavy care!" And the old woman sank back and shook her head from side to side, repeating continually—"a heavy care!"

"Come out with me, Ethne, and see the beauty of our orchard before it be all plucked," said Rachel. "Dear grandmother, I think you will not miss me for a little while. Is there aught you need before I go?"

"Need! I need nought. Do I ever trouble any one? Am I ever discontented at being left lonely and uncared for while you go gadding? There, go quickly, and shut the door. Haply I shall sleep a little."

Rachel obeyed, and we two went out into the orchard, where the warm autumn sun was reddening the cheeks of toothsome pippins, and warming the plentiful crop of those coarser apples which should make cider.

"Methinks *you* have 'a heavy care' in so querulous an old woman, Rachel," I said.

"She is old and sickly," said Rachel, with her sunny smile. "The end of her pathway of life is toilsome and weary, but she has been faithful. The least I can do is to bear with her lovingly."

"But oh, dear Rachel!" I cried, "sometimes I have thought—of late especially—that I should like to go where the *good people* cease from troubling. I would not irreverently alter Scripture, but Can you under stand?"

"I can, dear heart," said Rachel, a little sadly. "But if we do not recognise that we are children, learning many lessons from many teachers before we may go home to our Father's house, how much more than endurable every trial becomes. How welcome, rather! We need not go to seek our schooling, as recluses have vainly thought. It is here with us; our kinsfolk and friends are the means of teaching us patience, self-denial, and much more."

"If I could look upon it so," I said; and Rachel answered—

"But why not? Think of the joy and peace wo lose in failing to remember that *all things* work together for good for us who love God. And oh, Ethne! think of it, in this also *He* was made like unto us. Think of what *He* suffered in the faithlessness, and worldliness, and selfishness, not even of the world, but of His chosen. Not only of the one who was a devil, but of the eleven who were saints, and whose lives are examples to us."

"Saints," I repeated, "and examples. You speak as one who loves the blessed saints, Rachel, as I was taught to love and revere them. Father Ambrose was wont to say that the blessed saints are as the coloured rays of light, and that the different glories of each together made up the pure white light wherein God dwelleth. And since our eyes are too weak to comprehend that perfect light, he was wont to say that we do well to study their lives, and gather the rays of their various perfections into our hearts one by one."

Rachel did not for a moment answer, so I went on, feeling that to her at least I could speak of the thoughts that often oppressed my heart, of which I could not speak even to Roger.

"It is hard—I did not know how hard it would be— to leave the teachings of one's youth, the stars whereby one learned to steer on this tossing sea of life. Sometimes I feel adrift, adrift!"

Rachel turned her sweet face, full of tender love and pity, towards me.

"In truth life has storms, dear heart. But to us are given many days of calm and peace. The Lord's life was *all* storm till that last 'It is finished' brought Him into the haven where He would be. 0 Ethne, He was harder upon Himself than He ever is upon us!"

In so speaking she answered my thought rather than my words, and tears filled my eyes and choked my voice.

"Our *light* affliction—but for a moment—an eternal weight of glory. It is enough—0 Ethne, enough, far too much, for the disciple that he be as his Master." So she said, as Roger had once said to me in almost the same words. Her shining eyes were fixed upon the soft blue autumn sky, calmly bright, like her spirit.

"Yes," I said, thinking of old Mistress Eversley, and of myself then; "if only we could feel that our cares were making us, ever so slowly, a little like Him. "

"But that they surely do, if we will let them — changed from glory into glory—until at last, when I wake up after Thy likeness, I shall be satisfied with it. "

There was such a thrill in her voice, such a yearning in her eyes, that a sudden fear shot to my heart.

"Not yet; oh, not yet, Rachel! Stay in the world, if only for my sake."

She looked at me and smiled, and answered almost merrily—

"I shall not go home to play till I have learned all my lessons, dear Ethne. Meantime we can learn them cheerfully, you and I, can we not?"

"Truly I will try," I said, feeling already a cheerfulness in the thought.

"The more one tries, the less trying is needed. 'The joy of the Lord is your strength,' said Nehemiah right truly."

And with that Rachel and I went hand in hand through the orchard, and Rachel would have me see how God's fair sunshine fell alike on the good fruit and the poor, doing all that could be done, so that each should come to its own perfection; and then we talked of many things, and Rachel's sweet soul shed its own pleasantness over all, and my heart was lighter than it had been for many a day when I went back through the fields to Oldbury—for Rachel dwelt at Cowhill, a part of the hamlet that stood somewhat away from the rest.

CHAPTER XXVII. JFrom Stone's Diarj. jOR many days Rachel Eversley's good words dwelt with me, and upheld me in the chill atmosphere of the Standfast household. And indeed I needed upholding, for I who have ever been used to kindly ways and gentle words find it hard to do my best against continual chiding.

I seldom see Roger alone. In the daytime he is busy with the concerns of the farm, or with meetings for prayer, or with the charge of a few sick folk, for in his earlier days he studied to be a physician. At night he is weary, and lays his head upon the pillow to sleep soundly till early morning, when he rises to read the Word and pray in solitude before the business of the day. I have greatly longed for something of that happy seclusion of wedded folk which we two entirely lose, and for hours together I have pondered upon the happiness I should enjoy if I might be alone with Roger in even the smallest cottage.

Autumn has passed into winter. The days have grown shorter, the evenings grown longer—long evenings that are so pleasant in a pleasant home. I cannot make of this house a home. Yesterday, when one meeting me in the village asked, "Are you going home?" I returned the foolish answer, "I would I were!" thinking of my own dear home over seas. Alas, there is no home of mine left there now!

The thought and the longing have been so continually in my mind that at last I spoke of them to my husband, who, for a wonder, came in when I was alone in the living-room, my work on my lap, my eyes full of tears.

"What ails you, Ethne?" he asked. "Are you sick?" "Not in body, Roger," I said. "A little sick at heart, perhaps."

"And why?" asked Roger, speaking patiently, as if to a fretful child.

"I want a *home,* Roger," I said; and I stood up and laid my head on his shoulder. It was seldom a caress passed between us.

"A what, Ethne?" he asked; but his hand smoothed my hair, and I found courage to answer—

"A home, dear husband—oh, let us have a home, be it never so small! I would make it so pleasant for you. We should be so happy."

"Is my wife not content with her home?" Roger asked. "What ails it, Ethne? Do the windows not please you, or the walls, or the tables and chairs?" "I am not so childish," I answered, somewhat aggrieved. Though when I have a chance I set the furniture a little less stiffly, and free the poor flowers which Hester makes it her business to put in water and stuffs tightly into a bowl, cheek to cheek—blue, red, and yellow; yellow, blue, and red, with a fringe of green set evenly round the edge.

"I want to have a home of my own, like other wives," I said. "Here I am neither fish, flesh, nor fowl; neither mistress, nor servant, nor guest, nor anything."

"Here, as everywhere, you are my wife. Is not that enough, dear Ethne?"

"It *would* be enough"—I began; but Roger said gravely—

"My Ethne must study to be content. By having one home among us we save money, and have more to give to him that needeth. Is not that worth a little sacrifice? Though I cannot see that there is much sacrifice in being one of a Christian family who dwell together, rather than sitting solitary in your own house."

I lifted my face to his, and he kissed my brow and said—

"Let me see my Ethne give her mind to making our home as pleasant as she can." And what could I do but sit down again to my work and try to sing as I sewed. For if Roger could not understand, how useless to try and explain!

But indeed I would have bitten out my tongue sooner than speak of the matter at all, had I known how it would end.

I suppose Roger spoke of it to his mother, for the next evening as we sat at supper she lifted up her head after a long silence and said—

"I learn that my daughter-in-law is not content to take the second place in this household. If that be so, Ethne, I would gladly be relieved from the weight of care which even my experienced shoulders find heavy at times, and slip it on to yours, which are eager for a load, as it seems."

I looked reproachfully at my husband, but his eyes were fixed on his mother.

"No, no; it is not that at all!" I cried eagerly.

"What then?" asked Mistress Standfast, fixing her grey eyes, that have a steely look in them, upon my distressed face. "Let us at least hear wherein you are not content."

And she, looking at me, waited for an answer, and

Hester too looked and waited, and I in utter confusioD strove to speak with dignity—

"I only said to Roger, who might well have held his peace"

"Oh, truly, if I was to be kept in the dark about your wishes, I will say no more," said Mistress Standfast. "Yet it seems they concerned me and my rule here."

"Indeed I am grateful that you suffer me to be here," I said; "but, Mistress Standfast, I did but say that I could wish to have a little home of my own, as other wives have."

Mistress Standfast rose from her place at the head of the long deal table, and stood erect, pointing down at her seat.

"Hester and I had best therefore seek another home," she said, in a low deep voice. "Roger, I pray you, bring your wife to this place: it belongs to her. Hester, you and I will take the places of guests till we can find another shelter for our heads."

"I pray you—I entreat you, do not misunderstand me so!" I cried, in deep vexation; but it was long before all my apologies and all Roger's efforts at last prevailed upon his mother to take her seat again, and the evening passed in a painful constraint.

I needs must admire Mistress Standfast for her goodness. Often she works till late into the night to clothe the naked; ofttimes she denies herself food to feed the hungry, though I know her alms are given without a smile, and generally an exhortation is added, so harshly spoken that the recipients of her bounty turn away trembling.

Last week the strong stern woman was struck down by illness, and suffered evidently acute pain, so that though she uttered no word of complaint, her face was drawn into deep lines of anguish. Pity is akin to love, they say, and I felt so sorry for the sufferer that my heart went out to her, and I would willingly do all I could to ease her pain.

Her feet were cold as ice. I brought hot water and hot bricks, and would have made her comfortable, but she motioned them away.

"Not so; I will not pamper my wretched body," she said, " or suffer it to be pampered. Of good words that can help the soul I can never have too many, but these things I will not have!"

And as she continued firmly resolved, there was nothing for me but to carry the comfortable things away again. I dared not argue against her decision, but I thought of the Lord and His doings on Maunday Thursday; how with tender and loving care He not only washed the feet of the disciples, but wiped them with the towel wherewith He was girded. Surely *one* of the lessons of that great act is that we should care for the comforts of others, and be willing to receive their kindness in our own sufferings.

Mistress Standfast suffered with stern patience till her sickness abated; then she rose from off her bed and sternly gave thanks to God. Then she went about the house as usual, and all things were as before; and with grief I owned to myself that her illness had been to me something of a rest and respite, and it was as if for a few days a sharp east wind had ceased to blow and now began again, seeming the colder for the lull there had been.

Indeed at my heart there lies a deepening chill. Since the day I told my longing for a home to Koger and he could not understand, we two have drifted apart little by little. We have no quarrel; we speak no harsh words. I should not like to say we love each other less, but instead of growing nearer and dearer to each other as we were doing, our lives are lived every day a little more apart. If Roger seems glad or sad, I do not now ask him why; if I have a thought deep down in my heart, I do not tell it to him.

I think indeed that my heart is growing cold; and perhaps it is well, for if it be cold and hard I shall care less for harsh words, and I shall heed less if the love that Roger had for me should grow to be no greater than the affection he bears to his hard-faced sister Hester.

To-day he said to me—it is long since he has asked me to walk with him alone—

"Ethne, I am going down to Aust. Will you bear me company?"

I looked out of the window where I sat.

"The ways are wet and sodden, and it is cold," I said. "I thank you, Roger, but I would rather not go."

I did not look up as I spoke. He stood a moment as if hesitating whether to press me to come, then he turned on his heel and went, while I watched him go, and sat on stitching in a dull monotonous way till it grew dark, and Roger came back from his lonely journey.

I used to run and fetch him dry shoes, but to-day I only moved with my work to the table, where Hester had lighted the lamps.

Roger fetched his own shoes, as I suppose henceforward he will do, without even a glance at me.

But oh that wedded life should sink to this, or any life grow so flat as mine! Had any one foretold me this, I surely would not have believed him.

JFrom *QEtfynt'e* Diarg. ONOTONOUSLY, therefore, the days have gone on—the short, cold, winter days. When the snow happened to fall softly outside the window I wondered if it were falling thus also on my father's and mother's grave in the wild West—falling softly as my tears would do, could I, their sorrowful child, but go there to weep. When the broad Severn shone in the evening sun, I have thought of the light on the lakes at Lara—the sweet, soft evening light of my country. Sometimes, pacing alone on the shore, I have sung softly the melodies of my country—those melodies of which the most part have a minor note in them, as though the heart of the singer were more sad than he would willingly own. I have thought then of Malachy, and have wondered if the old man yet lived and sang among the desolation of which at least his eyes were spared the sight.

Within doors I have gone about so meekly and quietly that Mistress Standfast and Hester have often looked at me in surprise, and Roger, taking my pale face between his bands, asked a day or two since— "Ethne, are you sure you are not sick?"

"Only homesick, Roger," I said; and Roger dropped his hands and turned away with a sigh, and when nest he came I strove to be more cheerful, for after all he loves me and would fain make me happy—in his own fashion.

So matters have gone on, till a tearful spring began to follow winter—tearful, as if the weary old earth wept that she must needs deck herself again with flowers that she has so often before seen fade, and bring forth her harvests for storms to beat, her young birds to be the prey of hawk and falcon.

On one of these early spring days we sat at dinner, when there came a knock at the outer door.

A serving-maiden brought word that a strange gentleman was there, and craved a welcome as a kinsman of the mistress.

"Bring him in hither," commanded Mistress Standfast; and in a few moments there entered none other than Maurice Burke, at whom she gazed blankly, for she looked to see a kinsman of her own.

Maurice—but how changed! Maurice, in his cavalier dress, but with the need of a woman's hand to renew the ruffles. Maurice, pale and sunken about the eyes, and pinched about the mouth that used to smile as sweetly as a girl's.

Roger knew him, and rose from his seat with a greeting that was friendly though grave, and I rose too with a cry of—

"Maurice, 0 Maurice! how glad I am that you are come!"

I went to him and took both his hands in mine, pressing them with such gladness as I had not felt for many a day.

"Sit down and share with us," said Roger; and he turned to his mother and sister and told them this was my kinsman.

"As such he is welcome," said Mistress Standfast very stiffly, eyeing Maurice's dress the while—the cavalier dress that she hated.

Food and drink were given to Maurice, and Roger asked how he had come and whence, and Maurice told

T him of a stormy crossing, and of the weather in Ireland; and then a painful silence fell, and none seemed to know what to say next.

"I trust," said Mistress Standfast, breaking a painful silence, during which Maurice's eyes and mine had met, and we looked sadly one upon the other—" I trust that the good work has been going forward in Ireland, and will go on till all be done."

"If by the good work you mean the slow extinction of the Irish race, madam, and the rectifying of that mistake of Heaven, the giving of Ireland to the Irish, I think it goes forward as well as you could wish," said Maurice, somewhat bitterly.

"' Oliver Crom'ell did her pummel' to some purpose, as said the doggerel bard."

"Speak no ill of Oliver Cromwell, young man—of the Protector of England," said Mistress Standfast sternly.

"I have said no ill of him. I have but mentioned his great deeds," replied Maurice, the shadow of his old smile flickering about his mouth. "He is uppermost at present, as a log of wood is that seems uppermost because it is tossed to the top of some wild whirlpool."

"I understand you not, sir," said Mistress Standfast very sternly. "The Protector sits now in the place of the king whom the Lord overthrew for his sins and those of his father. The foolish race of Stuart are gone. The Lord hath given Israel a judge."

"Ay, but come what come will, the king shall enj jy his own again, and I shall live to see it!" cried Maurice. And I looked beseechingly at him, and he readily understood my glance, and turned his face with its most winning smile to the stern countenance of Mistress Standfast, to make what amends he could. How pleasant it was to be so readily understood!

"I crave your pardon, madam," he said. "I think my courtesy forsook me. I will do penance in an ugly white sheet, if you will spare me one, and a couple of candles for my penitent hands."

The apology unfortunately was a fresh offence, from its mention of a Romish custom. Mistress Standfast frowned, and was silent.

"Your kinsman would seem to be Papist as well as Royalist, Ethne," said Hester; and poor Maurice ventured a smile at her lowering face, and said as gaily as he could—

"Nay, I am what you will, if you do but forgive me;" and, alas, I knew that such a saying as this would but deepen the disfavour in which he was. So again the painful silence fell, and every mouthful seemed to choke me as I ate. I looked across at Roger, but he gave no answering look, and indeed since he is so slow to understand, such messages of the eyes cannot help much.

At last Maurice made another venture.

"My cousin has not asked after her old friends," he said, looking at me. "I am very sure she does not forget them."

I did not answer instantly, having grown used to weigh every word before I utter it, and Roger spoke for me.

"My wife has cast in her lot with the people of the Lord," he said. "Of the welfare of her old friends she would indeed be thankful to hear, if you have the good news that any of them have resolved to walk from henceforth in the true light."

There was no smile on Maurice's lips as he answered—

"Truly, Captain Standfast, your countrymen have not taken the best way of recommending their faith to our people. There are those who *have* joined them, and their worldly prospects have at once brightened, so that those who do not find it so easy to leave the faith of their fathers have good cause to think the motives of these converts not always pure. And as for the English themselves, there is too good ground for the saying of one who knows them well, that he has eaten and drunk, and gamed and ridden, but has never prayed with them."

So Maurice spoke, and Mistress Standfast pushed back her chair and rose, though she had not finished eating, and we all rose also and went into the family sitting-room. Roger set a chair for Maurice, but he would not take it. He stood upright and bowed to Mistress Standfast.

"Madam," he said, "I think you will gladly speed the parting guest. I thank you for your hospitable entertainment, and bid you farewell."

"Farewell, sir," said Mistress Standfast; but I stood up and spoke.

"Maurice, Maurice, you will not leave us thus! Roger, I pray you bid my kinsman welcome, as I and my kindred bade you welcome when you came as our guest, as a stranger, and more"

"Mother," said Roger, "hospitality is set forth as a Christian duty, as you well know. Master Burke, I pray you tarry with us so long as you have business, or desire to do so."

"For your *English* welcome," said Maurice, with a little pause upon the word, "I thank you. But since I have neither of the apologies for staying of which you have spoken, why then—
'Without more circumstance at all
I hold it fit that we shake hands and part;1
or, since in this house it may not be well to quote from a profane writer of plays, I will act on the words of the wisest of men—' Withdraw thy foot from thy friend's house, lest he weary of thee.'"

Now, beside me at the table where I sat there lay writing gear. Hastily, and with Hester's eyes upon me, I took pen and paper and wrote thus—

"Meet me at sundown between the church and the river."

"Farewell, my kinswoman Ethne," said Maurice, and went, but I followed him.

"Maurice, you let this paper fall."

"I thank you," said Maurice, and as he took it our eyes met. He went, and I turned back and silently took up my sewing.

"Ethne," said Roger, "I would speak with you;" and I followed him out of the room and up to our own chamber, where he closed the door and then came close to me, and my heart beat fast. I had ever respected Roger and looked up to him, but now I knew that I feared him with a trembling fear that belongs not to true love.

"Ethne," he said, "what paper was that you gave to Maurice Burke?"

"Did you not hear me tell him he had let it fall?" I said, striving to steady my voice.

"I fear that I heard my wife tell a lie," said Roger, in a grave, sad tone.

I made no answer.

"Ethne, was not that a lie?" he repeated.

"Slaves are mostly liars," I said; and I sat down and laid my hands in my lap and looked defiantly in his face.

"Slaves, Ethne—a *slave!*" said Roger. "Is that a fit name for a Christian woman?"

"What am I but a slave?" I said coldly, not even feeling afraid now, but only utterly wretched; "when I must see my kinsman insulted before my face—sent away. Said I not well that I have no home?"

"Ethne," said Roger, coming nearer and looking down into my pale set face, "does it repent you that you wedded me and not Maurice Burke?"

"Yes," I said, without moving or flinching from his searching gaze, "it *does* repent me. He would have shown me kindness—you are cruel. O Roger Standfast, you are doing your best to break my heart."

"Ethne," began Roger, "look in my face again," for I had dropped my eyes. I would not lift them at his bidding, but sat still as a stone.

"Argument is useless. I can but pray for you," said Roger, and every tone of his voice shut my heart more firmly against him. "But as you are my wife, and owe me obedience, I lay upon you my commands not to speak again with Maurice Burke. You hear me?"

"To hear is to obey; that is how slaves make answer in the East," I said, the words seeming to drop like icicles from my lips. Roger turned and went, and I was left alone.

I fell on my knees—I have been used to pray in all times of need. But no prayer would come, and I rose again.

"I am too wicked to pray," I said

aloud, and the words echoed in the empty room. I went down and sat at my work—a long white seam, long and dull like the life that lay before me. No tear fell on the work; I sat as one petrified, only every now and then I looked at the sky to see how the day wore on.

A wild wet day it was. Into that furious driving rain Maurice had gone forth—our guest suffered to go away in weather in which one would not willingly drive a dog forth!

I might seem like a stone, but at my heart was a bitter, burning anger, that seemed to swallow up every emotion—every thought almost.

The drops covered the window and ran down ceaselessly; the wind moaned in the leafless trees and about the house like a homeless thing that would fain be made welcome. Homeless, lonely, unhappy, it sounded, and I longed to go out and be with it—to take its wings and wander blindly through the world, wailing for anguish as it wailed.

"How cold it is!" said Hester, and stirred the fire, and as I made no answer she looked sharply at me.

"Why, Ethne, you are white as death, and your hands are surely numb. Bring your work to the fire. Are you not cold?"

"I had not noticed it," I said, feeling that I must indeed look pale and numb if Hester could take notice of my looks.

The longest and most weary day comes to an end at last. From the window I could see that the wild black clouds were parting a little in the west. The rain had almost ceased; the clouds flew before the furious wind; an angry orange light glowed about the path of the setting sun. I rose and put aside my work and went to my chamber, where I put on my saffron gown and my long hooded mantle.

When I came downstairs, Hester stood at the door. She looked at me with wide-open eyes. "Whither go you, Ethne?"

"Out!" I said, and looked her straight in the face. "Will you bear me company?" "*I* am in my right mind!" said Hester, for a wild rush of rain swept down as I spoke. She looked narrowly at the fastenings of my mantle, through which it may be the paler saffron silk peeped.

"Heaven help the people down below if this goes on," she said. "There will be a spring tide to-night. I know not what will happen!"

"Thank Heaven then that you are high and dry!" I said.

"Hester!" called Mistress Standfast from the livingroom, "why is the house door open in this bitter weather?"

"Because Ethne has a fancy to walk," rejoined Hester; and Mistress Standfast called loudly—

"Ethne, are you mad? Come back at once; do you hear? Come hither to me!"

"Do you hear, Ethne?" repeated Hester. "My mother may well call you mad. Go to her as she bids."

"Tell her I will be back shortly," I said, and passed her, and went out into the storm, and as I went I heard Hester's voice above the wild wind calling to her mother—

"Ethne will come when she has finished the important business which calls her forth."

But I stayed not. I wrapped my mantle closely round me, and fought my way against the storm to the mound whereon the church stands—the best trysting-place I could think of to give Maurice.

There between the church and the water I found him. It was not high tide, yet the muddy waters were lapping greedily almost against the summit of their low green dyke. The grey hills of Wales were almost hidden by the sweeping rain which hissed as the wind beat it against the walls of the old church and upon the troubled breast of the river.

Maurice drew me into the shelter of a high mass of thorn and bramble. Were ever such blackberries as those which grow at Oldbury in the low lands by the Severn, so large and sweet and splendid? They were sodden though now, and spoiled.

"You are come, Ethne—my dear Ethne—my poor Ethne!" said Maurice. "Oh dear my lady, whom I cannot choose but love, how I thank you for coming!"

"Nay, Maurice," I said; "speak not of love, or I shall repent me that I came. Speak of friendship if you will, for that I sorely need—0 Maurice, I cannot tell you how sorely!"

"My loved one!—nay, I must speak what is in my heart. You must hear me, Ethne. I love you with a love which I cannot stifle though I have tried. My mother is deaa, Ethne. She lay dead one morning in the wretched place in which you saw her, without a farewell—I think it is what she would have wished. Well, when she was gone, I felt I must see you once more, Ethne—you, the one thing left that I have loved. And I thought' if I can see her and know that she is happy, I can go away content—I love her well enough for that.' But I have come to find you miserable, Ethne, with a husband who is cruel to you."

"Nay," I said again, "speak no ill of my husband, Maurice. He is kind to me—that is, he would be, if"

"If he were not a heartless dog!" broke in Maurice. "It is like you, Ethne; like you to be so good and kind, so patient with him. But I tell you he is not worth your patience. Tell me, is not the breach between you widening daily?"

I could not answer.

"I know it is," said Maurice. "Love makes us wondrous sharp of sight. You know you can never hope to be happy with him, Ethne. It is useless to try; the gazelle cannot mate with the jackal. Leave him, Ethne—it is a lighter punishment than he deserves—and come away with me to Spain. There, among the orange trees and gently plashing fountains, mingled with the sweet tones of the guitar, with song and laughter in place of these droning hymns and this forbidding piety, we will dwell. Surely God is not served by this dwelling in gloom. He made the earth and called it good— in Spain you shall find splendid temples to His honour and the noblest music breathing His praise. No, no; hear me to the end. For your marriage a dispensation can easily be had, making it null and void, and you yet may shake off this life which is crushing you and be young and blithe and happy once again, as the God who made you meant that you should be. Ethne, my love, come!"

And Maurice clasped my hands in his, and looked beseechingly in my face, and drew me more closely into the shelter, for the rain and storm grew wilder and wilder. A tree close by was uprooted by a frantic gust, the wind screamed as if with triumph as it tore the roots from their earth and then flung the tree like a broken toy upon the earth. Wild as was the war of the elements, it seemed as though the strife in my heart was yet more fierce.

"0 God!" I cried aloud, "pity me, guide me, or I shall lose my reason!" and I looked despairingly into the sunset, which shed a lurid glare upon ns as we stood.

"When thou passest through the waters I am with thee, and the rivers they shall not overflow thee." Out of the deep I called upon God, and He heard my cry, and in all my despair one thing became plain to me.

If we would follow the Lamb we must follow Him *whithersoever* He goeth — though it be to Calvary. "Father," He said, "if it be possible, let this cup pass." But it passed not. Only strength was given Him to drink it.

I might follow Maurice; my father's Church would dispense me from my marriage with a heretic; I might be pronounced not only sinless but right in what I did.

But before the bar of the Almighty! At that thought a horror came over me, and a deep shame that I had ever suffered such a thought to enter my heart at all—the thought of disloyalty to my husband. A vile wretch and utterly humbled I felt, and it was without the slightest doubt or hesitation that I made answer to Maurice.

"No, Maurice, never! It is better to do the will of God, however hard it may seem—better, did I say? it is the only hope of happiness. After all, life is not very long; we toss on an angry sea and must toil all night, but He stands on the shore to welcome us at last."

"Then you have courage to give up all hope of happiness in life, Ethne?" said Maurice, in a low, choking voice. "For yourself, and for me?"

"There may yet be some happiness—at least there may be *peace* for us," I said. "Forget yourself, Maurice —live for others; that is the only hope. Pray, like St. Austin in his extremity, 'Save me from myself.' The Cross replaceth all, my mother used to say, but nought replaceth the Cross."

Thus I said in the effort to cheer Maurice, and to my own heart there came a ray of comfort as I spoke.

But his voice had a hollow and hopeless sound in it as he said—

"Farewell then, Ethne; farewell all hope, all joy." He bent towards me and kissed me passionately twice and thrice, lifting my face to his; and as he kissed me I looked and saw Hester standing above us under the wall of the church, looking down upon us from the mound.

I uttered a faint cry, and Maurice looked and saw her too. She turned and went away while we watched.

"Ethne," said Maurice, "what will you do now? Come with me, or bid me stay with you. I am yours to do your will."

"Nay," I said; "I entreat yon leave me. "

He made one last appeal in a voice choked with sobs, but since I would not hear he left me at last, and fled as one possessed along the wet meadows towards Aust Cliff by the river, that stood up darkly against the fading sky.

And I, with a blank sense of utter hopelessness, went back homewards through the wild twilight, for the storm had not lessened with sundown.

Woe betide the fishers at sea to-night. Yet I thought as I walked that I would rather be with them, and face the winds of God, than face, as I must now do, the anger and scorn of men—and of women, who are severer judges of their sisters than men.

CHAPTER XXIX. JFrotn *tetfynt'e* iDtatg. jflE door of the living-room stood open when I came in.

"Ethne!" called Mistress Standfast. "I am coming," I said. I closed the house-door and walked into the room, where, all wet as I was, I stood before them—Mistress Standfast in her high-backed chair by the fire, and Roger seated at the table, and Hester standing between them, her wet mantle thrown aside upon a chair.

I put back my hood and stood as I was, looking at Roger. For his sake I had stood before another tribunal; I wondered if he remembered that day as he looked upon me now.

I think he did, for it was in a gentle voice that he asked—

"Where have you been, Ethne?'

I had rather he had spoken harshly; then my voice would not have trembled as I answered—

"Beside the river, below the church."

Hester nodded her head, as though she would say, "In this at least she has not lied."

"With whom were you there?" asked Roger.

"With Maurice Burke," I answered, feeling as though my breath caught, so that I could scarcely speak.

Hester nodded again.

"Did I not forbid you to speak with him?" asked Roger; and now indeed he spoke sternly.

"Yon did; but in this matter I could not obey you," I said. "However, I will obey you now, for I have sent him away, and he comes no more."

"Hum!" said Hester aloud. "Ask her, Roger"

"What need to ask me, Hester?" I said. "I shall not lie; I will tell Roger that it is true that he kissed me thrice before he went."

"She confesses it!" cried Mistress Standfast, and Hester almost shrieked—

"Not a blush on her face, the brazen thing! 0 Roger, what a creature have you brought us?"

"Silence, Hester!" I said, moving from where I stood; and Hester stepped back as I came near, dismayed as it seemed by such new courage in me. But my business was not with her, and I heeded her not, but went to my husband and stood before him.

"Roger," I said, "when we were wed, you promised to love and to cherish me. I pray you think how you have kept that promise of tender care and kindness. For me, I promised to love you—I have done that as long as you would let me; to obey you, which I have never but in this one thing failed to do; and to honour you, which I have done to-night in very sore temptation. If your heart held yet a spark of love for your wife you could not have humbled her as you have now done. May God forgive you, as I will strive to do." I turned to the two women. "And for you, my mother and sister as you might have been, I say to you, may God Almighty never judge you as you have judged me, the stranger within your gates."

They made no answer, but gazed at me in utter dismay, and I turned and went from the room, closing the door behind me, and passed to mine own chamber, where, forgetting my wet clothes, I sat down to think what I should do next, and strive to calm the tumult of my spirit.

I heard Roger's step come upstairs presently. He came to the door, and put his hand on the latch, but I had fastened it within. He did not knock, nor did he call, but stood irresolute, and presently went away, and slowly down the stairs again. Then came a long silence. All three were doubtless in the room below while I sat still, but apparently none spoke. As Roger entered I heard his mother speak, but there was no answer from him, and they three sat silently below, as I sat above.

I could not stay in that house, so ran my thoughts. To fly with Maurice had been sin, but to leave my husband who loved me not would be kindness to him, and perhaps the best thing I could do. Then all at once I thought of Rachel Eversley.

"Rachel—to her I will go!" I said aloud, and I pushed away the curtains and looked out. The night was inky black. It was not now raining, but I think I had never seen so dark a night; it seemed to me as dark as the future that lay before me.

Yes, I would go to RacheL I gathered together a little bundle. A miniature of my parents I took from the table, and slipped it inside my dress. The touch reminded me how wet I was. Should I make myself dry before I went?

It mattered so little what became of me now! Why should I take so much trouble about myself? I took up my bundle and went downstairs as I was, stepping lightly, in the hope that I should not be heard.

I was not heard. The inner door was shut. The latch of the outer door clicked as I lifted it, and I made haste to pass through and shut it as quietly as I could, and then went forth into the blackness of the night.

So dark was it that I had to feel about for the garden gate. My hand touched a stake that leaned against the fence, and I took it, thinking I might be glad to grope my way with it as the blind use to do. So I went out and took my way towards the pleasantly wooded spot that is called Cowhill, to seek Rachel and throw myself on her compassion.

I passed the church that gleamed faintly above me through the pitchy blackness, and went on, keeping not far from the sound of the river, since I feared to lose the path across the common land if I should keep too far from the shore.

I felt each step carefully with the stake I carried, nevertheless more than once I plunged ankle-deep into water. Not that that mattered much to one already so drenched and bedraggled as I was. It was very still. I could hear the washing of the full river, and a distressed bleating now and then, as of sheep that had stuck fast in the mire. Up the stream, where there are many houses, I could faintly see lights going to and fro, once when I turned to look. But I had but time for a glance.

For suddenly there came a seething sobbing sound in the grasses at my feet, and my heart turned sick, for I remembered what Hester had said of the fear of a flood if the tide should rise high to-night.

Again it came, that sobbing sound; and this time the water flowed above my ankles, and I heard it rush far beyond me, and the next moment I was almost carried off my feet, for the flood was as high as my knees, and but for the chance, or the leading of Providence, which made me take that stick, surely I had been lost then—drowned alone and in the dark!

Blindly and helplessly I tried to move forward; but the tide was now deep—my wet raiment clung about me. I splashed a step or two, then hope and strength alike failed me. I cried once, twice, for help, but the wind carried my voice away. And indeed it wonld be hard, I felt, for any to help me. Faint and dizzy at last, I let fall my stake, or rather it was washed from my hands, my knees gave way under me, and crying upon God's mercy I fell forward into the flood!

Most truly man's extremity is His opportunity. As I fell my right arm encircled something firm, and with the strong grasp of desperation I clung to it, and found it to be the trunk of a crooked thorn tree, which, thank God, was old and firmly rooted in the low pastureland. Its crookedness was to me another mercy, for I clung to it the better, and pulled myself, exhausted and drenched as I was, to a secure resting-place among the branches.

There I sat, breathless and dripping, but thankful that life was spared me, and looked round. There was nothing to see that could give me much comfort—the greedy waves lapping below me, and trees and hills standing darker against the sky.

Dimly I could see the distant lights moving to and fro. The flood must have filled the lower rooms of those houses, I thought. Doubtless there was much consternation there; boats would go out, but how could they steer in this darkness? The houses they might reach; but here, on this lonely common, there was little hope that any would find me. Certainly no one would seek me here; till bedtime I should not even be missed.

I had not felt it cold as I walked, but now the wind blowing upon my wet clothes sent a deathly chill through me, and my limbs began to grow numb and my head heavy.

Had I been saved from a sudden death only to die more slowly? Well, so it might be, and it might well be also that longer time for repentance was being granted me.

I drew myself up as far among the branches as I could, lest from sheer exhaustion I should let go my hold and fall into the water. Then I lifted up my face into the wild blackness of the night and strove to pray.' It should have been easy to pray. It seems harder when our cold hearts, rooted to the world, are basking in its sunshine and finding no special need, to cry to God for help. Give us this day our daily bread has much meaning for the poor man living from hand to mouth—to the rich it seems but a pleasant formula, or one chiefly to be applied to spiritual needs. But now in the darkness and storm my heart seemed so dazed, my brain so bewildered, that I knew not how to pray. Even so, I thought, must they feel who, after a careless life seek to make their peace with God in a time of sore sickness, when agony of body, and worldly care concerning business left undone, and spiritual distress overwhelm their whole spirit, and all is dismay and confusion.

Death was very near me—death and burial. I thought how it would be to lie still and straight, with my hands, that have ever been busy, crossed idly on my bosom, never to work more; and then my thoughts followed my body laid in the chill and darkness of the earth, and how the summer flowers would spring presently above my grave. I was very young to die!

Doubtless our body is not our real self. Still it is hard to help thinking that it is in some manner we ourselves who are laid in the ground. And as I thought of this there came back to my mind the words of supplication that are written in grand and noble English, with a stately cadence as of solemn music, in that Prayer-Book which the Church of England made for herself, purging her ritual in the words and manner of it in the days of King Edward VI.

And as fitly as though they had been made for me sounded those words as I spoke them aloud—
U
"In the midst of life we be in death: Of whom may we seek for succour but of Thee, 0 Lord, which for our sins justly art moved? Yet, O Lord God most holy, 0 Lord most mighty, 0 holy and most merciful Saviour, deliver us not into the bitter pains of eternal death. Thou knowest, Lord, the secrets of our hearts; shut not up Thy merciful eyes to our prayers: But spare us, Lord most holy, 0 God most mighty, 0 holy and merciful Saviour, Thou most worthy Judge eternal, suffer us not at our last hour for any pains of death to fall from Thee!"

Thus I prayed, and then my whole consciousness seemed to grow more dim.

"Into Thy hands—Thine—I commend my spirit," I said, and I remember not how the time passed after that!

I suppose I fell asleep, though I knew how perilous such sleep ever is, for I dreamed a dream.

I dreamed that I struggled through the dark waters of Death, and fell breathless and exhausted upon the further shore at the pierced feet of the Lord Himself. I dreamed that I looked up at His face and saw no welcome there, but only sorrow, and that He said to me—

"Ethne, where is your husband?" and I found no words wherewith to answer. And He said, "I set thee beside him to be a helpmeet to him, and in thy blind impatience at his imperfections thou hast forsaken him and left him to struggle on alone. My child, in the little 1 gave thee to do thou hast not been found faithful."

And as He spoke, I heard Roger's voice calling me in a tone of bitter anguish from beyond the dark river, and I cried aloud—

"Lord, let me go back to him; even through the sharpness of death I will go, if Thou wilt send me."

A smile came upon the blessed face; and as Roger's voice called again, I thought that I sprang up to go, and I opened my eyes and found that a pale light was in the sky, and that Roger's voice was no dream, but a reality, for over the waste of waters he was rowing in a little boat seeking me, and calling my name with a heartbroken cry.

Whether he heard the faint answer I made, or whether he caught sight of me, I know not; but I know that my stiffened limbs were soon safely held in his strong arms, and I was lifted into his boat, and a strong cordial held to my lips, while he whispered—

"Ethne, my love! my life! thank God I have found you! My wife, say you forgive me!"

I had not strength to speak; I looked in his face and smiled, and leaned back as he had laid me in the stern, looking at the scene of dreary desolation round us.

Fire and flood, the two things in Nature that wreck men's homesteads, I have seen. Fire is terrible to see, but I think a flood ten times more horrible. The dark slimy waters that lap so greedily are ill to look upon, and loathsome are the shapeless, nameless, sodden things that come floating down their turbid course. The gentle beasts of the field are carried away and become repulsive carcasses that drift by—a sight to make one shudder. Sodden household gear, also sadly useless and spoiled, is sadder to look on than any heap of grey, smouldering ashes. At least so it seemed to me in the chill of that dismal dawn, and in truth the peril was not even yet at an end, for a heavy piece of wreckage, floating almost under water, bore suddenly down upon us, and though Roger saved the boat from the shock, yet one oar was caught and snapped like a reed. So we were helpless, and the receding tide in its strength caught our little boat, and swept us out upon the wide tide of the Severn.

"Courage, sweet heart," said Roger, bending over me. "We shall yet be saved, please God; and if not, at least we will die together. Oh, my wife, the anguish of this night has taught me how I love you. Forgive me, and let nought come between us again."

"Forgive me too, Roger," I said; and he stooped and kissed me, and even in that hour of peril I was happy as I had not been for many a long day.

Then Roger, steering with the one oar that remained, shouted aloud for help, and before long there came an answering shout, and a larger boat, rowed by strong arms, came over the wan waters towards us.

I remember little more. I know Roger's strong arms carried me at last to my own chamber, and last of all I remember that Mistress Standfast stood by me and kissed not my brow bat my lips, while Hester brought pillows and smoothed my bed with a kindness such as I could never have hoped for from her JFtom ti)E Secort of &ooer StanDfaot.

E, Roger and Ethne Standfast, do thank the
Lord.

Thus, at my dear wife's bidding, I, Roger, close this record of a part of our lives, which we, having each read the record of the other, since now there are no secrets between us, have resolved to keep, that perhaps our children may hereafter read them and take warning and counsel from them.

"Thou shalt remember the way that the Lord thy God led thee."

Yea, Lord, we do remember it, and therefore, with thanksgiving for the past, we give our future lives to Thee. We and our household will serve the Lord.

Somewhat yet remains to be briefly recorded before we tie these scattered leaves together. Namely, how, while yet my wife lay prostrate from the fever which followed that terrible night of the flood, a man and his wife came to our house and asked to see her. How I went down and found to my surprise that it was Teague O'Ruark and Nora, now his wife, who besought me to let them stay with us as servants, for that their own country was rendered terrible to them by that which had passed, especially of late.

Then it was that I learned a thing which will for ever cast a stain upon the record of English dealings with that sad island over which she has rule.

The departure of so many swordsmen for Spain left many widows and orphans, and maidens for whom there were no husbands. Women were much needed in the West Indian sugar plantations, and the sugar merchants of Bristol treated with those in authority, who appointed agents, and gave them orders upon masters of workhouses and others to deliver grown women, those who were not too aged, to them, and young girls, together with men who were prisoners and young boys, who were shipped in such numbers that the supply began to fail, some six and a half thousand having been shipped in four years. For presently any who could not prove that they had a settled course of industry were seized, and then agents were employed to delude people by one pretext or another into their power, being given money for each person so deluded, so that women were kidnapped from their husbands, and children from their parents.

Now Teague, among his band of Tories, swept down upon a party of these men-stealers, who, however, proved too strong for them, and beat them back, but not before Teague had discovered to his horror that Nora, his beloved, was among the prisoners.

He therefore, forsaking the robber band, followed her secretly, and finding that the party were to be taken to Bristol, there to be shipped for the Barbadoes, concealed himself on board the ship. After they reached Bristol a looser watch was kept on the captives in the strange city, and he contrived her escape. They were wedded by a priest of their own faith, who kept them concealed till the ship had sailed. One captive more or less made little difference, no doubt. They fled now to us, and besought that they might dwell with us in safety; and never among many faithful and diligent workers have I seen any so faithful or so diligent as these two poor souls.

Another matter not as yet set down is the strange and wonderful dealing of God with the soul of Maurice Burke, who, flying from my Ethne in despair, went hurrying and stumbling on to the summit of Aust Cliff, where he looked down on the troubled waters, and would have cast himself in, and so have made an end together of his sorrow and his life.

But Rachel Eversley, who walks with God, felt that night an impulse she could not resist, and heard a voice speaking plainly through the storm, and saying—

"Go to Aust, to the top of the cliff."

They may doubt her word who list; for me I humbly and reverently believe that the Lord spoke plainly to her that night. Wild as such an errand seemed, she went forth in the twilight as swiftly as she could, and reached Aust Cliff in time to save the desperate man—in time to save a soul from despair, and bring back a wanderer to the fold.

For Maurice, being grateful to the gentle maiden, presently learned to love her, and how she, being won by his exceeding gentleness, after much prayer felt that the Lord had called her to be his wife, I must also here record.

In days past I myself would fain have wooed and won Rachel Eversley. But first she feared my wild and unconverted spirit, and after the Lord had touched my heart she feared me still—because of the harshness that is natural to me, as I think. Against that I daily strive and pray, for I find in the Christ a marvellous example of gentleness, and perfect courage withal.

For my Ethne, her eyes may have lost something of their youthful sparkle, but it is no loss, for now they shine like two fixed stars, with a calm and peaceful light, gladdening all who come near, and me her husband above all.

"He that findeth a wife findeth a good thing." Day by day I thank God for her from the very depths of my heart.

But hark! a hand is lifting the latch of our door, the door of that little home which Ethne calls her Eden, and would not change, so she says, even for the fair castle that once was hers.

And there are the voices below of Maurice and Rachel —of their little Rachel who shall hereafter wed our eon Gerald, as Ethne will say, building fairy castles for our little son, in whose face I see daily his mother's eyes and his mother's smile.

I am coming, Ethne. Wait but a moment. Only let me write the last words of my record. They shall stand at the end as they stand at the beginning, in fair large writing—

I, ROGER Standfast-on-the-rock, do thank the Lord.

ADAMS.—WORTHIES OF THE CHURCH OF ENGLAND: A Series of Biographies. By W. Davenport Adams. Crown 8vo. extra, cloth boards, y. 6d. 'Mr, Adams has spared no pains to give an impartial view to his " Worthies' and his work will be a very useful addition to the parish library and the home book-shelf of the young Churchman.'—Publishers' Circular. AINSLIE.— INSTRUCTION FOR JUNIOR CLASSES IN SUNDAY SCHOOLS. By the Rev. A. C. AlNSLIR, M.A., LL.D., Vicar of Langport, Somerset, Prebendary of Wells. Fcap. 8vo. cloth boards, Is. each.

A packet of Lesson Leaflets for a class of ten, price $s.

Vol. I. The Story Of The Gospels In Fifty-two Lf.ssons.

Vol. II. Fifty-two Lessons On The Acts Of The Aiostles.

'Clear, concise, and graphic'—GUARDIAN.

These books are specially designed to help those who have not been trained as Teachers. For more advanced scholars, see Bishop Carpenter's ' Outline Lessons,' and Canon Daniel's 'Daily Offices' AMERICAN CHURCH REVIEW.—Edited by the Rev. II.

Mason Baum. Monthly, *is. 6d.*

ANDERSEN, HANS.—The Snow Queen.. s«pym.

THE ARTIST: A Journal Of Home Culture.

Monthly, price 6./.; post free for a year, *Js.* The yearly Volumes form a complete history of the Art World. 4to. cloth boards, *Us. 6d.* 'The only newspaper of the Art World publishel; and a very good one too.'

Journals And Journalism. 8AIRD.—Works by the late Rev. William Baird, M.A. THE DAYS THAT ARE PAST: A Manual of Early Church

History. Fcap. 8vo. cloth boards, *2s. 6d.*

A BAIRD.— *Works by the late Rev. Wm. Baird, M.A.—Continued.)* THE INHERITANCE OF OUR FATHERS: Plain Words about the Book of Common Prayer. Fcap. 8vo.doth boards, *y.6d.* WATCHING BY THE CROSS: Prayers, Readings, and Meditations for Holy Week. Royal 32mo. *6d.*; cloth boards, red edges, *is.* Fourth Edition.

BELL.—FROM PHARAOH TO FELLAH. By C. F. Moberlt Bell, Author of ' Egyptian Finance,' &c. With upwards of 130 IUuitrations from Drawings by Georges Montbard. Engraved by Charles Barbant. Crown 8vo. fancy cloth boards, *16s.*

'*Few will resist reading to the end when they have begun it. Mr. AfeSerly Bell has one knack which not a few historians would be thankful to possess; he knows how to put the facts of Egyptian history into true perspectizv.*' AThEN-ECM.

'*Written with singular and most captivating hightncss and humour. Mr. Moberly Hell and Mr. Georges Montbard have made as bright and readable a book as has ever been written upon Egypt past and present.*'

Manchester Examines.

'*At once original, fresh, and amusing.*—STANDARd.

'*Mr. Moberly Bell has a minute knowledge of Egyptian history and ajfiiir?; he does not let slip the opportunity to convey a deal of interesting and valuable information.*'—SCOTSMAN.

BIDDER.—WESTMINSTER CLOISTERS: The Story of a Life's Ambition. By M. Bidder. With Illustrated Frontispiece, Title-page, and Initial Letters. Crown 8vo. appropriate cloth boards, *£r.*

'*The pictures of ecclesiastical life are wrought with a good deal of force and picturesque realism, and the principal historical characters are clearly depicted .... Decidedly interesting and well told.*'—SATURDAY Review.

'*A very graceful and touching story of life in the great monastery of Westminster, during the time when Richard La-ur de Lion was held captive in Germany. The book will certainly be a favourite, both with girls and boys.*' Guardian.

BlRLEY.— Tales by Miss Caroline Birley. THE LINEN-ROOM WINDOW; or, 'What the Snow conceals the Sun reveals.' Illustrated. Square t6mo. cloth boards, *is. 6J.*

WE ARE SEVEN. A Tale for Children. Coloured Illustrations by T. Pym. Square i6mo. extra cloth boards, *is. 6d.*

'*The children are real children, many-sided little mortals, and their joys and sorrows are such as children can understand.*'—Manchester Examiner.

'*This is a tale for children and children's occupations, which children will like. Ptor little Birdie and her wonderful dolls are sure to be favourites.*' The Queen. BLOOM FIELD.—THE FAKENHAM GHOST. By Robert Bloomfiei.d. With numerous Illustrations by J. L. Wimbush. Small 4to. cloth bevelled boards, gilt edges, *2s. 6d.* The Illustrations have been drawn on purpose, and are not in any zoay a reproduction of the Illustrated Edition published by Darton and Harvey in 1812.

BLUNT. — A THOUSAND YEARS OF THE CHURCH IN CHESTER-LE-STREET. By the Rev. William O. Blunt, M.A., Rector; Hon. Canon Durham. Illustrated, crown 8vo. paper boards, *Js.6d.* '*A model of parish history.*'—Church Bells. BOEVEY.—TOPSY TURVY. By S. M. Crawley Boevey. With numerous Illustrations by H. J. A. Miles. 4to. extra cloth boards, *3. 6d.*

Second Edition.

A most original tale for children from ten to fourteen; full of adventures and teeming with fun and humour. 'The illustrations deserve particular mention, as they add largely to the interest of this amusing volume for children. Jack falls asleep with his mindfull of the subject of the fish-pond, and is very much surprised presently tofind himself an inhabitant of Water-iuorld, where he goes through wonderful and edifying adventures. A handsome and pleasant book.'—The LITERARY World. BOURDALOUE. —EIGHT SERMONS For Holy Week AND EASTER. Translated from the French of the Rev. Father Louis Bourdaloue by the Rev. G. F. Crowther, M.A., of St.

John's College, Oxford. Crown 8vo. cloth boards, *y. 6d.*

'*His Bourdaloue style is exceedingly clear and flowing; his reasoning—granting his premises—is often powerful; his appeals to the conscience of his hearers are fervid and impassioned. The sermons here reproduced are most-*

ly as though they had been written in English.'—The SCOTSMAN.

BRADLEY. — A Selection From The Sermons By THE LATE REV. CHARLES BRADLEY. Edited, with
Memoir, by the Rev. G. J. Davies, Author of ' Successful Preachers,' &c. Crown 8vo. cloth boards, y. 6d.
'The prince of sermon writers'—CANON HAVERGAL. 'May be thought to be the flower of evangelical preaching.'—SatURDAY REVIEW.

BROOKS.—LECTURES ON PREACHING. By the Rev. Phillips Brooks, Rector of Trinity Church, Boston, U. S. A. Crown 8vo. cloth boards, 3. 6d. BU LLEY.—Works by Eleanor Bulley. GREAT BRITAIN FOR LITTLE BRITONS. With numerous Illustrations of Places and People. Large crown 8vo. cloth, bevelled boards, y.Cxl. 3rd Edition, thoroughly Revised, with additional Illustrations.
'A very pleasant device for making geography agreeable.'—GUARDIAN.
'Great pains have been taken with this book, and it contains abundance of information.'—Spectator.
'It will give "Little Britons" a better idea of their native land than they will obtain from a dozen dry geographies.'—LITERARY WORLd.

THE FIRST LADY OF THE LAND. Illustrated. Small crown 8vo. cloth boards, 1. *A popular Life of the Queen.* BURNE AND MILES.—Tiles From Dame Marjories CHIMNEY-CORNER AND CHINA FROM HER CUPBOARD. By F. S. T. Burne andH. J. A. Miles. A new and origiml book for Children. Printed in various shades of blue. Oblong papa boards, y. 6d. 'They form a charming collection, very delicately executed.'—The Times.
'The figures in the large Tiles are done with character, sweetness, esti grace, and the reproduction in tints resembling the old Dutch tiles ccuid not k surpassed for delicacy and softness of rendering.'—The Decorator. BURROWS.— *Works by the Rev. H. W. Borrows, B.D. Canon of Rochester.*
THE EVE OF ORDINATION. Fcap. 8vo. cloth limp, *Is. 6d.*
Third EditkB.
LENTEN AND OTHER SERMONS. Fcap. 8vo. cloth boards, *is. 6d.* Third Editim.

'They are striking, simple, brief, and impressive.'—Christian World. 'A brevity, born not of poverty, but of fulness.'—Church Times. CALTHROP.— *Works by the Rev. Gordon Calthrop, M.J. Vicar of St. Augustine's, Highbury.* THE BRAZEN SERPENT, and other Sermons, preached before the University of Cambridge. Crown 8vo. cloth boards, 51
MEMORIALS OF THE LIFE AND MINISTRY OF THE
REV. W. B. MACKENZIE, M.A., late Vicar of St. James's,
Holloway. With Portrait. Crown 8vo. cloth boards, fa.

Second Edilica.
'His distinctiveness lay in the piety of his personal character, the dezvtedness of his pastoral consecration, and the simplicity, earnestness, and success of his preaching.'—British Quarterly Review. CARPENTER.— Short Outline Lessons For Each SUNDAY IN THE CHRISTIAN YEAR. By the Right Rev.
V. Boyd Carpenter, D.D., Bishop of Ripon. i6mo. *8d.;* cloth boards, *is.*
CENTRAL AFRICA.—A Monthly Record of the Work of the
Universities' Mission. 8vo. Monthly, *id.* Volumes, cloth boards, *is.*
Cloth cases for binding the year's numbers, *Sd.*
CHATTERBOX.—Weekly, One Halfpenny; Monthly, in Wrapper,.
Annual Volumes,containing about Two Hundred Full-page Illustrations,
Illustrated paper boards, cloth back, *y.;* extra cloth, bevelled boards,
gilt edges, 5. Cloth cases for binding the year's issue, *is.* each.
A few copies of the following Volumes are still in print:— y. Edition—1883, 1884, i88s, 1886. 5. Edition—1883, 1885, 1886.
This is the most popular children's magazine ever published. In artview ofchildren's books the Times *says of the volume edition:* 'Chatterbox is one of the best children's books we have seen.'
CHATTERBOX CHRISTMAS-BOX.-Edited by Santa Clads. It contains an Oleograph, two Chromos, four Monochromes, besides Stories from Fairyland, Tales, Sketches, Songs, Puzzles, Games, &c Price *is.*

£j —11 LD-NATU RE.—By One of the Autrirs of Child-World.' Illustrated. Small square 16mo. cloth boards, gilt edges, 6d. CHILD'S OWN STORY-BOOK.—In Short Words and Large Type. With Coloured Plates by T. PYM. Square i6mo. extra cloth boards, *is. 6d.* Second Edition.
'Six dozen capital stories. Will amuse little ones who are just beginning to feel an interest in reading to themselves.'—Literary WORLd.
CHORISTER'S ADMISSION CARD.—Contains Reasons and Motives for joining the Choir, with space for name, &c. On Card in Red and Black. *2d.* CHURCH CONGRESS REPORTS. NOTTINGHAM, 1871. *Out of print.* BRIGHTON, 1874. 8vo. paper covers, *$s. 6J.;* cloth boards, *6s. 6d.* STOKE-ON-TRENT, 1875. 8vo. paper covers, 5. *6d.;* cloth boards, dr. 6. /. PLYMOUTH, 1876. 8vo. paper covers, 5. *6d.;* cloth boards, *6s. 6d.* CHURCH WORK.—A Record of Home and Foreign Church Work. Monthly, &/. Post free for a year to all parts of the World, *"Js.* Cloth cases for binding six months' numbers, *is.*
The following Volumes *of Mission Life* are still in print:— 1867-1870, reduced to *y. 6J.* each; 1871 (Part II. only), 1872-1886,3. 6d. each vol. of six months. *KA well-edited repository of news from every part of the Mission field.'*

Nonconformist. CLARKE.—COMMON-LIFE SERMONS. By the Rev. J. Erskine Clarke, M.A., Vicar of Battersea, Hon. Canon of Winchester. Fcap. Svo. cloth limp, *2s.;* cloth boards, *2s. 6d.* 6th Thousand.
Works edited by the Rev. /. Erskine Clarke, M.A. CHILDREN'S HOME HYMN-BOOK. Royal 32mo. *id.;* cloth, *2d.* CHILDREN'S SCHOOL HYMN-BOOK. Royal 32010. *id.;* cloth, *2d.* GOOD STORIES. The earlier numbers, consisting of 180 Complete
Stories. Illustrated, in an Ornamental Cover, *yi.* each. A List forwarded on application.
The following Volumes, strongly bound in cloth boards, *Is. 3d.* each, will be found most useful in Village and Lending Libraries:—
ALICE AND HER CROSS, and Other Sto-

ries (Temperance).
COLONEL ROLFE'S STORY (Soldiers).
CONSULTING THE FATES, and Other Stories (Young Women).
FOUR LADS AND THEIR LIVES, and Other Stories
(Confirmation).
GREGORY OF THE FORETOP, and Other Stories (Sailors).
JACK STEDMAN, and Other Stories (Young Men).
MARTIN GAY THE SINGER, and Other Stories (Temperance).
NETHER STONEY, and Other Stories (Temperance).
CLARKE.— *Works edited by Rev. J. Erskine Clarke, M.A.— (Continued.)*
RHODA'S SECRET, and Other Stories (Young Women).
THE FORTUNE-TELLER, and Other Stories (Young Women).
THE RAINHILL FUNERAL, and Other Stories (Tradesmen).
THE PARISH LIBRARY. Illustrated. 18mo. cloth boards, price
is. each.
CAN SHE KEEP A SECRET? DEB CLINTON, THE SMUGGLER'S DAUGHTER. LUCY GRAHAM. OLD ANDREW THE PEACE-MAKER.
THE CLOCKMAKER OF ST. LAURENT.
THE PARISH MAGAZINE. Illustrated, Monthly, *id.;* cloth uses for binding the year's numbers, *id.;* post free for a year, *is. 6d.*
The following Volumes are still to be had, and will be found very popular for School Libraries, Prizes, and for Lending to Sick Folk:— *ix. 6d.* Edition— 1861, 1864, 1866, 1879, 1884, 1885, 1886.
2s. Edition—1859, 1861, 1862, 1864, 1866, 1867, 1868, 1869, 1870, 1871, 1873, 1874, 1877, 1879, 1882, 1883, 1884, 1885, 1886. *This was the first and the most popular Magazine adapted for localisation. Both the Archbishops, and nearly the whole of the Bishops, have from time Is time contributed to its pages. 'Hints on Localising the Parish Magazine' will be forwarded on application.* THE PRIZE. For Boys and Girls. Monthly, *id.;* illustrated with numerous Engravings and one Coloured Picture. Cloth cases for binding the year's numbers, *is.* Post free for a year, *is. 6d.* Each Volume contains about One Hundred Illustrations.
Volumes, *is. 2d.* paper cover; *is. 6i.* Illustrated paper boards; *2s.* cloth boards; *2s. 6d.* extra cloth boards, gilt edges.
Some copies of the following Volumes are still in print:— *is. 2d.* Edition—1881, 1882, 1884, 1885, 1886.
is. 6d. Edition—1871, 1877, 1883, 1884, 1885, 1886. *2s.* Edition—1874, 1883, 1884, 1885, 1886. *2s. 6d.* Edition—1868, 1879, 1883, 1884, 1885, 1886. *A New Series, with Coloured Illustrations, commenced with the fartwy issue for* 1882. *The Volumes are most attractive, and contain Thirtet Coloured Plates and numerous Engravings. 'A well-illustrated monthly serial of such literature as is calculated to pleas' and benefit the younger boys and girls of our Sunday-schools. "The Children's Prize" is a meritorious and useful publication. For its special purpose— reward and encouragement of industry and intelligence in the classes of schxls for poor children—no better work lies upon our table.'*—Athen.eum. COBB.— *Works by James F. Cobb.* MARTIN THE SKIPPER. A Tale for Boys and Sea-faring
Folk. Illustrated. Cr. 8vo. cloth boards, *3s. 6d.* 8th Thousand.
'We should imagine those queer folk indeed who could not read this st&J with eager interest and pleasure, be they boys or girls, young or old. We comfit sufficiently commend the style in which the book is written, and the religions spirit which pervades it.'— CHRISTIAN World. COBB.— *Works by James F. Cobb.—Continued!)* OFF TO CALIFORNIA. A Tale of the Gold Country.
Adapted from the Flemish of Hendrik Conscience. Illustrated by
A. Forestier. Crown 8vo. cloth boards, *y. 6d.*
'The scene of this story is laid in exciting times. The adventurers go through the greatest perils; and though they find a wonderful treasure in the pool of a mountain .... This is a good story of its kind, told with spirit, and admirable in tone and moral.'— SPECTatOR.
'This is a capital story for boys, full of adventure and stirring incident, but of excellent tone and good moral tendency. There are half-a-dozen spirited illustrations, and the book is attractively bound.'—NONCONFORMIST.
THE WATCHERS ON THE LONGSHIPS. A Tale of Cornwall in the Last Century. Illustrated by Davidson Knowles. Crown 8vo. cloth boards, *y. (id.* 16th Edition.
'A capital story, and one we heartily commend to boy readers, both gentle and simple.'—Guardian. THE CONFIRMATION SERVICE. — With Prayers for Candidates, to be used during the Service. With Commendatory Note by the Bishop Of Bedford. Fcap. 8vo. *d.; 6s.* per 100.
30th Thousand. // is believed that this will supply a long-felt want, and will be very helpful in supplying the Candidates with suitable thoughts during the pauses in the Service. CONVOCATION REPORTS. THE SALE OF ADVOWSONS AND THE AUGMENTA-
TION OF SMALL LIVINGS. Second Report of the Lower
House of the Convocation of Canterbury, July 1879. *qd.*
THE RELATIONS OF CHURCH AND STATE. —A Full
Report of the Committee of Convocation of Canterbury, July 1879. *$d.*
THE RUBRICS OF THE BOOK OF COMMON PRAYER.
The Report of Convocation of Canterbury, as presented to Her
Majesty the Queen, in obedience to the Royal Letters of Business, on
July 31, 1879. *is.*
THE CORAL MISSIONARY MAGAZINE.— A Record of
Missionary Work among the Working Classes and in the Church Missionary Schools and Stations abroad. Monthly, *id.;* Post free for a year to all parts of the World, *u. 6d.;* Volumes, cloth, *is. 6d.* each; cloth cases for a year's numbers, *8d.* COWPER.—HELP AT HAND; or, What shall we do in Accidents or Illness? By Countess Cowper. Numerous Illustrations. Fcap. 8vo. paper cover, *3d.* cloth, *6d.* Second Edition.

'The directions are adequate, concise, and unmistakably clear.'—ThE WORLd. *'Thoroughly sensible and practical in tone.'*—ThE SCOTSMAN.
CROMPTON.—A TALE OF THE CRUSADES. By Sarah Crompton. Fcap. 8vo. cloth boards, is. *Sir W. Scott's 'Talisman' in Short Words.* CUTTS.— THE BREAKING OF THE BREAD: An Explanation of the Holy Communion, with Notes on the Communion Service. By the Rev. E. L. Cutts, B.A., D.D., Vicar of Holy Trinity, Haverstock Hill. 18mo. extra cloth boards, red edges, 2s. *'A valuable aid to the pastor in preparing lectures to communicants'*
The Living Church. DANIEL.— *Works by the Rev. Evan Daniel, M.A., Principal of the National Society's Training College, Battersea; Hon. Canon of Rochester.* THE DAILY OFFICES AND LITANY. Being an Introduction to the Study of the Prayer-Book. Specially designed for the Use of National Schools and Sunday Schools. Fcap. 8vo. *SJ.*; cloth boards, *lat.* 8th Thousand.
THE PRAYER-BOOK: Its History, Language, and Contents.
Crown 8vo. cloth boards, *6s.* Twelfth Edition.
'So large, wide, and speedy a circulation is proof at once of the interest which the subject possesses, and of the high merit of this treatise on it The "glossarial notes" on the Prayer-book version of the Psalms are a peculiar and valuable ingredient in this scrz:iceable volume; so also are the condensed, but pregnant, remarks upon the "Propria" for each of Me Sundays and festivals, which will often furnish most valuable hints and references for the Sunday-school teacher and the preacher.'— Guardian. Second Notice. DE TEISSIER.
—The Parables Of Our Lord Jesus CHRIST PRACTICALLY SET FORTH. By the Rev. G. F. De Teissier, B.D., Rector of Church-Brampton. Fcap. 8vo. cloth limp, 2s. *6J.*; cloth boards, 5. DICTIONARY OF THE ENGLISH CHURCH, ANCIENT AND MODERN. Crown 8vo. cloth boards, *ys. 6d.* 'Besides containing much information, ecclesiastical and historical, is also of considerable practical utility. The writer is impartial and trustworthy'
Spectator. DIVINE FELLOWSHIP.—A Daily Text-Book. 18mo. cloth boards, gd. DIX.— *Works by the Rev. Morgan D/.y, Rector of Holy Trinity, New York.* SERMONS, DOCTRINAL AND PRACTICAL. Crown 8vo.
cloth boards, 2s. 6d. THE GOSPEL AND PHILOSOPHY. Six Lent Lectures. Crown 8vo. cloth boards, *y. 6d.* 'A book calculated to be eminently useful. .... Space will not alloz? us t give any more quotations, as we should gladly do, but we most earnestly rciommctnt this work for general use.'—Guardian. THE DRIVER'S BOX, and Other Stories. With Ten Full-pe Coloured Illustrations. Crown 8vo. cloth boards, 3. *6J.*
This volume contains the lollowing Stories:—
The Driver's Box.
St. Christopher.
Mrs. Milsom's Supper Party.
Sir Arnold.
The Young Recruit.
The Escape.
The Last Will And Testament.
Rock Cottage.
A Superior Girl.
The Olive Gleaners.
Guv's Secret.
Conscience Monev.
John's Mistake.
DUMBLETON.— *Works by the Rev. E. N. Dumbleton, M.A. Rector of St. James's, Exeter.* FORMS OF PRAYER to accompany Sermons and Instructions, for use in Churches and Mission Rooms with the approval of the Ordinary. Crown 8vo. o/.
PRAYERS AND MEDITATIONS FOR THE MORNING
AND EVENING OF EACH DAY OF THE WEEK.
Chiefly in the Words of Holy Scripture. Fcap. 8vo. cloth boards, *1s. 6d.*
SPECIAL SERVICES FOR THE CHURCH SEASONS, for use in Churches and Mission Rooms with the approval of the Ordinary. Advent, 2d; 6s. per 50. Lent, 2d.; 6s. per 50. Easter,
2d; 6s. per 50. Ascensiontide and Whitsuntide, 2d.; 6s. per 50.
EDITH VERNON'S LIFE-WORK.—By the Author of 'Harry's Battles,' 'Susie's Flowers,' &c. &c. Crown 8vo. extra cloth boards, 3s. *6d.*
Twelfth Edition. *'A very pretty story, very well told.'*—liter Ary Churchman.
EDMUNDS.—SIXTY SERMONS: Adapted to the Sundays and Principal Holy-days of the Christian Year. By the Rev. John Edmunds, M.A., formerly Fellow of the University of Durham. Fcap. 8vo. cloth boards, 3. *6d.* ELLISON. — HOLY MATRIMONY: the Married Life of the Christian Man and Woman. By the Rev. Henry T. Ellison, M.A., Rector of Haseley, Hon. Canon of Christ Church, Chaplain-in-Ordinary to the Queen. Fcap. 8vo. cloth boards, is. *6d.* New Edition.
'jfust the thing to put into the hands of a newly-married couple. The chapters are simple and to the point, and the book is prettily got up.'
Ecclesiastical Gazette. EWING.—A WEEK SPENT IN A GLASS POND, by the Great Water-Beetle. Written by the late Mrs. Ewing, Author of 'Six to Sixteen,' &c-With Illustrations in Colours by R. Andre. 4to. Pictorial Cover, cloth back, paper boards, *y. 6d.* 'A clever little fantasia on the keeping of an aquarium, by Afrs. J. H. Ewintf, than whom a better qualified author on the subject could not have been found.—Morning Post.
THE FAMILY LESSON-BOOK. — Being a Selection of Morning and Evening Readings for the Christian Year. Based upon the Church's Lectionary. Crown 8vo. cloth boards, with silk registers, *1s. 6d.*; leather, *y. 6J.* Upwards of 450 pp.
Each Reading is complete in itself, and ajfoids a simple subject for meditation. Every Holy-day will be found to be conveniently noted, and the Reailings to correspond with its proper teaching. The cheapest book of the kind ever published.
'Those who read portions of the Scriptures in family devotions could not have a better book to guide them. The Festivals of the Church are taken into account, which is not a common feature in books of Daily Readings. It has also another great advantage—it is cheap.'— LITERARY ChUrChMAN.
FAMILY.WORSHIP FOR BUSY HOMES. On Folding

Card, in plain type, *2d.* FARRAR.—THE CHRISTIAN MINISTRY: A Manual ot Church

Doctrine. By the Rev. Thomas Farrar, Rector of St. Paul's, Guiana.
Crown 8vo. cloth boards, *6s.* Third and Enlarged Edition.

'*Mr. Farrar s book is one which we would gladly see in the hands of all Readers, District Visitors, Teachers, and young men preparing for Holy Orders; for the selections have, for the most part, been made from writers who are both learned and clear.*'—Church Times. THE FAVOURITE STORY-BOOK.— A Book for the Little Ones. Profusely Illustrated with Large Pictures, and Easy Reading. The Illustrations are printed in Sepia. Small 4to. cloth boards, *2s.* '*A most attractive volume for juvenile readers. The stories would do very well to read out in school as exercises in composition. The book is handsome enough, however, to deserve a place on the drawing-room or parlour table, where even the older folk might dip into its contents with satisfaction.*'

The Schoolmaster.

Fl ELD.— *Works by Mrs. E. M. Field.* ETHNE.—"Being a truthful historic of the gteat ano final.&cttle» mcnt of jl-relann bp ffHiuer Crointoefl, ant) certain other notcrnortto; Ctienta, from trjc 3lournal» of Ctlne ©'Connor, ano of Soger fetanofast, Captain in the 3rmj of the Commons of CnglanB. Edited by Mrs. E. M. Field. Etched Title and Frontispiece. Large crown 8vo., appropriate cloth boards, *6s.* '*The interest of the story is admirably kept up from beginning to end.*'

Standard.

'*Mrs. Field has succeeded very well; and what is more, she has produced a very attractive and interesting book.... delightfully fresh and picturesque*'
Guardian.

'*Mingled with a certain amount of romance, the story is full of historical detail, shilfully woven together; the interest is maintained throughout. The reader, whatever his religious views, is bound to be charmed with the character of Bthne .... Bui beyond all this we can recommend the book, as being of great merit.*'—Church Times.

'*This is, without exaggeration, one of the most beautiful stories of ancient Irish life that has ever come under our notice. The character of Ethne is a masterpiece.*'—Public Opinion. MIXED PICKLES; A Story-Book for Children. With Illustrations by T. Pym. Square 16mo. fancy cloth boards, *is. 6d.*
'*One of the prettiest records of juvenile pranks*'—GRAPhIC.
FLORAL FANCIES.—A Book of Designs, with Mottoes for Colouring or Drawing. From Designs by G. W. Rhead. 4to. fancy boards, *is.*; cloth, *is. 6d.* '*An ingenious and useful attempt to provide a quiet and rational entertainment for the busy fingers of children.*'—SPECTAtOR.
'*A novelty among children's books.*'— Saturday Review. FLYING LEAVES.— With Prefatory Note by the Rev. the Earl OF

Mulgrave. 32mo. fancy cloth boards, *)d.* '*These little leaves are sent out into the world with the earnest prayer that one of them at least may be wafted to some weary soul, and carry with it one little ray of comfort and hope.* — Introductory' Chapter. FOLLOWING CHRIST: Short Meditations for Busy People.

Adapted from the French. 18mo. cloth limp, *is.* '*Thoroughly practical.*'— SPECTAtOR.
FORDE.—THE OLD SHIP; or, Better than Strength. By H. A.
Forde. With Full-page tinted Illustrations. Cr. 8vo. cloth boards, *y. 6d.* FULTON.— *Works by the Rev. John Fulton, D.D., LL.D. Rector of St. George's Church, St. Louis.* INDEX CANONUM. The Greek Text, an English Translation and Complete Digest of the entire Code of Canon Law of the undivided Primitive Church. Imp. 8vo. cloth boards, Io. 6J. '*We do not know any book on the subject to compare with this in fulness and completeness.*'—GUARDIAN.
THE LAWS OF MARRIAGE: Containing the Hebrew Law, the Roman Law, the Law of the New Testament, and the Canon Law of the Universal Church, concerning the Impediments of Marriage and the Dissolution of the Marriage Bond; Digested and Arranged with Notes and Scholia. Crown 8vo. cloth boards, 7. *6d.* GOOD STORIES.— New Series. Each with a Coloured Frontispiece, Monthly, *3d.*; Series, containing four numbers, bound in extra cloth boards, *is. 6d.*; Seven Volumes, extra cloth boards, gilt edges, 51. each. *The ' Series' are most popular in Village and School Libraries. The 'Volumes' as Prizes or Presents. A complete list forwarded on application.* GORE.— THE CHURCH OF ENGLAND, PAST AND PRESENT. By the Ven. Archdeacon Gore. Crown 8vo. paper cover, *Sd.* Second Edition.

'*Both interesting and helpful .... with an entire absence of controversial temper.*'—Guardian. THE GOSPEL MISSIONARY. — Containing Missionary News, Anecdotes, and Verses suited for Young People. Illustrated. Monthly, One Halfpenny. *Published under the Direction of the S. P. G.* THE GRAIN OF MUSTARD SEED; or, Woman's Work in Foreign Parts. Monthly, *id.* Cloth cases for binding a year's numbers, *id.* Post free for a year to all parts of the World, *Is. 6d. Published by the S. P. G. Ladies' Association for the Promotion of Female Education among the Heathen.* HARRIS. —GOLDEN STEPS: Lectures to Communicants' Classes. By the late Rev. G. C. Harris, M.A. Royal 32mo. *6d.*; cloth boards, red edges, *is.* Third Edition.
HAPPY SUNDAY AFTERNOONS.—A Series of Bible Outlines, printed on Superfine Lined Paper, for the Little Ones to colour and write about. Crown 4to. *is.*; cloth boards, *is. 6d.* '*The publishers improve on the educational idea, which is at the root of the Kindergarten system, of making children teach themselves in their amusements. In "Happy Sunday Afternoons for the Little Ones" this firm, so pleasantly associated with a long history of juvenile recreation, supplies the means of selfimprovement by a series of simple Bible outlines, to colour or write about either from memory or by reference to the Scriptures themselves.*'
The Daily Telegraph. HAPPY SUNDAY AFTERNOONS. —Second Series.

Crown 4to. *is.*; cloth boards, *is. 6d.* HELEN MORTON'S TRIAL, And TIMID LUCY.

With Coloured Illustrations. 18mo. extra cloth boards, *1s. 6d.* HELPS BY THE WAY,—

I. MY MORNING HYMN. I III. MY WEEKLY QUESTIONS. II. MY DAILY RULES. IV. MY CONFESSION TO GOI).

Printed in red and black, 8vo. *id.* Second Edition.

HER GREAT AMBITION.—A Story for Little Boys and Girls. With Thirty Illustrations. Small crown 4to. cloth, bevelled boards, *2s. 6J.* 'A delightful story delightfully told. A little orphan girl comes to live with her uncle, a widower with several boys. At first her cousins dislike the idea of Dolly coming to live with them, because she is a girl. But she makes herself so pleasant and useful that they soon can do nothingwithout her kelp. Dolly s "great ambition " is to do something heroic for her uncle, whom she loves very much. At last the occasion she so ardently desired comes,' etc.—Saturday Review. HIGH WAGES AND OTHER STORIES. Ten Full-page coloured Illustrations. Crown 8vo. cloth, bevelled boards, 3. *6d.*

This volume contains the following popular Stories:—

High Wages.
Look To The End.
Saving And Spending.
Jean Ross.
Spilling Water.
The Last Straw.
'Bet.'
Twenty Minutes Late.
Diki Iculties Of A Business Woman.
Tittle-tattle.
Gipsies.

HOBART.— *Works by the Hon. Mrs. C. Hobart, nee N. P. W.* THE CHANGED CROSS. With Outline Illustrations by H. J. A.

Miles. Square 16mo. cloth, bevelled boards, gilt edges, *is. 6d.*

Twentieth Edition.

THE CHANGED CROSS. Set to Music by George Carter. 4.

THE CLOUD AND THE STAR. With Outline Illustrations by

H.J. A. Miles. Square i6mo. cloth, bevelled boards, gilt edges, *is. 6d.*

Second Edition.

HOBSON.—AIDS TO THE STUDY OF THE BOOKS OF SAMUEL. By the Rev. Edwin Hobson, M.A., Principal of St. Katharine's College, Tottenham. Fcap. 8vo. cloth boards, 2 vols. I. *6d.* each, or I vol. complete, with Map, *2s. 6d.* 'No difficulty is left unexplained, and the contents of the book are admirably summarised.'—The Schoolmaster. HOLINESS TO THE LORD; The Character of the Christian

Priest. Adapted from the French of the Abbe Dubois for the use of the

English Clergy. With an Introduction by the Bishop Ok Carlisle.

Crown 8vo. cloth boards, *Js. 6d.*

'A volume of practical teaching, which every member of the Church will be the better for applying practically,'—John Bull. HOME.—THE WRATH OF THE FAY, By F. Wyville Home. Author of 'Songs of a Wayfarer,' 'Lay Canticles,' tc. Illustrated. Small 4to. cloth, bevelled boards, *2s. 6d.* 'The great charm of this pretty little gift-book lies in the hoice of the simplest words. It is one of the purest specimens of English rhyme.'—Schoolmaster. HONOR BRIGHT; or, The Four-Leaved Shamrock. By the

Author of 'One of a Covey,' 'Robin and Linnet,' &c. Illustrated Frontispiece and Title-page. Large crown 8vo. cloth boards, *y. 6d.*

Fifth Edition.

'A cheery, sensible, and healthy tale.'—The Times. HOPKINS.— *Works by the Rev. W. B. Hopkins, B.D., Vicar of Littleport, Cambridge.*

HOLY SCRIPTURE: Temperance and Total Abstinence. Fcap.

8vo. cloth boards, *is.* Third Thousand.

'// will repay study either by the total abstainer or moderate drinker.'

Daily Review. THE POSITION AND DUTY OF NON-ABSTAINERS WITH REFERENCE TO THE TEMPERANCE CAUSE.

8vo. 4//. Second Edition.

HOW TO ENSURE A HAPPY NEW YEAR. On Card, *u.* HOW.—*Works by the Right Rev. W. Walsh Am How, D.D. Bishop of Bedford and Suffragan of London.*

THE BALLAD OF THE CHORISTER BOY. Illustrated by H. J. A. Miles. With Floral Decorations by E. C. Gardner. Small

4to. Illustrated cover, delicately bound with silk ribbon, gilt edges, *ls.6d.* THE BOY HERO. A Story founded on Fact. Illustrated by II. J. A. Miles. Oblong, paper boards, ir. *6J.*; fancy cloth, bevelled boards, gilt edges, *2s.* 'A pathetic story, founded on fact, of a boy of six .... The incident occurred not lung ago at Bristol.'—Spectator.

'*The illustrations are very well drawn.*'—Saturday Review.

A PRAYER FOR THE PARISH. On Card, in red and black, *id.*

A SERVICE FOR THE ADMISSION OF A CHORISTER.

In red and black. *2d.* CANTICLES POINTED FOR CHANTING, WITH APPROPRIATE CHANTS. 410. paper covers, *is.*

CONFIRMATION SERVICE. Directions for the Clergy and

Churchwardens. Free on application.

DAILY FAMILY PRAYER. Fcap. 8vo. cloth boards, *is. 6d.*

Twelfth Edition.

IS" A Sixpenny Edition, in large type, cloth boards, is now ready. This volume will be found most suitable for parochial distribution, and is the cheapest book of Family Prayers yet published. HOLY COMMUNION. For those who need Encouragement. W. per Packet of Twenty. 185th Thousand.

HYMNS. Complete Edition. Fcap. 8vo. paper cover, *6d.* MORNING AND EVENING PRAYER FOR A CHILD.

Cloth, *Id.* NOTES ON THE CHURCH SERVICE. Fcap. 8vo. cloth, *ji.*

The Goon Shepherd.
A Fresh Start.
The Bread Of Life.
Christ Knocking At The Door.

HOW.— *Works by Right Rev. W. Walsham How.—Continued.)*

LETTER BOOKLETS.

Crosses.
Despondency.
How To Prepare For Holy Communion.
Repentance And Faith.

Each in Packets, 20 per *6ii.* A specimen set, 3'/.

PASTORAL WORK. Fcap. 8vo. cloth boards, *2s.* 6rf.

'The Bishop of Bedford's long and varied experience as a clergyman gives him a right to publish a volume on "Pastoral Work."... The volume contains some practical suggestions which have the merit of freshness, and some practical hints about preaching; and as they are given with the homely simplicity which is part of the charm of the Bishop's character, they are likely to stick in the memory. We refrain from giving extracts because the book is short, and cheap, and worth buying.'—Saturday Review.

'There is not a dull page in "Lectures on Pastoral Work." '—Guardian. PASTOR IN PAROCHIA. With the Appendix. Fcap. 8vo. cloth boards, red edges, 3. 6/.; leather limp, Jr.; calf limp antique, lor. 6d. Also morocco plain, and best flexible morocco, red under gold edges, 12s. 6d. Fifteenth Edition.

PLAIN WORDS. First Series. Sixty Short Sermons for the Poor, and for Family Reading. Fcap. 8vo. cloth, turned in, 2s.; cloth, bevelled boards, red edges, 2s. 6d. Large-type Edition, cloth boards, y. 6d. Forty-ninth Edition.

PLAIN WORDS. Second Series. Short Sermons for the Sundays and Chief Holy-days of the Christian Year. Fcap. 8vo. cloth, turned in, 2s.; cloth, bevelled boards, red edges, 2s. (xi. Large-type Edition, cloth boards, y. 6d. Thirtieth Edition.

Vols. I. and II., in one vol. cloth boards, 4. 6r/.

PLAIN WORDS. Third Series. Forty Meditations with a View to the Deepening of the Spiritual Life. Fcap. 8vo. cloth limp, 2s.; cloth, bevelled boards, red edges, 2s. 6d. Large-type Edition, cloth boards, 3-f. &/. Seventeenth Edition. PLAIN WORDS. Fourth Series. Forty Readings for those who desire to Pray Better. Fcap. 8vo. cloth limp, turned in, 2s.; cloth, bevelled boards, red edges, 2s. 6J. Seventh Edition.

Vols. III. and IV. in one, cloth boards, 4s. 6d. PLAIN WORDS, as Tracts. Series I.-III., in Large Type, 21. 6J. each Series.

A Selection from 'Plain Words,' for Parochial Distribution, in smaller type, u. per packet: three kinds. PLAIN WORDS TO CHILDREN. Fcap. 8vo. cloth limp, turned in, 2s.; crown 8vo. cloth, bevelled boards, 2s. 6d. Third Edition. POEMS. Complete Edition. Fcap. 8vo. cloth boards, gilt edges, y. 6J. Without the Hymns, 3. Tree calf, or calf half extra, Js. f£/.

PRIVATE LIFE AND MINISTRATIONS OF THE PARISH

PRIEST. Royal 32mo. cloth, 6d.

RESOLUTION.0. FOR THOSE RECOVERING FROM

SICKNESS. On Card, in red and black, 12 copies in packet, /.

REVISION OF THE RUBRICS. An Historical Survey of all

that has been done since the issue of the Ritual Commission in 1867.

Demy 8vo. ix.

HOW.— Works by Right Rev. W. Walsh Am How.—Continued.) SCRIPTURE READINGS. Selected Passages for Reading to the Sick. The Appendix to 'Pastor in Parochia.' Fcap. 8vo. cloth boards, is. 6d. SEVEN LENTEN SERMONS ON PSALM LI. Fcap. 8vo.

cloth limp, turned in, is. Thirteenth Edition.

SUGGESTIONS FOR OBSERVING THE DAY OF IN-

TERCESSION FOR FOREIGN MISSIONS. I,/.;6. per

ICO. loth Thousand.

THE EVENING PSALTER POINTED FOR CHANTING.

Oblong cloth limp, 6d.

TWENTY-FOUR PRACTICAL SERMONS. Fcap. 8vo. cloth limp, turned in, 2s.; cloth boards, red edges, 2s. 6d. Twelfth Edition.

TWO ADDRESSES ON HOLY MARRIAGE. id. VESTRY PRAYERS WITH A CHOIR. On Card, in red and black, id.

'WAS LOST, AND IS FOUND.' A Tale of the London Mission,

1874. With Outline Illustrations by H. J. A. Miles. Square 16mo.

cloth, bevelled boards, gilt edges, is. 6d. 'A really spirited religious ballad, artistically, yet gracefully illustrated.'

The Times. WORDS OF GOOD CHEER. Fcap. 8vo. cloth limp, Is. 6d.; small crown 8vo. cloth, bevelled boards, 2s. 6d. HOW.—WEEK-DAY SERVICES IN COUNTRY CHURCHES.

By the Rev. F. Douglas How, M.A. 6d. HOW TO PRAY THE LORD'S PRAYER. —32TM. id. 6s. per 100. loth Thousand.

'In the plainest type and language. We can earnestly commend it for distribution, as likely to be most useful. '—Guardian. HUTTON.—THE SUN OF RIGHTEOUSNESS: Meditations on the Earlier Ministry of our Lord. By the Rev. Vernon V. Hutton, M.A., Prebendary of Lincoln. Crown Svo. cloth boards, e,s.

Second Edition.

IN A QOOD CAUSE. — A Collection of Stories, Poems, and Illustrations. Edited by Mrs. Tyssen Amherst. Fcap. 4to. bound in white, $s. net.

'" In a Good Cause " they will find Mr. Quaritch enlisted with a pleasant little tale; Mr. Oscar Wilde with a poem in which philanthropy accompanies agreeable fancy; Mr. Anstey with a comically distressing tale about a kitten; Mr. Kider Haggard with a hunting story Jrom Zululand; and other writers. All illustrated by Mr. Caldecott, Mr. Carter, Mr. Tristram Ellis, and other artists. '—Daily News.

'The literature includes stories by Mr. W. R. S. Ralston, Mr. Anstey, Mrs. Cashel Hoey, Lady Augusta Noel, Lady Constance Howard, and others. Mr. H. Rider Haggard tells a capital hunter s yarn of the most thrilling description, and Mr. Andrew Lang contributes a characteristic poem.'—Saturday Review.

'One of the prettiest books of the season. Seldom has an Editor been so successful in enlisting the aid of distinguished authors.' — EDINBURGh

Daily Review. INGELOW.— Works by Jean Iageloiv. MOPSA THE FAIRY. Illustrated. Crown 8vo. cloth boards, y. 6J.

A SISTER'S BYE-HOURS. Illustrated. Crown 8vo. cloth boards, 3r. 6d. Third Edition.

STORIES TOLD TO A CHILD. Illustrated. Crown 8vo. cloth boards, 3. 6ti.

STUDIES FOR STORIES FROM GIRLS' LIVES. Illustrated.

Crown 8vo. cloth boards, 3. 6V/. Sixth Edition.

JACKSON.—BALLADS OF LIFE AND

HOME. By the Rev. E. Stanway Jackson. Crown 8vo. cloth boards, *y. 6d.* JENYNS.—A BOOK ABOUT BEES. Their History, Habits, and Instincts; also the First Principles of Modern Bee-keeping, for Young Readers. By the Rev. F. G. Jenyns, M.A., Rector of Knebworth. With numerous Illustrations. Crown 8vo. cloth, bevelled boards, 3. 6d. School Edition, *is. txi.* 'As a reading-book we may call it excellent. It is written in the most interesting style, full of information, and well graded. It should be in all our country schools especially, for the knowledge obtained can be turned to practical account there. Mr. fenyns has done sen-ice, both to the School and the State, in bringing out this book, and 70c wish it a very wide circulation, not only for its intrinsic value as a reading-book, but for the benefit it is capable of conferring upon our agricultural labourers.'—SCHOOLMASTER.

'The style is simple and clear, and Mr. Jenyns' pages hare that indescribable charm sometimes met with in books on natural history, which is the outcome of a deep and real sympathy on the part of the writer with his subject. The book is abundantly supplied with good engravings. It is educational in the best sense of the term, and wilt be found no less interesting to the general reader than to those for whom it is particularly intended. A capital rewardbook for Day and Sunday-school Scholars, and we trust that it wiltfind a place on the shelves of many a parish library.'—School Guakdian. JONES.— *Works by C. A. /ones.*
COUNT UP THE SUNNY DAYS. A Story for Boys and Girls.
Illustrated. Large crown 8vo. cloth, bevelled boards, *y. 6J.*
FOUR LITTLE SIXES: A Story for Boys and Girls. Illustrated. Square 16mo. cloth boards, *is. 6d.*
LITTLE JEANNETON'S WORK: A Chronicle of Breton Life, with upwards of Thirty Illustrations. Crown 8vo. cloth, bevelled boards, 3.5. 6d. 'This " Chronicle of Breton Life" is a story of the old regime. Jeanneto is a farmer's daughter, and being taken up by the great people at the Castle *tf* Kerlionik, is not a little spoilt by their favcur.... It is a pretty little story, well put together, and brought round at last to a satisfactory endtny.' Spectator.

'The little woodcuts scattered about the text increase the attractions of tit volume.'—Daily News. JONES.— *Works by C. A. Jones.—Continued.)* ONLY A GIRL: A Story of a Quiet Life. A Tale of Brittany.
Adapted from the French. With upwards of Forty Illustrations.
Crown 8vo. cloth, bevelled boards, gilt edges, *y. 6d.*
'We can thoroughly recommend this brightly written and homely narrative.'
S Al U KDAY R KVIEW.
UNDER THE KING'S BANNER. Stories of the Soldiers of
Christ in all Ages. With Introduction by the Bishop Of Bedford.
Outline Illustrations by John Sadler. Square 161110. cloth boards,
2s. 6d.
'Miss Jones has hit upon an excellent idea, and quite dcserz'cs the commendation bestowed on her design by the Bishop of Bedford.... The book is one which the children will read, probably with interest, and certainly with edification.'—Saturday Review. JOSA. —'THE APOSTLE OF THE INDIANS OF GUIANA.' A Memoir of the Life and Labours of the Rev. W. H. Brett, B.D. For Forty Years a Missionary in British Guiana. By the Kev. F. P. L. Josa, Rector of Holy Trinity, Essequibo. With Portrait and Illustrations. Crown 8vo. cloth boards, *6s.* KING.—ADDINGTON VENABLES, BISHOP OF NASSAU.
A Sketch of his Life and Labours for the Church of God. By the Rev. W. F. H. King, M.A., Commissary to the late Bishop. With Portrait, Map, and Illustrations. Crown 8vo. cloth, bevelled boards, *y,* 6V.
'His life was one of utter self-denial and sheer hard work for God and His Church.'—John Bull. KIP.—THE DOUBLE WITNESS OF THE CHURCH. By the Right Rev. W. Ingraham Kin, D.D., LL. D., Bishop of California.
Crown 8vo. cloth boards, *2s. 6d.*
This edition of Bishop Kifls' fofttlar Lectures on the Principles of the Church is the authorised reprint of the 22nd American edition.
THE LAND OF LIGHT: A Transcript from the Rhythm of Bernard de Morlaix. With Outline Illustrations by H. J. A. Miles. Square 16mo. cloth, bevelled boards, gilt edges, *Is. bti.* Uniform with 'The Changed Cross.' 'We have seldom seen a more beautiful little booklet.'—ChURCh TIMES.
LAY.—STUDIES IN THE CHURCH; Being Letters to an Oldfashioned Layman. By the Right Rev. Henry C. Lay, D.D., LL. D., Bishop of Easton, U.S.A. i8mo. cloth, bevelled boards, *2s. 6d.* 'Full of clear sound common sense and manly piety, which cannot but enlist the reader s sympathy. The Bishop deals with his subject from an intellectual, doctrinal, and practical point of view.... Laymen cannot but appreciate his broad sympathies.'—GUARDIAN. LEE.—PRAYERS FOR CHILDREN. By the Rev. HENRY W. Lee. i8mo. cloth boards, I.
B
'LEFT TILL CALLED FOR.'—By the Author of 'From Donothing Hall to Happy-Day House.' With Outline Illustrations by J. Sadler. Oblong, cloth boards, *is.* The story of a little boy left at a railway station on Christmas Eve.
LETTER OF COMMENDATION: A Card in Red and Black for giving to Parishioners on leaving a Parish. *6d.* per packet of 12.
LETTERS TO OUR WORKING PARTY.—By the Author of ' Miss Toosey's Mission,' &c. Fcap. 8vo. cloth boards, I. *6J.*
'11 'hether hopeful or the contrary, they show genuine feeling and deep sympathy with the sufferings of the poor, and a desire to excite the sympathies of others in their behalf.'—Morning Post. LEWIS. —YOUNG MEN'S BIBLE CLASSES AND HOW TO MANAGE THEM. By M. A. Lewis. Paper covers, *6d.* LITTLE FABLES FOR LITTLE FOLKS, which Great

Ones may Read. With Nineteen Illustrations. 18mo. cloth boards, *is* LITTLE HELPS FOR DAILY TOILERS.—By a working

Associate of the Girls' Friendly Society. With Prefatory Note by the Bishop Of Bedford. Royal 32010. fancy cloth boards, *gd.*

LITTLE LAYS FOR LITTLE LIPS.— With Outline Illustrations by H. J. A. Miles. Square 16mo. cloth, bevelled boards, gilt edges, 11.

Seventh Edition.

LITTLE PAINTER'S TEXT-BOOK.—Simple Outlines to Colour or Illuminate. 410. coloured boards, is.; cloth, ir. fsd.

A LOST PIECE OF SILVER. By the Author of 'Edith Vernon's Life-Work,' &c. Illustrated. Large crown 8vo. cloth boards extra, JJ. 6V.

'This is a simple, pathetic little story, which has the look of being true: tnu, that is, in the sense of being faithful to life.... Told without exoggeratim, without any fine writing, but with very considerable power.'—SpfcCT At OR.

LOVING COUNSELS TO A YOUNG FRIEND: Before and After Confirmation. Fcap. 8vo. cloth boards, is. 6d. MACLAGAN.—Words Of Counsel Addressed To CONFIRMATION CANDIDATES ON THE EVE OF

CONFIRMATION DAY. By the Right Rev. W. D. Maclagan, D.D., Bishop of Lichfield. Fcap. 8vo. 3'/.

MACRITCHIE.—BV THE SEA OF GALILEE. A Poem. By Margaret S. Macritchie. Tinted Outline Illustrations by H. J. A. Miles. Square 16mo. cloth, bevelled boards, gilt edges, i. 6d.

MARRIAGE SERVICE.—Printed in Red and Black with Illustrations, and a Marriage Chorale. Bound in white and gold, 6'/.; or white silk, $s. MAY.—THE CHRISTIAN COURSE; or, Helps to the Practice of Meditation. By the Rev. Thomas May, M.A., Vicar of Leigh, Tunbridge. With Preface by the Bishop Of Bedford. Royal 8vo. cloth boards, %s. Fourth Edition, Corrected and Enlarged. IVIILES.— Works Illustrated by H. J. A. Miles. OUTLINE PICTURES FOR LITTLE PAINTERS. 4to. in chromo-lithographic wrapper, I.; cloth, ix. 6d. Printed in sepia on grey paper specially made for the purpose.

'The idea is excellent, and the style of work good. Some of the pictures are thoroughly well drawn.'—Journal Of Education. TILES FROM DAME MARJORIE'S CHIMNEY-CORNER, AND CHINA FROM HER CUPBOARD.—See Burne, p. 3.

MISSION FIELD.— Containing a variety of Missionary Information, with a Record of the Proceedings of the S. P. G. Monthly, 2d. Post free for a year to all parts of the World, y. MISSIONARY CONFERENCES.—Report Of The MISSIONARY CONFERENCE HELD AT LONDON, 1875.

Crown 8vo. paper, 2s. 6d.; cloth, y.

REPORT OF THE MISSIONARY CONFERENCE HELD

AT OXFORD, 1877. Crown 8vo. paper, 2s. 6d.; cloth, 3s.

MISSIONARY PRAYERS For The Extension Of CHRIST'S CHURCH AT HOME AND ABROAD. For

Private and Family Use. 18mo. paper covers, 6d.; cloth boards, is. MITCHELL. —THE SUFFERER'S GUIDE. By Elizabeth Harcourt Mitchell, Author of 'The Beautiful Face,' &c. Edited by the Rev. T. T. Carter, M.A. Crown 8vo. cloth boards, y. 6d. This Volume consists of Three Parts:—On Suffering in General—On Spiritual Sufferings—Suffering a Means of Perfection. Second Edition.

MONTH BY MONTH.—Poems for Children. With Twelve Illustrations by T. Pym. Sq. 16mo. cloth, bevelled boards, gilt edges, is. 6d. 'We hardly know which to praise most, the quaint little illustrations or the poetry '—Church Times. MOORE.—SIMPLE GUIDE TO CHURCH DOCTRINE: Being an Explanation of the Church Catechism in Question and Answer, with Notes and Scripture Proofs. By Blanche Moore. 16mo. $d. Third Edition. MORNING STAR: Daily Texts for Little Children. Printed in red and black, 32mo. extra cloth boards, gd. The texts selected are specially simple and plain. MOTHER'S UNION.—Containing Morning and Evening Prayers and Four simple Resolutions, in red and black, id.; ts. per loo.

N. OR M.—By the Author of 'Honor Bright,' "Peas-Blossom," One of a Covey,' &c. With numerous Illustrations by H. J. Miles. Large crown 8vo. cloth, bevelled boards, y. 6d. 'It is possible that objection may be taken to the somewhat touching end with which the author of "Honor Bright" closes her new story. If so, it will be the only fault that is likely to be found with a most thoroughly charming and delightful tale.... Nolly and Molly are two bright, luppy girls, full of fun and merriment, and not too good to be altogether acceptable to youthful readers. ... The illustrations are plentiful, and are of a quality that will prove entirely satisfactory to young readers. In every way an acceptable gift-book.'—GUARDIAN.

NORTON.— Works by the Rev. J. G. Norton, M.A., Rector of Christ Church Cathedral, Montreal. HEARTY SERVICES: or, Revived Church Worship. Crown 8vo. cloth, bevelled boards, y. 6d. Third Edition. WORSHIP IN HEAVEN AND ON EARTH: Responsive, Congregational, Reverent, Musical, and Beautiful. Demy 8vo. cloth boards, iZf. 6d. 'Canada has just afforded us, in Mr. Norton's " Worship in Heaven and on Earth," a good instance of Evangelical Churchmanship, united with learning and toleration. His work will prove attractive to those who take an interest in liturgical studies. It is certainly very thorough, as it deals with the worship and ritual of Greeks, Romans, Jews, Buddhists, and Devil-Worshippers, as well as of Christians of every church and denomination.'—CONTEMPORARY Review.

O'BRIEN.—Stories by Mrs. Charlotte O'brien. MARGARET AND HER FRIENDS. With Coloured Frontispiece. Fcap. 8vo. cloth boards, is. MOTHER'S WARM SHAWL. With Coloured Frontispiece. Fcip.

8vo. cloth boards, is.

OLIVER DALE'S DECISION. With Coloured Frontispiece.

Fcap. 8vo. cloth boards, Is.

THE OLD, OLD STORY. By the Author of ' Heart to Heart,' &c With Outline Illustrations by H. T. A. MILES. Square 16mo. cloth, bevelled boards, gilt edge:, ts. 6d. ONE OF A COVEY.—By the Author of 'Honor Bright,' 'PeasBlossom,' &c. With numerous Illustrations by H. J. A. Miles. Large crown 8vo. extra cloth boards, gilt edges, 3. 6d. 'Full of spirit and life, so well sustained throughout that grown-up readers may enjoy it as much as children. This "

Covey" consists of the twelve children of a hard-pressed Dr. Partridge, out of which is chosen a little girl to be adopted by a spoilt,fine lady.... It is one of the best books of the season.'—GUARDIAN.

'We have rarely read a story for boys and girls with greater pleasure. One of the chief characters would not have disgraced Dickens' pen.'
Literary World.

O'REILLY.— *Works by Mrs. Robert O'reilly.* CHILDREN OF THE CHURCH: or, Short Lessons on the Church Catechism for Infant Children. 18mo. cloth boards, *is. 6d.* Eighth Edition.
CHILDREN OF THE CHURCH. Second Series. Lessons on the Collects. i8mo. cloth boards, IX. *6d.* Second Edition.
SUE AND I. Illustrated Frontispiece and Title. Large crown 8vo. cloth, bevelled boards, 3. *6d.* Third Edition. *'A thoroughly delightful book, full of sound wisdom as well as fun.'* ATHENiEUM.
OUR FRIENDS IN PARADISE; or, Sanctorum Dulcis Memoria. With Introduction by the Right Rev. W. D. Maclagan, D. D., Bishop of Lichfield. Sm. 4to. fancy cloth boards, jr. *(xi.* Second Edition.
'Constructed after the model of a birthday text-book, and designed to recall the memory of those wh» have entered into their rest, and thus assist in realising more fully the doctrine of the Communion of Saints.'

The Year-book Of The Church.
'A very elegant volume externally and internally. To every page three days are allotted, those on the left bearing dates, texts, and choice quotations, the opposite pages being spacedfor records and remarks.'—ThE QUEEN.
OUR BOYS AND GIRLS BOTH GOOD AND BAD.—
Edited by the Author of ' Great Britain for Little Britons.' With Thirty Illustrations. Small crown 8vo. cloth, bevelled boards, 2s. 6d.
OWINDIA: A Tale of the Mackenzie River Indians. With Frontispiece. Square i6mo. bound in white cloth boards, *is.*
PANTON.—LISTEN! Poems for the Children's Hour. By J. E.
Panton. With Frontispiece by W. P. Frith, R.A. and Outline Illustrations by Helen Miles and T. Pym. Square l6mo.

fancy cloth boards, *is. 6d.* 'The pretty little poems in this pretty little boot will be sure to find ready listeners.'—Morning Post. THE PAINTED SAIL, and Other Stories. Each Story has a Fullpage coloured Plate. Crown 8vo. cloth, bevelled boards, 3. *6d.*

This volume contains the following Stories:—
The Mother's Christmas Gift.
On The Hazel.
Little Brava.
The Painted Sail.
The Turning-point Of Life.
Rich And Poor.
Wrong In His Head.
The Midnight Summons.
Nobody's Darling.
Mother Holkokd's Ladder.
Rosalie's Lovers.
'In Keeping."
Kathleen's Choice.
Needs Must.
PALMER.—*Stories by Mrs. Palmer.*
DOGGED JACK. With a Full-page Coloured Illustration. Crown 8vo. clotn, levelled boards, *y. 6d.* Second Edition.
TRUE UNDER TRIAL. Illustrated Frontispiece and Title-page.
Large crown 8vo. cloth, bevelled boards, *y. 6d.* Fifth Edition.
'A well-written story.'—The Times.
'One of the best boys' books we have seen for a long time. The adventures of little Edward Forbes, who was "true under trial," are written with such knowledge of the details of London life among the destitute orders; with such rare
combination of religious spirit with a perfect abstention from cant, and so well
put together, that we believe no reader who once took up the book would put it down without finishing it.'—STANDARd.
PAPAL CLAIMS Considered In The Light Of SCRIPTURE AND HISTORY. With an Introduction by the
Bishop Of Bedford. Fcap. 8vo. cloth boards, *2s.*
'This short treatise provides valid arguments enough to satisfy all who really desire to understand the right and wrong of the case. Its tone is calm and

dispassionate: it is free from anything like flippancy or prejudice. It ought to be a useful book to the parochial clergy.'—GUARDIAN.
PAPERS FOR MEN. Price One Penny each. *Published under the direction of the Church of England Purity Society.*
PARABLES OF THE KINGDOM.—Our Lords Parables Simply Told for Children. By the Author of 'Voices of Nature," 'Earth's Many Voices.' With 46 Illustrations in Outline by H. J. A. Miles. Square 16mo. cloth, bevelled boards, zr. *6d.* 'Teachers will find this a valuable help.'—ChUrch BELLS. THE PARISH GUIDE.—A Complete Handbook, giving Information concerning every kind of Parochial Institution and Organization, in both Town and Country Parishes, for the use of the Clergy and Lay-Helpers. Edited by the Rev. Theodore Johnson, Diocesan Inspector of Schools for Rochester, Author of ' The Clergyman's Ready Reference Register,' &c Demy 8vo. cloth boards, *6s.*
P EAS" BLOSSO M.—By the Author of' Honor Bright,' ' One of a Covey,' &c. With numerous Illustrations by H. J. A. Miles. Large crown 8vo. cloth boards, gilt edges, 3. *6d.* '"Peas-blossom " may be described as a rollickingly respectable Irish story, tkt names of the juvenile pair of heroes being Pat and Paddy. Like the young Anthony Trollope, they are sent to a schoolfive miles away from their home, across country, and are even more regardless than he of personal appearance. On one occasion they swim a river when a bridge has been washed away, and walk onwards in their wet clothes .... and so we are carried on to the end of Ike chapters, through an exceptionally readable volume.'—ThE Times.
'A delightfully written book for boys about twelve. The best book of the season.'—Sta N D Ard. PENNY.—TEN YEARS IN MELANESIA. By the Rev. Alfred Penny. With Chart and Illustrations by the Author and H. J. Rhodes. Crown 8vo. cloth boards, *$s.* Second Edition.
'A most interesting and charmingly written description of Melanesian life.' Pall Mall Gazette. 'A distinct contribu-

tion to our knowledge of Melanesia.'—SatURDAY Review. *'Freshly written .... Full of interest.'*—GUARDIAN.

PLAIN TEXTS FOR DAILY USE.—With Introduction by the Bishop Of Bedford. 64mo. cl.boards,4/.; Persian limp, *gd.*; caldp., *is.bd.* PLUNKET.— *Works by the Hon. Emmeline M. Plunket.* MERRIE GAMES IN RHYME, FROM YE OLDEN TIME.

Printed in red and black. Crown 4to. cloth boards, *y. 6d.* Each Rhyme is accompanied by a rubric indicating how the game is played, and a musical score of the traditional tune to which it is chanted. 'A collection of value, and a work of art as well. Many of the rhymes are very ancient, as are not a few of the melodies to which they are set; and the quaint and graceful illustrations chime in harmoniously with the venerable music'—The Times.

'// will supply amusement to children for many an evening. This book would be a treasure indeed at a party for little children.'—STANDARD. 'Miss Plunket will be welcomed, and her book be voted prime—

There's a fund of rare amusement in her "Merrie Games in Rhyme."'

Punch. VERY SHORT STORIES IN VERY SHORT WORDS.

With numerous Illustrations by T. Py. m. In large type. Square l6mo. cloth boards, *Is. 6d.* POTTER.— A PRESENT CHRIST: Daily Ten Minutes'Readings for Four Weeks on the Incarnation. By the Rev. J. Hasloch Potter, M.A., Vicar of Holy Trinity, Upper Tooting. Fcap. 8vo. cloth boards, *2s. 6d.* Second Edition.

Specially suited for use at Daily Services or Family Prayer. POTTER.—SERMONS OF THE CITY. By the Rev. Henry C. Potter, D.D., Secretary to the House of Bishops, U.S.A. Crown 8vo. cloth boards, *2s. 6d.* PRESCOTT.— *Works by the Rev. G. F. Prescott, M.A., Vicar of St. MichaeFs, Paddington.*

COUNSELS ON PRAYER. Royal 32mo. *6d.* ; cloth boards, *is.*

HINDRANCES TO SPIRITUAL LIFE: A Course of Lent

Lectures. Crown 8vo. cloth boards, *is. 6d.* Fourth Edition.

THE 'PRIZE' BIBLE.—Numerous Illustrations. Twelve Coloured Chromo Plates. Large-type Letterpress, and printed on Toned Paper. 4to. extra cloth, bevelled boards, gilt edges, izt. *6d.* PYM.— *Works Lllustrated by T. Pym.*
A. B. C.

A new Children's Alphabet, beautifully printed in colours. Each letter is accompanied with an explanatory verse. Square l6mo. fancy boards,
2s. 6d.

'*Such graceful drawing and delicate colouring are not often expended on an A. B. C*—Daily News.

'*The prettiest alphabet we have ever seen.*'—SchoOLMASTER.

'*One of the very best picture-books of the season; there is a refined delicacy about the drawing and colouring of these pictures which makes this a really charming and artistic little book.* —NONCONFORMIST.
PYM.— *Works Illustrated by T. Pvm.— (Continued.)* CHILDREN BUSY, CHILDREN GLAD, CHILDREN NAUGHTY, CHILDREN SAD. With Stories by L. C. An Illustrated Book of Child-life, printed in the best style of Chromo-Iithography. Bound in an Illustrated cover, paper boards, cloth back, 3. 6. '*A most charming book for children. The pictures are very pretty, and Ike children represented in them look like real children as they are seen in nurseries, which is not always, nor even often, the case in books of this sort. The stories display a delicate fancy, and will be read with real pleasure for their literary merit by grown-up people as well as children. '*—The Times. OUTLINE ILLUSTRATIONS FOR the LITTLE ONES

TO COLOUR. Fcap. 4to. *is.*; cloth, *Is. 6d.* MORE OUTLINES for the LITTLE ONES TO COLOUR.

Fcap. 4to. *is.* ; cloth, *is. 6d. These Outline Picture-books are printed in sepia, on tinted paper expressly made for the purpose.* PICTURES FROM THE POETS. A Book of Selected Extracts from Ancient and Modern Sources, illustrated by Child-life, carefully printed in Chromo-Iithography in brown and red tints. Oblong 4to. Illustrated cover, cloth back, 3. *6d.* '*This volume will afford pleasure to every one who can admire good artistic work.'*—Scotsman. THE SNOW QUEEN. By Hans Christian Andersen. Beautifully printed in the best style of Chromo-Iithography. Fcap. 4to. Illustrated cover, cloth back, coloured edges, 5.

THE QUIET HELPER. Text, Prayer, and Hymn for Four Weeks, and for the principal Holy-days. Printed in large type for hanging on the wall. On roller, 3. READINGS AND DEVOTIONS FOR MOTHERS, With

Introduction by the late Bishop Of Salisbury. Fcap. 8vo. cloth limp, *is.* &/.

'*This little book certainly seems to supply a want which has not exactly been supplied before, and as the Bishop of Salisbury observes, it has done it in a way most likely to prove useful.'*—Church Times.

A REMEMBRANCER OF MY SPONSORSHIP FOR MY GODCHILDREN. Printed in red and black, with blank spaces for names. *2d.* RIDGEWAY.—FOUNDATION TRUTHS: A Course of Instructions, by the Rev. C. J. RlDgeWAY, M.A., Vicar of Christ Church, Lancaster Gate. Small crown 8vo. cloth boards, *is. 6d.* Second Edition.

'*We rejoice to see these useful Lectures have come to a second edition. They will be useful not only for private reading, but as helps in giving addresses at missions and the like.'*—Church Bells. ROBIN AND LINNET. By the Author of 'Honor Bright,' &c. With Coloured Illustrations by T. Pym. Square l6mo. extra cloth boards, *is. 6d.* '*The adventures are very amusing, and the story will be a favourite with children, who will delight to fancy themselves roaming on the beach, or dabbling in the pools in such liberty.'*—GUARDIAN.

'*It requires a special talent to describe the sayings and doings of very little children, and the author of "Robin and Linnet,' and "Honor Bright," cVv. possesses that talent in no small degree. '*—Literary Churchman. ROCHESTER DIOCESAN DIRECTORY FOR 1888.

Published by Authority. Small crown 8vo. paper boards, cloth back, *is. 6d.* net.

A ROUGH DIAMOND and other Stories. — Each Story has a Full-page coloured Illustration. Crown 8vo. cloth, bevelled boards,

This volume contains the following Stones:—

A Rough Diamond.
Three Heroines.
A Hard Man.
Strange Landlady.
In A Chalet.
Wove Wire.
Yes Or No.
The Ring Of Fiends.
Wanted—A Gardener.
What's In A Name? ROWLEY.— Works by the Rev. Henry Rowley. THE RELIGIONS OF THE AFRICANS. Fcap. 8vo. cloth boards, *p. (xi.*
TWENTY YEARS IN CENTRAL AFRICA. The Story of the
Universities' Mission, from its Commencement under Bishop Mackenzie to the Present Time. With Map. Crown 8vo. cloth boards, 3. *6d.*
'The volume abounds in thrilling incidents.'—AMERICAN CHURCHMAN.
RULE.—THE PARENTS' MANUAL. By the Rev. U. Z. Rule.

Fcap. 8vo. cloth, *is.* Third Edition, Enlarged and Revised.

'By far the best book of the kind we know; so simple are its earliest prayers, hymns, and instructions. —GUARDIAN.
RUTH HALLIDAY; or, The Adopted Daughter. A Tale founded on Fact. Fcap. 8vo. cloth boards, *is.*
"ST. AUSTIN'S COURT; or, The Grandchildren. With Coloured Frontispiece. 18,110. cloth boards, I .
SHADOWS OF TRUTH; or, Thoughts and Allegories in Prose and Verse. By G. M. C. Fcap. 8vo. cloth boards, gilt edges, *2s. 6d.*
Third Edition.
SHELFORD. — TWENTY YEARS AT S. MATTHEW'S,
UPPER CLAPTON, 1866-86: A Record and Sermons. By the
Rev. Leonard E. Shelford, M.A., Rector of Stoke Newington.
Fcap. 8vo. cloth boards, *2s. 6d.*

'SHERLOCK.—THE AMETHYST: A Selection of Temperance Readings in Prose and Verse. By Frederick Sherlock. Crown 8vo. cloth boards, *Is.* Second Edition.

"SIDEBOTHAM.—THE DISCIPLINE OF TEMPTATION, and other Sermons. By the Rev. H. Sidebotham, M.A., Canon of Gibraltar and Chaplain of St. John's, Mentone. Fcap. 8vo. cloth boards, I;. 64. Second Edition.

'A wholesome, thoughtful, and right-hearted little book, fit for those who call a halt in the nt'ift march of life, and "consider their ways' as soldiers of Christ.'—Church Bells. SILVERMERE ANNALS; Tales of Village Life. By C E. B. With Coloured Frontispiece. Fcap. 8vo. cloth boards, *is.* SISTER LOUISE. The Story of her Life-Work. With Portrait. Fcap. 8vo. cloth boards, *2s. 6d.* Second Edition.

THE 'SISTER DOHA' OF AMERICA. 'The memoir of Sister Louise shows what a self-denying woman can do ' the way of helping those who are incapable of helping themselves,... she wtmld not be happy unless she was engaged in practical philanthropy. Her relifio was that of faith working by love. Many were her trials.. .. The story is full of practical suggestions.'—ThE ROCK. SKEY.— DOLLY'S OWN STORY. Told in her Own Words. By L. C. Skev. Illustrated in Outline by J. Sadler. Square 16mo. cloth boards, *is. 6d.* SLATTER.—STUDENTS' GOSPEL HARMONY. Being the Four Gospels in the Original Greek, arranged in parallel columns so as to show the consentient portions together, with a Preface and Analytical Tables. By the Rev. John Slatter, M.A., Vicar of Streatley, Berks, and Hon. Canon, Christ Church, Oxford. Demy 8vo. cloth boards, *12s. 6d.* 'Although, in many cases, the assignation of a passage to a particular place in the "Harmony "must involve a choice of difficulties, there is evidence through"1 that all the conditions of the problem have been fully considered. In short, « student who follows Canon Slatter will hardly go wrong.'—Daily News. SNOWDON.— Works by the late Jasper W. SmivDorr. DOUBLE NORWICH COURT BOB MAJOR. Crown 8vo. paper covers, *is.* ROPE-SIGHT: An Introduction to the Art of Change-Ringing.

Crown 8vo. paper cover, *is. 6d.* Second Edition.

'Very much wanted.... Mr. Snowdon is peculiarly filled for the post of teacher.'—ChURCh BELLS. STANDARD METHODS in the ART of CHANGE-RINGING. With a Book of Coloured Diagrams. Crown 8vo. paper cover, *2s. (sd.*

'In each of the methods selected instructions and examples of the different calls used are given, and to render the book more complete when in the hands of sixbells ringers, a peal of each of the-five and six-bells methods is given.'
'Church Bells.

A TREATISE ON TREBLE BOB.

Crown 8vo. paper cover. 2 vols. *y.* SONGS AND LYRICS FOR LITTLE LIPS. With Musical

Contributions by W. H. Cummings and others. Illustrated by G. L. Seymour and others. 8vo. cloth extra, bevelled boards, gilt edges, *6s.*

'A collection of some of the choicest little poems for children that we possess— some old, some new—with appropriate music and charming "pictures." We can imagine no more delightful present to a child six or seven years old'

Guardian. SPECIAL SERVICES. SPECIAL SERVICE OF INTERCESSION FOR THOSE

AT SEA. *id.;* 6s. per ico.

Approved by the late Archbishop of Canterbury. SPECIAL SERVICES FOR USE IN CHURCHES AND

MISSION ROOMS.

Advent, *2d.*
Lent, *2d.*
Easter, *2d.*
Ascensiontide and Whitsuntide, *2d.*

A SPECIAL SERVICE OF PREPARATION FOR HOLY

COMMUNION. 50 copies for *2s.*
Many churches have adopted this Service for use on a meek-day evening. It is now published with the view of an extended circulation, and is sanctioned by the Bishops of London, Winchester, and others. FORM OF INSTITUTION AND INDUCTION, *y.* per 100.

As prepared by a Committee of the Lower House of the Convocation of Canterbury.

FORM OF SERVICE FOR THE DEDICATION OF

CHURCH BELLS, zr. *6d.* per packet of 50 copies.

AN OFFICE FOR NEW-VEAR'S EVE. *id.*; 6s. per 100copies.

Approved by the Bishop of Winchester. STEVENS.— LOVE IS OF GOD, and other Sermons. By the Right Rev. W. Bacon Stevens, D.D. LL.D., Bishop of Pennsylvania. Crown 8vo. cloth boards, *2s. 6d.* STOKES.—THE TEACHERS' GRADUAL: Lessons on the Church Catechism. By the Rev. Louis Stokes, M.A., late Assistant Diocesan Inspector for London, and Carapden Lecturer of St. Lawrence, Jewry. Fcap. 8vo. cloth boards, *2s. 6J.* *'He has made the Catechism as clear as words can make it.'*—Guardian.

'There is no better workpublished.'—Chvrch Times.

'Teachers will find it most useful. — Saturday Review. STONE.—DEARE CHILDE. A Village Idyl. By the Rev. S. J. Stone, M.A., Vicar of St. Paul's, Haggerston. With Outline Illustrations by H. J. A. Miles. Square i6mo. cloth, bevelled boards, gilt edges, *is. 6d.*

Third Edition.

STORIES & EPISODES OF HOME MISSION-WORK.

With a Preface by the late Archbishop Of Canterbury. Crown 8vo.

cloth boards, *y. 6d.*; paper, *2s.* 'As both the Archbishops and several of the Bishops write to commend this book, it does not seem to need other patronage.'— Spectator. STRACHAN.—FROM EAST TO WEST; or, Glances at the Church's Work in Distant Lands. By the Right Rev. J. M. Strachan, M.D., D.D., Bishop of Rangoon. Illustrated. Crown 8vo. cloth boards, %s. 6d, SUNDAY.— Weekly, One Halfpenny; Monthly, in Wrapper, *yi.*

Annual Volumes, with upwards of Two Hundred Illustrations. Illustrated paper boards, cloth back, *y.*; cloth, bevelled boards, gilt edges, *$s.*

Cloth cases for binding a year's issue, *is.*

A few copies of the following Volumes are still to be had:—

Sr. Edition—1882, 1884, 1886, 1887.

y. Edition—1882, 1883, 1884, 1886, 1887.

'Well written, well illustrated, well printed.'—Morning Post.

'We know of no better magazine of its kind, and we imagine no handumer gift at Christmas time to bestow upon a child.'—ChuRch TIMES.

'There are no fewer than 240 Illustrations in the volume, and they do great credit to Mr. Gordon Browne and his fellow-artists. The sketch of the children and their pets is exceedingly clever and spirited. Many of the tittle girls, whether rich or poor, are very pretty and engaging; and now and again, in a tiny vignette or initial letter, is a dash of humour that is irresistibly droll. As for "Sunday" itself, with its blending of stories, poems, "Good Words" in simple language, it seems well suited to the little people-for whom it is written.'

Times. SWAYNE.—THE MINISTER OF CHRIST IN THESE LAST DAYS. Five Addresses to Candidates for Ordination. By the Rev. Robert S. Swayne, M.A., Chancellor and Canon Residentiary of Salisbury Cathedral. Crown 8vo. cloth boards, *2s.* 'It will, we think, be a welcome volume to the Bishops of the Church, who will desire to place it in the hands of their young men who are looking forward to the sacred ministry. '—New Yokk Churchman. TAYLOR.— OUT OF THE WAY. A Village Temperance Story.

By H. L. Taylor. With numerous Illustrations by A. H. Collins. Large crown 8vo. extra cloth boards, gilt edges, *3j. 6d.* 'A favourable specimen... . We were half way through the book before we found out that it was a Temperance tale at all.'—GUARDIAN.

'The book deserves warm praise; we wish there were more Temperance tales like it.'—Christian World. TEMPERANCE HYMNS AND SONGS. With Accom panying Tunes. To which is prefixed a short Opening Service. Demy8vo. paper covers. *Is. (xi.*; cloth boards, *2s. 6d.* Words only, paper covers, *2d.*; lim cloth, *yd.* New and Enlarged Edition.

Published under the Direction of the Church of England Temperance Society. This is the most comprehensive and the cheapest book of its kind yet issued. THORNE. —A SELECTION OF SINGLE AND DOUBLE CHANTS. Selected and Edited by E. H. Thorne, late Organist of Chichester Cathedral. Oblong, cloth limp, *is.* Twenty-fourth Edition. THOUGHTS FOR THE SICK AND INFIRM ON THE DAY OF INTERCESSION. With Commendation by the Bishop Of Bedford, *id.*; *6s.* per ioo. THREE CUPS J or, The Girls of St. Andrews. By the Author of 'Marty and the Mite-Boxes. ' Illustrated. Crown 8vo. cloth boards, *y. 6d.* 'It appears there is a Chinese proverb, "When you have three cups to drink, drink your three cups," and this gives the quaint title of "The Three Cups" to a pleasant little American book.'—Guardian. TITCOMB.—PERSONAL RECOLLECTIONS OF BR.'TISH BURMA. By the late Right Rev. J. H. Titcomb, D.D., First Bishop of Rangoon. Illustrated. Demy 8vo. half cloth, *2s. 6d,* TROYTE.— CHANGE-RINGING. An Introduction to the Early Stages of the Art of Church or Handbell Ringing, for the Use of Beginners. By Charles A. W. Troytr, of Huntshara Court, Devonshire; Member of the Ancient Society of College Youths, London. Crown 8vo. paper covers, up to 'Six Bells,' *is.* Complete Edition, cloth limp, *2s. 6i.* THE CHANGE-RINGERS' GUIDE TO THE STEEPLES OF ENGLAND. With an Appendix, containing information on many subjects interesting to the Exercise. Compiled by Rev. R. Acland-troyte and J. E. Acland-troyte, Members of the Ancient Society of College Youths, the Oxford University Society, &c. Crown 8vo. *is. 6d.* TUCKER.— *Works by the Rev. H. W. Tucker, M.A., Secretary to the Society for the Propagation of the Gospel.* MEMOIR of the LIFE and EPISCOPATE of EDWARD

FEILD, D.D., Bishop of Newfoundland, 1844-1876. With Prefatory

Note to the Author by the Right Hon. W. E. Gladstone, M.P.

With Map of Newfoundland. Cr. 8vo. cloth boards, *y.* Third Edit.

'A record of a devoted life.'—Pall Mall Gazette. MEMOIR of the LIFE and EPISCOPATE of GEORGE

AUGUSTUS SELWYN, D.D., Bishop of New Zealand, 1841-

1869; Bishop of Lichfield, 1867-1878. With Two Portraits, Map,

Facsimile Letters, and Engraving of the Lady Chapel of Lichfield
Cathedral. Two vols. 8vo. 800 pp., cloth boards, 24.
Popular Edition, 2 vols, crown 8vo. cloth boards, 12/.
'Of more than ordinary interest.'—Quarterly Review. TUTTIETT.— *Works by the Rev. La Wrence Tuttiett.* COUNSELS OF A GODFATHER. Fcap. 8vo. cloth, bevelled boards, *2s. 6d.* Or in Five Parts. Second Edition. HOUSEHOLD PRAYERS FOR WORKING MEN. i8mo. cloth, *6d.* loth Thousand. PLAIN FORMS OF HOUSEHOLD PRAYER for Four Weeks.
Chiefly for those Engaged in Necessary Business. In targe type, fcap.
8vo. cloth boards, *2s. 6d.* Seventh Edition.
THE TRUE PENITENT: Reflections on the Penitential
Psalms. Fcap. 8vo. cloth, *is. (td.*
TURNING-POINT OF LIFE, and The Double War FARE: Two Confirmation Stories. Illustrated. i8mo. cloth boards, *is.*
TURNOCK. — A MANUAL OF ENGLISH CHURCH HISTORY. By the Rev. J. R. TuRNOCK, Vicar of St. Mary-le-Tower, Ipswich, Hon. Canon of Norwich. Fcap. 8vo. cloth boards, *is. 6d.* UNDER MOTHER'S WING. By L. C, Author of the Stories irv 'Children Busy.' With Coloured Illustrations on every page by J. K. 4to. Illustrated Cover, *$s.* 'The letterpress is full of originality.'—Saturday Review. , One of the most charming of the Christmas books is " Under Mothers I Ving," by L. C, illustrated remarkably well by J. K. The stories are more than usually piquant and graceful.'—GUARDIAN.
THE VANGUARD.—The Monthly Paper of the Church of England Purity Society. Price *id.;* A Yeai's Subscription, post free, I. 6V/. VENABLES.— *Works by the Rev. George Vekables, S.C.L. late Vicar of Great Yarmouth.* CHURCHMAN'S MANUAL. 32mo. cloth boards, *is.* 6,/.
Third Edition, enlarged. FIVE OFFICES FOR PAROCHIAL USE.—Sunday-school Teachers, Opening and Closing Schools, Meeting of District Visitors, Mission-room Services, Cottages, &c. Fcap. 8vo. *6J.* OUR CHURCH AND OUR COUNTRY. Crown 8vo. paper covers, *is.* Sixth Edition.
THREE EXTRA SERVICES FOR USE IN CHURCH — an Office for Communicants, a Service of Song, and an Office for a Catechetical Service. 241110. *$,!.*
VERNON.—KALENDAR NOTES: Short Devotional Comments for Every Sunday and Holy-day of the Christian Year. By the Rev. J. R. Vernon, M.A., Rector of St. Audrie's, Somerset. Fcap. 8vo. cloth boards, *y.* 'Brief readings—terse and thoughtful.'—Literary Churchman.
VI DAL.— *Stories by Mrs. Vidal.* LUCY HELMORE. Coloured Illustrations. Fcap. 8vo. extra cloth boards, *2s. 6d.*
THE TRIALS OF RACHEL CHARLCOTE. With Coloured
Frontispiece. Fcap. 8vo. cloth boards, *is.*
VOICES OF NATURE. By the Author of 'Parables of the Kingdom,' 'Earth's Many Voices,, £:c. With Illustrations. Square 16mo. extra cloth boards, *is. 6d.*
WAYNE.— OLD PATHS: Sermons on the Apostles' Creed. By the Rev. E. F. Wayne, M.A. Fcap. 8vo. cloth boards, 3. WHITWORTH.— *Works by the Rev. W. Allen Whitworth,*
M.A., Vicar of All Saints', Margaret Street.
A BIBLE-CLASS MANUAL—Offices, Prayers, and Intercessions for
Members of Bible Classes. Royal 32-mo. *$d.;* extra cloth, red edges, *6d.*
Third Edition.
THE CHURCHMAN'S ALMANAC FOR EIGHT CEN-
TURIES (1201 to 2000), giving the Name and Date of every
Sunday. Small folio, *Ss. 6d.*
A HELP TO SELF-EXAMINATION. Fifty copies in packet,
is. gd.
THE DIVINE SERVICE. Holy Communion according to the Use of the Church of England, with Explanatory Notes and Helps to Private Devotion. Fcap. 8vo. paper boards, *&/.;* cloth boards, *is.* 8th Thousand.
The same book, in cloth boards, bound with Mv Private Prayer-book, containing spaces for notes of Special Intercession, *is. 6d.* complete.
'The office is printed in larger type at the top, and the notes and kelps in smaller at the bottom of each page. There is careful instruction on preparation and thanksgiving. A book we can recommend.'—Literary Churchman. IS IT PEACE? Words of Encouragement for Anxious Souls. 16mo. *6l.;* extra cloth, *is.* 'A rousing little book.'—Guardian.
MY PRIVATE PRAYER-BOOK. Containing spaces for notes of
Special Intercession. Fcap. 8vo. *3d.*
'The best thing of the kind we have seen. '—Church Bells. SEVEN PRAYERS ON THE SEVEN WORDS FROM THE CROSS. For Distribution on Good Friday, or for Use during 'The Three Hours.' Fifty copies in packet, *is. sjd.* WILBERFORCE.—SPEECHES ON MISSIONS. By the Right Rev. Samuel Wilberforce, D.D. Edited by the Rev. Henry Rowley. 8vo. cloth boards, *Js.* Second Edition.
'This book may be considered an instruction-book. It teaches the speaker or the preacher how to provide himself well with materials, and then haw to infuse life and warmth into them.'—Church Bells. WILKINSON.— *Works by the Right Rev. G.H. Wilkinson, D.D. Bishop of Truro.* ABSOLUTION: A Sermon. 8vo. paper covers, *i.*
BE YE RECONCILED TO GOD. *id.; 6s.* per ioo. New Edit. CONFESSION: A Sermon. 8vo. paper covers, *is.* FIRST STEPS TO HOLY COMMUNION. The Substance of Four Simple Instructions after Confirmation. Fcap. 8vo. *6d.;* leather, *is. 6d.* A Superior Edition in Old Style, bound in white, *is.* FOUR MISSION PRAYERS, *id. ; Js.* per too. HINDRANCES and HELPS to the DEEPENING of the
SPIRITUAL LIFE AMONG CLERGY and PEOPLE. *3d.*
HOLY WEEK AND EASTER. Fcap. 8vo. cloth boards, *Is.;*
leather, *is. 6d.* 17th Thousand.
HOW TO BEGIN A NEW LIFE. Fcap. 8vo. paper covers, *6d.;*
leather, *is. 6d.* A Superior Edition in Old Style, cloth, bevelled boards, *is.*
HOW TO KEEP LENT. Notes on Quinquagesima Sunday
Address. *3d.* nth Thousand.
HOW TO DEAL WITH TEMPTATION. A Lenten Address.
Fcap. 8vo. *3d.* INSTRUCTIONS IN THE

DEVOTIONAL LIFE. Fcap. 8vo. price *6d.* Cloth boards, *is.;* leather, *is.* *6d.* 54th Thousand.

INSTRUCTIONS IN THE WAY OF SALVATION. Fcap. 8vo. price *6d.* Cloth boards, *is.;* leather, *is.* *6d.* 30th Thousand. LENT LECTURES. Fcap. 8vo. cloth boards, *is.;* leather, *is.* *6d.* 18th Thousand. MORNING AND EVENING PRAYERS FOR CHILDREN. On Card, *id.* PENITENTIARY WORK: Its Principles, Method, Difficulties, and Encouragements. Fcap. 8vo. price *td.* PRAYERS FOR CHILDREN. 32010.*2d.* PRAYERS FOR CHILDREN. On Card, *id.* SOME LAWS IN GOD'S SPIRITUAL KINGDOM. Fcap. 8vo. cloth, bevelled boards, 3;. 6.7.

THE CHASTENING of the LORD.' Four Bible Readings given at St. Peter's, Eaton Square. Fcap. 8vo. cloth boards, *is.;* leather, *is.* *6d.* 13th Thousand.

C WILKINSON.— *Works by the Rt. Rev. G. H. Wilkinson.*— (Continued.) THE COMMUNION OF SAINTS.' A Help to the Higher Life of Communicants. Fcap. 8vo. cloth boards, Is.; leather, *is.* *6d.* THE POWER OF SUFFERING: A Thought for Holy Week.

6d. per Packet of Twelve. THE POWER OF WEAKNESS: A Thought for Good Friday.

Fcap. 8vo. 3/.

THOUGHTS for the DAY of INTERCESSION. *id.;* *6s.* per too. 15th Thousand. THOUGHTS ON CALVARY. The Substance of Two Good Friday Addresses. Fcap. 8vo. *yi.*

TWO ADDRESSES TO COMMUNICANTS. Fcap. 8vo. *6J,;* leather, *is.* *6d.* WILKINSON.— Edited by the Rt. Ren. G. H. Wilkinson. BREAK UP YOUR FALLOW GROUND. A Help to Self Examination. Price *3d.*

SELF-EXAMINATION QUESTIONS. Founded on the Ten Commandments and the Church Catechism. Price *2d.*

SIMPLE PRAYERS FOR DAILY USE FOR YOUNG

PERSONS. Price *2d.* WILLIAMSON.— *Works by the Rev. Arthur Williamson, M.A., Vicar ofSt. James', Norlands.*

THE OUTSTRETCHED HANDS: Good Friday Addresses.

Fcap. 8vo. cloth boards, *is.*

DISESTABLISHMENT; or, The Crisis in Church and State.

Four Sermons. Fcap. 8vo. cloth, *is.* *6d.* 'Deals with the subject exhaustively, and yet he does not go into details whuk would be out ofplace in the pulpit. He very properly avoids politics.'—Figaro. IN THE KING'S SERVICE. A First Manual of Instruction on

Confirmation and Holy Communion. Fcap. 8vo. *(sd.*

THE WONDERFUL VOICE, and other Stories. With

Ten Coloured Plates. Crown 8vo. cloth, bevelled boards, *y. 6d.*

Eighth Edition.

WOOD.—NUMBER ELEVEN, and Other Stories. By Frances H. Wood. Illustrated. l8c:o. cloth boards, *is.* *6d.* WOODHOUSE.— *Works by the Rev. F. C. Woodhovse, M.A. Author of 'The Life of the Soul in the World,'* cW.

A MANUAL FOR ADVENT: a few Thoughts for Every Day, and for Christmas and the New Year. Crown 8vo. cloth boards, *y. 6d.* Third Edition.

'*The book is pithy and sensible as well as devout, and capable of being used not only for its primary purpose of private meditation, but for reading at family prayer; by the clergy, as supplying materials for sennonets a good deal above the average.'*—ChUrch TIMES.

A MANUAL FOR LENT: A few Thoughts for Every Day, and for the Sundays and Eastertide. Crown 8vo. cloth boards, 3. *6d.* Sixth Edition.

Besides several notices from the Church papers, the Christian World says: '*This is a remarkably good book; thoughtful, striking, earnest, and deeply interesting. It is not scrappy and incoherent, but really full of power andsuggestiveness. The style is always clear and cultured. We believe it to be a book which preachers and intelligent laymen will prize greatly, and read with profit and pleasure.'* WYNNE.—SPIRITUAL LIFE IN ITS EARLIER STAGES. Five Lectures for Lent. By Rev. G. R. Wynne, A.M., Vicar of Holywood. Fcap. 8vo. cloth boards, *is.* *6d.* '*It is written in an earnest, thoughtful, and thoroughly honest spirit .... cannot fail to be helpful to those whose religious feelings, al-*

ready awakened, need to be stimulated and guided in a right direction.'—Daily Express. THE YOUNG STANDARD-BEARER. An Illustrated Temperance Magazine for Children. Price One Halfpenny Monthly. Volumes, cloth boards, *is.* *6d.* each. 1881-1886. Cloth cases for binding a year's numbers, *8J. Published under the Direction of the Church of England Temperance Society.*

Pan

A. B. C, a New Children's Alphabet. 23

Absolution, A Sermon.... 33

Acts, Lessons on the 1 Advent, Special Service for...27

Aids to the Study of the Books of Samuel 12

Alice and her Cross 5

American Church Review

Amethyst, The 26

Artist, The 1

Ascensiontide and Whitsuntide, Special

Services for 27

Ballad of the Chorister Boy... x3

Ballads of Life and Home... 16

Be ye Reconciled to God.... 33

Belts, Form of Service for Dedication of. 27

Better than Strength (Forde)... 11

Bible-Class Manual, A.... 3a

Book about Bees, A 16

Boy Hero, The 13

Brazen Serpent 4

Break up your Fallow Ground.. 34

Breaking of the Bread, The... 8

British Burma, Personal Recollections of 29

By the Sea of Galilee 18

Can She keep a Secret?.... 6

Canticles Pointed for Chanting.. 13

Central Africa 4

Change-Ringing 30

Change-Ringer's Guide to the Steeples of

England 30

Changed Cross, The....19

,, ,, The, with Music.. 12

Chants, A Selection of Single and Double 29

Chastening of the Lord, The... 33

Chatterbox 4 series) 21 the

Chatterbox Christmas-box

Chester-le-Street, A Thousand Years in

Child-Nature.
Child's Own Story-book.
Children Busy, Children Glad
Children of the Church (rst and 2nd
„ of the Old Testament Children's Home Hymn-book.
School Hymn-book. Chorister's Admission Card Christian Course, The H Ministry, The.
Church Catechism,
(O'Reilly).
Church Congress Reports
„ Work Church of England, Past and Present
The.
Churchman's Almanac for Eight turies, The....
Churchman's Manual.
Clockmaker of St. Laurent
Cloud and the Star, The.
Collects, Lessons on the (O'Reilly)
Colonel Rolfe's Story
Common-Life Sermons
Communicants, Two Addresses to
Communion of Saints, The
Confession: A Sermon..
Confirmation Service, The
Consulting the Fates
Convocation Reports
Coral Missionary Magazine
Counsels of a Godfather.
„ on Prayer. Count up the Sunny Days
Crisis in Church and State (Williamson)
Cen
Page
Daily Family Prayer....13
„ Offices and Litany... 8
Day of Intercession, Suggestions for Observing the 15
Day of Intercession, Thoughts for the. 34
„ „ Thoughts for the Sick and Infirm...... 29
Days that are Past x
Deare Childe a8
Deb Clinton 6
Dedication of Church Bells, Form of. 27
Devotional Life, Instructions in 33
Dictionary of the English Church.. 8
Discipline of Temptation, The . 26
Disestablishment 34
Divine Fellowship 8
„ Service, The.... 32
Dogged Jack 22

Dolly's own Story 26
Double Norwich Court Bob Major. 27
„ Warfare, The.... 31
„ Witness of the Church.. 17
Driver's Box, The, and other Stories. 8
Early Church History, Manual of (Baird) 1
Easter, Special Service for 27
Edith Vernon's Life-Work... 9
Ethne 10
Evening Psalter Pointed for Chanting,
The 15
Extra Services for Use in Church, Three 31
Fakenham Ghost, The...-. a
Family Lesson Book, The... 9
H Worship for Busy Homes.. 10
Favourite Story-Book xo
Feild, Life of Bishop.... 30
First Lady of the Land.... 3
Floral Fancies 10
Flying Leaves 10
Following Christ u
Forms of Prayer to accompany Sermons &c. 9
Fortune-Teller 6
Foundation Truths 25
Four Lads and their Lives... 5
„ Little Sixes x6
Mission Prayers 33
Page
Four-leaved Shamrock, The... 13
From Pharaoh to Fellah.... 2
„ East to West t8
Glances at the Church's Work in Distant
Lands (Strachan) 28
Golden Steps 11
Good Stories 5
„ (New Series). xx
Gospel and Philosophy.... 8
„ Missionary, The.... 11
Gospels, Story of the 1
Grain of Mustard Seed, The...11
Great Britain for Little Britons. 3
Gregory of the Forctop.... 5
Happy Sunday Afternoons.. ix, is
Hearty Services ao
Helen Morton's Trial, and Timid Lucy. ia
Help at Hand 7
Helps by the Way 1a

Help to Self-Examination, A...3a
Her Great Ambition....is
High Wages xa
Hindrances and Helps.... 33
„ to Spiritual Life... 23
Holiness to the Lord....is
Holy Communion, First Steps to. 33
„ Communion (How).... 13
Marriage, Two Addresses on. 15
„ Matrimony (Ellison). . 9
Scripture: Temperance and Total Abstinence 13
Holy Week and Easter (Wilkinson). 33
„ „ and Easter (Bourdaloue). 3
Honor Bright 13
Household Prayers 30
How to Begin a New Life 33
„ to Ensure a Happy New Year. 13
„ to Keep Lent 33
„ to Deal with Temptation.. 33
„ to Pray the Lord's Prayer.. *1$*
Hymns (How) 13
In a Good Cause 15
Index Canonum xx
Inheritance of our Fathers.. a
Parish Magazine 6
„ Priest, Private Life, &c... M
Parents' Manual, The.... 25
Pastor in Parochia.... 14
Pastoral Work M
Peas-Blossom.....22
Penitentiary Work 33
Pictures from the Poets.... 24
Plain Forms of Household Prayer.. 30
Texts for Daily Use... 23
Words, x, a, 3, 4. Series... 14
„ „ as Tracts.... 14
„„, to Children... 14
„ Words about the Book of Common Prayer (Baird).... 2
Poems (How) 14
Position and Duty of Non-Abstainers. 13
Power of Suffering, The.... 34
„ of Weakness, The.... 34
Practical Sermons (how).... 15
Prayer for the Parish, A....13
Prayer-book, its History, Language, and Contents.... 8
Prayers and Meditations for each Day of the Week 9
Prayers for Children (Lee)... 17
„ „ (Wilkinson).. 33
„„, on Card 33

Preaching, Lectures on.... 3
Present Christ, A 23
Prize Bible, The 23
„ for Boys and Girls.... 6
Quiet Helper, The 24
Rainhill Funeral 6
Readings and Devotions for Mothers. 24
Religions of the Africans, The.. 25
Remembrancer of My Sponsorship, A. 24
Resolutions for those recovering from
Sickness 14
Revived Church Worship (Norton).. 20
Revision of the Rubrics.... 14
Rhoda's Secret 6
Robin and Linnet 25
Rochester Diocesan Directory... 25
Rope-Sight 97
Rough Diamond, A 25
Ruth Halliday 25
Sanctorum Dulcis Memoria... 21
St. Austin's Court 26
Scripture Readings 15
Selection from Sermons by Bradley. 3
Self-Examination Questions... 34
Selwyn, Life of Bishop.... 30
Sermons, Doctrinal and Practical.. 8
„ of the City.... 23
Service for the Admission of a Chorister. 13
Seven Prayers on the Seven Words. 32
Shadows of Truth 26
Silvermere Annals *26*
Simple Guide to Church Doctrine.. 19
„ Prayers for Young Persons.. 34
Sister Louise 26
Sister's Bye-Hours, A.... 16
Sixty Sermons 9
Snow Queen, The.... 24
Some Laws in God's Spiritual Kingdom. 33
Songs and Lyrics for Little Lips.. 27
Special Services for Use in Churches, &c. 27
„ tl for Church Seasons. 9
„ „ (Holy Communion). 27
n„ (Intercession for those at Sea)....
Spiritual Life in its Earlier Stages.
Standard Methods in Change-ringing
Stories and Episodes.... 28
„ told to a Child.... 16
Students' Gospel Harmony... 26
Studies for Stories from Girls' Lives. 16
„ in the Church.... 17
Sue and I (O'Reilly),.. 21
Sufferer's Guide, The....19
Sun of Righteousness.... 15
Sunday 28
Tale of the Crusades, A.... 7
Teachers' Gradual, The.. 28
Temperance Hymns and Songs 29
Ten Years in Melanesia.... 22
Thoughts on Calvary.... 34
Three Cups...29
Page
Tiles from Dame Marjorie's Chimney-
Corner 4
Timid Lucy 12
Topsy Turvy 3
Treble Bob: A Treatise on... »7
Trials of Rachel Charlcote... 31
True Penitent, The.... 30
„ under Trial 22
Turning-point of Life, The... 31
Twenty Years in Central Africa.. 25
„ at St. Matthew's.. 26
Under Mother's Wing.... 31
„, the King's Banner... 17
Vanguard, The 31
Venables, Life of Bishop...17
Very Short Stories in Very Short Words 23
Vestry Prayers with a Choir... 15
Voices of Nature 32
Psse
'Was Lost, and is Found"... 15
Watchers on the Longships... 7
Watching by the Cross.... «
Way of Salvation, Instructions in the. 33
We are Seven a
Week-day Services in Country Churches 15
Week Spent in a Glass Pond, A.. 9
Westminster Cloisters.... a
What shall we do in Accidents or Illness? (Cowper) 7
Wonderful Voice, The.... 34
Words of Counsel 18
„ Good Cheer.... 15
Worthies of the Church of England. 1
Worship in Heaven and on Earth.. 20
Wrath of the Fay, The....12
Young Men's Bible Classes.. 1 8
„ Standard-Bearer, The... 35
WELLS GARDNER, DARTON, & Co., Paternoster Buildings, E.G.

CPSIA information can be obtained at www.ICGtesting.com
Printed in the USA
BVOW09s1049010515

398583BV00013B/121/P